AMERICAN EXTREMES
(Extremos de América)

The Texas Pan-American Series

The Texas Pan-American Series is published with the assistance of a revolving publication fund established by the Pan-American Sulphur Company and other friends of Latin America in Texas. Publication of this book was also assisted by a grant from the Rockefeller Foundation through the Latin American translation program of the Association of American University Presses.

AMERICAN EXTREMES
(Extremos de América)

BY DANIEL COSÍO VILLEGAS

Translated by Américo Paredes

Introduction by John P. Harrison

EXTREME: that which is the most intense,
loftiest, or most active of anything
        (*Diccionario de la Academia*)

UNIVERSITY OF TEXAS PRESS AUSTIN

Library of Congress Catalog Card No. 64–11188

Copyright © 1964 by Daniel Cosío Villegas

Printed in the United States of America

CONTENTS

INTRODUCTION

This introduction is essentially informational as its purpose is to present to an English-reading audience the perceptive and sophisticated mind of the influential Mexican intellectual, Daniel Cosío Villegas. The fact is that Cosío is already well known to many historians, economists, and other social scientists who read Spanish, as well as to a considerable number of persons, both in and out of government, whose decisions affect the course of action of the United States toward Mexico in particular and Latin America generally. It is equally a fact that whether the man has been experienced through personal confrontation, through the written word, or through a combination of both, he is but partially known to anyone in the United States or Europe. The description of his accomplishments that follows should help explain this, just as the mention of his publications should make understandable why his typically long and specialized books have not been translated into English.

The increased concern within the English-speaking world about the recent past in Latin America resulted, in 1963, in the publication in English of one of Cosío's few short historical monographs, a case study of the recognition of Porfirio Díaz by the United States as affected by border difficulties immediately following his accession to authority in 1876 (*The United States Versus Porfirio Díaz,* University of Nebraska Press, 1963). None of his other writings have appeared in English in book form, nor is it likely that his detailed, multivolume studies will be thus published. It is probable, however, that he is better known throughout Latin America for his brilliant essays than for anything else he has written. Certainly, the essay is a literary form ideally suited to his cutting intelligence and his ability to perceive what is central to basic new directions within society and government before these new directions are recognized by others. It is the combination of these two talents that makes these essays, written as they were for particular purposes at particular moments in time, important and illuminating for us today. It also explains why they were chosen as the best vehicle for making the complexity 1) of Latin America and 2) of Daniel Cosío Villegas more readily understandable to the English-speaking world.

It is a difficult task to write briefly of Cosío without making the account sound either like an exaggerated parody or a lengthy obituary in the *New York Times*. This is because he has had an active career just a year or two shy of half a century, one that began when he was 17, teaching ethics in the National University of Mexico, and which, now that he is 64, gives no indication of abating either in volume or significance. He has been a sociologist, economist, historian, although for the past sixteen years he has confined his scholarly efforts to history. He has been diplomat, banker, teacher, publisher, his efforts in each of these fields having been characterized by conceptual originality and successful implementation. He has published in every literary form save drama and poetry, his earliest and perhaps least successful ventures being with the novel. This protean professional life, however, has had a clear unifying theme. Everything that Cosío has done has had as its primary purpose to serve the needs of the developing Mexican state and its society within a changing twentieth-century world. Also, his every action has been characterized by imagination and—above all—by sheer intelligence. This last, indubitably, is his distinguishing hallmark.

Nearly a year ago, in an Austin, Texas, hotel, Cosío and the poet Robert Lowell met for the first time. At that meeting neither was familiar with the other's work, and Lowell asked Cosío what kind of books he wrote. The answer "big books" let Lowell know that he was probably not talking with a fellow poet. Cosío, then 63, was working on the last volume of an eight-volume history of

Mexico covering the period from the triumph of Benito Juárez over the monarchist forces of the Emperor Maximilian in 1867 to the end of Porfirio Díaz's thirty-four-year rule in 1911. This history is the product of the Seminar on Modern History at El Colegio de México (an influential Mexican center of training and advanced research in the social sciences and humanities); and, of the seven published volumes, the three written entirely by Cosío total 2,697 carefully documented pages. There is every reason to believe that the eighth volume, like its companions, will have a beam of nearly three inches, will be extremely detailed and full of bite, and will become the standard point of departure for future studies relating to the subject dealt with—in this instance the internal affairs of Mexico under Porfirio Díaz.

This history of the Porfiriato and the constitutional republic that preceded it was begun in July, 1948. By the time the last volume is published in 1965 or 1966, it will have been the main scholarly effort of Cosío for more than fifteen years. During these years he wrote, in addition to his "big books," four of the essays in this collection; published four monographs—*En el centenario del Congreso Constituyente de 56, La Constitución de 1857 y sus críticos, Porfirio Díaz en la Revolución de la Noria,* and *Estados Unidos contra Porfirio Díaz;* served for three years as the Mexican delegate to the Economic and Social Council of the United Nations, and was president of that Council; started two professional journals of high quality and distinctive format—*Historia Mexicana,* which he edited for several years, and *Foro Internacional;* organized and directed for its beginning years the Seminar on Contemporary Mexican History (1910 to the present) at El Colegio de México; established at this same institution, with financial support from the Mexican government and United States foundations, a history program leading to the Ph.D. and a three-year advanced-level course in international relations for Mexicans and other Latin Americans (many of whom are now employed by their respective foreign offices); and, together with Victor Urquidi, was responsible for establishing the Faculty of Economics at the University of Nuevo León. During these years, Cosío filled a series of diplomatic assignments to international organizations for the Mexican government and was either director or president of El Colegio de México (he held one of these two positions from its founding in 1939 until his resignation in January, 1963).

This incomplete listing of Cosío's activities since 1948 indicates that his response to Lowell, while accurate, was at best partial. It was further misleading in that from 1932, when he published his study on Mexican tariffs in five fat volumes, until 1949 his writings consisted solely of essays, the principal ones of which were collected in a volume entitled *Extremos de América,* from which the title and all but four of the essays in this book were taken. During this seventeen-year period, Cosío devoted himself, as he remarks in his preface to *Extremos de América,* to the task of making it possible for other authors to have their books not only published but well distributed throughout Spanish America. The significance of this achievement thirty years ago can be fully appreciated only by those familiar with today's publishing industry in Latin America—above all with the distribution of books.

The mechanism that produced this near miracle was the Fondo de Cultura Económica, a publishing house with complete autonomy in the selection of titles published, but operating with the advantage— very necessary at the start—of a government subsidy. Like the many other professional and intellectual ventures that Cosío began and directed during their formative years, the Fondo de Cultura has continued to flourish since his departure, although the editorial line may have taken somewhat different directions than would have been the case under his leadership. It is today, as it has been throughout its existence, the principal outlet for important contributions by Latin Americans in the social sciences, and is one of the major publishers in other areas of scholarship and literature. Being published by the Fondo is a distinction—perhaps somewhat less so now than formerly because economists and sociologists have many new and satisfactory professional publishers available to them (such as university presses and organizations like the Economic Commission for Latin America and the Inter-American Development Bank). But even more, due to the exceptional distribution system that Cosío organized throughout Spanish America, it assures writers of a broad and important audience wherever Spanish is read. The Fondo provided the small but important group of professionally trained Spanish American social scientists with an effective podium when none other existed. It also made available to policy makers throughout the area, analyses of regional problems prepared by trained professionals who were a part of the society being dissected. During the years 1932–1948, Cosío further helped the Spanish American economist make his voice heard by establishing and editing what has become the leading professional economic journal in the Spanish language: *El Trimestre Económico.*

A different type of contribution to the contemporary intellectual life of Mexico was the primary role Cosío played in making Mexico, among the Spanish American countries, the strongest magnet for the Spanish intellectuals and professionals who migrated from Spain during and following the Civil War. From his vantage point as Mexican ambassador to Portugal in 1936 he saw the desolation resulting from the Spanish Civil War in Estremadura. Conversations with Spaniards who sifted through the frontier to Lisbon made more acute his awareness of what the chaos in Spain meant to her creative and professionally trained men. Cosío knew the variety and quality of these men from his 1933 stay in Madrid as a visiting professor at the Central University, an experience that had put him in a close personal relationship with many of the leading Spanish intellectuals.

In 1936 the universities and most, if not all, of the research institutes were closed. Those who had staffed these institutions were not professionally active nor was there any way for them to lead creative lives. Cosío accompanied his report of the situation to President Lázaro Cárdenas with the suggestion that the Mexican Government should offer these men the opportunity of leading productive lives once again by the simple expedient of providing them with transportation to Mexico and assuming responsibility for their resettlement. The need of Mexico for such men was too apparent to need extended comment. With the President's approval Cosío left Lisbon for Valencia, where he met with the Foreign Minister and the Under Secretary of Public Education of the Republican Government. A list of approximately fifty Spanish intellectuals was drawn up as a result of this meeting and the personal interviews that followed. Arrangements were made individually with the men selected, about their transportation and that of their families to Mexico. The first of these to arrive in Mexico was the philosopher José Gaos, whose influence on a generation of Mexican *universitarios* has been extraordinary. The variety of

Spanish intellectuals who have enjoyed productive careers in Mexico as a result of this simple and imaginative arrangement can be illustrated by the following brief list of names: Antonio Madinaveitia, Luís Recasens Siches, Adolfo Salazar, Enrique Díaz Canedo, Juan de Encina, Pedro Bosch Gimpera, and Gonzalo Lafora.

When the Republicans lost the war, many more professional men and scholars quite naturally made their own way to Mexico as the Spanish-speaking country with the most congenial climate for their talents and opinions. To provide an intellectual home for many of these men and to provide a bridge between Spanish and Mexican institutions, Cosío was instrumental in founding the Casa de España which, under the presidency of Alfonso Reyes, soon changed its name to El Colegio de México while continuing as a meeting ground for Mexicans and Spaniards engaged in writing and research. The injection of this sizeable body of highly trained talent into Mexican society provided a major stimulus to the economic diversification as well as to the intellectual development of the country.

In the essay "Background of Tyranny" Cosío states his belief that the crucial quality in society is the existence of personal and public freedom and not the fidelity with which electoral results reflect the will of the people. To use this electoral test would be to say that the Colombia of Laureano Gómez was a perfect democracy while the contemporary Mexico of Miguel Alemán lived under a tyranny. The count down, country by country, and an attempt at classification of degrees of democracy at the time of writing, illustrates, when compared with 1964, the fruitlessness of trying to make long-range forecasts or to base policy decisions on a composite picture of situations in each of the twenty Latin American nations. Although the immediate picture has changed drastically in many of the republics in the two decades since the essay was written, the emphasis on the total lack of tangible democratic progress still applies. The probing of the question to which the essay devotes itself, "What forces condemn or seem to condemn Latin America to fall time and again under tyranny, to remain sunk in it up to the neck like an animal in a bog?" remains as timely as when it was written. This ability to examine political, economic, and social questions in their immediate circumstances, yet with an uncanny eye for what is transitory and what is lasting, is one of Cosío's trademarks, and is why these essays written intermittently over a span of nearly twenty-five years are being presented in book form for the English-reading audience concerned with Latin America. They are as needed and helpful today as they doubtless will be for the indefinite future.

These essentially policy-directed political essays are in one sense history at its best, for by drawing specifically from the past in support of generalities, they will orient the careful reader toward a fundamental understanding of the present in Latin America and protect him from the shock of too great surprises in the future. At the same time, they are written with the pungency and urgency of an active intelligence which has never wavered from its concern for bringing material and moral growth into balance as the only way to achieve liberty—that is, something approaching equal options for all—and for satisfying the material wants of the peoples of Latin America.

Perhaps a final observation or two might help prepare those readers who are going to be confronted with Cosío for the first time. It is axiomatic that any continuously active man with a cutting intelligence is going to wound someone. In Cosío's case he has been able to rankle at one time or another individuals of all political persuasions in all American countries. His method is so direct and fundamental that many if not most readers take what he says as somehow being directed at them personally. While Cosío is intimately a part of what he writes about, his observations are so intellectually cold and clean—and in retrospect so right—that one gets the impression they must have been made from some vantage point of separateness in outer space. And, indeed, for many North Americans they may as well have been, for these political essays, with a single exception, were directed with a sense of immediate urgency not to those who speak English but to his fellow Mexicans and other Latin Americans. The reader in the United States thus has the unusual opportunity of seeing his own country's social values, economic interests, and political direction diagnosed from within Latin America as they have affected specific situations in that area over the past quarter century.

En garde!

JOHN P. HARRISON

AMERICAN EXTREMES
(*Extremos de América*)

MEXICO'S CRISIS*

FOR SEVERAL YEARS NOW, Mexico has been in a crisis which worsens day by day; but, as in those cases in which the patient is mortally ill, the members of the family will not talk about it, or they do so with an optimism that is tragically unreal. The crisis stems from the fact that the goals of the Revolution have been exhausted, to such a degree that the term *revolution* itself has lost its meaning. As is their custom, the official political groups continue to guide their acts according to their most immediate ends, while no one seems to care about the distant future of the country.

To understand the crisis, to gauge and resolve it, these primary questions should be considered: what were the goals of the Revolution, when were they exhausted, and why?

The Mexican Revolution never had a definite program, nor has it attempted to formulate one now, *in articulo mortis*, though tomorrow, *post mortem*, there will be many programs, especially those expounded and interpreted by conservative writers. Some goals or theses, however, were established, at least in the mechanical form which is the result of reiteration. Furthermore, as in all prolonged historical processes, not all the initial aims were preserved to the

* First published in *Cuadernos Americanos*, Año VI, 2, March 1947, Vol. XXXII.

end. On the contrary, some of the original goals lost their force and finally gave way to new ones—some primary, others secondary— which because they were new had some initial vigor. By these juxta- positions the ideological trend of the Revolution became even more confused, for these new propositions did not replace the old; rather, both old and new coexisted, superficially at least. Then beside the really fundamental theses appeared designs of less importance and magnitude: for example the solution of the agrarian problem runs neck and neck with the desire to promote the tourist trade.

At any rate, one of the main goals was that the indefinite tenure of power by one man or one group of men should be condemned; another, that the lot of the many should prevail over that of the few, and that in order to improve the fortunes of the many the govern- ment should become an active element of change; finally, that the country had interests and tastes of its own, which must be safe- guarded, and that in cases of conflict they should prevail over foreign interests and tastes. The reaction against the Porfirio Díaz regime and its ultimate overthrow was the application of the first goal; agrarian reform and the labor movement of the second; while to the third belongs the nationalist tone of the Revolution, exalting what was Mexican, distrusting, or openly fighting, what was foreign. Some would include among the principal goals of the Revolution the necessity for vigorous educative action on the part of the state, though this objective notoriously has been approached in a weaker and less consistent manner than have the other three. In fact, be- cause the Revolution was not carried into the schools it very soon lost the support of Mexican youth.

Those propositions seem commonplaces today, and ingenuous be- sides; and such they are for the very few who still believe in them, especially for those who would admit them on the printed page of a book but never in the reality of Mexican history. In their time, however, not only were they innovations but they corresponded so genuinely and so deeply to the country's needs that they changed its course for more than a quarter of a century, and they may still change it until mid-century is reached.

The ideological content of the Porfirio Díaz regime was poor in- deed. Suffice it to say that the guiding principle behind one of General Díaz' revolts was condemnation of the stamp tax, that is in addition to the principle of no-reelection, so faithfully observed later by Díaz himself. On the other hand, national and world realities gave him two magic words: "order" and "progress." The necessity for order, for peace after three-quarters of a century stained with blood and plagued with misery and hunger, was in the minds of all Mexicans. As for progress, Mexico until then had not even shared in the crumbs of the Industrial Revolution, which had begun in England at the end of the eighteenth century. Thus the Porfirio Díaz regime ended by dispensing in Mexico the medicines of order and progress, which had been accepted as panaceas for every ill suffered by the Western world during all of the nineteenth and the first years of the twentieth centuries. The Díaz regime, in sum, gave the country a philosophy which had been imposed upon it by the Western world, and which like all philosophies exalted some values to the detriment of others.

Madero's action in rising against this philosophy in 1910 was a daring novelty; for, the world situation then being what it was, its basic tenets did not suffer serious defeat until 1917, in Russia, and not until years afterwards in Europe proper. Madero's attack upon the old regime was partial, and everyone has said that it was directed upon the least vulnerable flank, since it sustained a thesis that was merely political, without any social or economic content. Madero's simple slogan, "Effective suffrage, no reelection," meant two things. First, the recognition of a biological fact, the most compelling of all facts: in the country during the Díaz regime there had arisen a whole new generation that was denied access to political power, to wealth, and even to social standing. Second, the belief that political life, liberty, and democracy were of greater value even than material progress and that because of this it did not matter if this last were compromised in order to achieve the former. Now, after the catastrophe of the second World War, we must recognize and remember that it was Madero's innocent thesis which threw into the flames of war several million men, who died defending an idea identical with his.

The second goal of the Mexican Revolution was to put the status and betterment of the many before that of the few; and the belief was that this end could not be secured without the active initiative and support of a Revolution-made government. To attack the problems instead of hoping they would be resolved of themselves some

day; to attack them at their base and not at the summit—the problems of the masses, not those of the elite—all this may seem almost
a commonplace today. Then it was the most glorious act of the
Revolution, and the highest lesson it could teach. The first objective
was no theoretical novelty, though it was new to Mexico's historic
realities. The second was a theoretical innovation, for the Mexican
Revolution—like the Russian, which was engendered without any
ideological relationship to ours—was the first great assault upon the
bastion of liberalism, at least in its aspect of *laissez faire, laissez
passer*. No further effort is necessary to show that these goals were
well chosen.

No one can doubt that in the Díaz regime, as in all systems that
have outlived themselves, the few had prevailed over the many. And
consider who were the many: all the agricultural workers of the
country, three-fourths of the total population; the workers in industry, mining, transportation; even those employed in household
shops; everyone who was "small," the merchant, the bureaucrat, and
such. The Díaz regime in its last days was a pyramidal organization.
On the apex were the "one hundred families"; the rest were desti-
tute, in greater or lesser degree. A movement that would destroy the
"hundred families" and, after doing so strengthen the economic,
social, and political status of the peasant and the worker, that of the
poor in general—such a movement had great novelty and tre-
mendous force in the Mexico of 1910 or 1916. Aside from this, agrarian reform, which sought above all the destruction of the politico-
economic power of the great landowner, is a fact that appears in the
"natural" evolution of every country: in England since the sixteenth
century and definitively in the eighteenth; in France with the Revolution of 1789; in Germany about 1848; in Russia in 1904–1907; and
in the countries of Eastern Europe at the end of the first World War.
In Argentina Perón has stated the issue, and it is one of the forces
he manipulates; in Brazil and in Chile the first symptoms of this
tragic but seemingly necessary disease are becoming manifest. As
for the labor movement, one could write a history of nineteenth-
century Europe—as well as of twentieth-century United States—
around the sole theme of the frictions and readjustments provoked
by the appearance of this new third estate.

In what might be called its third thesis, the Mexican Revolution
also was original and sure. It is true that after the first World War a

nationalistic storm was loosed throughout the world, and perhaps something may have reached us from this source, but even so, one thing cannot be disputed, and this is that we were in tune with the world and not against it. As to the wisdom of such nationalism, small doubt appears to exist. Mexico has had only two other nationalist fevers before that of the Revolution: the first created the necessary climate for Independence; the second gave the victory to Juárez' Reform and finished off foreign intervention. The nationalism of 1910 not only identified itself with the economic and cultural elevation of the Indian but exalted his physical and spiritual gifts: his dances, songs, costumes, and domestic arts, for example. First it repudiated the Europeanizing pomp of the Díaz regime; then, with greater clarity and determination, it rejected "imperialism," that is to say, all foreign influences—from politico-economic ideas to trends of fashion. In fine, it showed a passionate preference for all that was Mexican.

This nationalism, for the rest, was as wholesome as nationalism can be; in truth it never degenerated into xenophobia. Let us remember, for example, that Carranza, for the first time in our recent history, attempted serious diplomatic measures to bring about a *rapprochement* among all Latin American countries, and that Mexico, especially from 1920 to 1924, became a true home for Latin Americans, whom it welcomed and protected. It is true that both of these actions had an anti-North American origin, like, among others, Vasconcelos' program of scholarships for great numbers of Central American students to study in Mexican schools; but neither this nor other "anti's" ever defiled Mexican nationalism in those times. In fact, it can be said that one of its fruits, certainly not the least nor the most insignificant, was to make Mexico the first Spanish-speaking country aware of its culture, of its language, and of its Indian and mestizo race: a spirit and attitude which had been lost to Spanish America for a long century.

When and why the program of the Mexican Revolution was exhausted is a very painful chapter in our history; for not only has the country lost its motive force, which until now it has failed to replace, but the failure is one of the most definite tests to which the undoubtedly creative genius of the Mexican has been subjected—and the conclusions, unfortunately, could not be more discouraging.

Let us begin, then, with the following statement: without exception all the men of the Revolution were inferior to its demands; and
if, as may be argued, these demands were quite modest, one must
rightly conclude that the country, in a whole generation and in the
depths of one of its three major crises, could not produce one leader
of great stature, of the kind who deserve to be remembered in
history. The extraordinary thing about the men of the Revolution, in
magnificent contrast to those of the Díaz regime, was that, bursting
forth as they did from the soil itself, they seemed capable of giving
the country something as solid, as well founded, and as genuine as
are all things which sink their roots deep into the earth to nourish
themselves directly from it, profoundly, perennially. If the Mexican
Revolution was after all a democratic, popular, and nationalist
movement, it seemed that no one but the men who had made it
could lead it to success, because they were of the people and had
been so for generations. They had felt the whiplash of injustice on
their own flesh, and on that of their sons and fathers—the political
boss, the priest, and the lawyer—they had known loneliness, misery, ignorance, the dense and heavy mists of uncertainty, if not complete subjection. How could one fail to hope, for example, that with
Emiliano Zapata agrarian reform would be achieved—he, a poor
peasant belonging to a people who had lost their lands centuries
before and who had for generations demanded in vain their return?
The very fact that the men of the Revolution were ignorant—the
very fact that they governed by instinct rather than reason—this
seemed a promise, perhaps the best, for while reason makes distinctions instinct hits straight to the mark.

But what has been said is the truth: all the revolutionaries were
inferior to the task which the Revolution had to accomplish. Madero
destroyed the Díaz regime but he did not create democracy in
Mexico; Calles and Cárdenas ended the great landed estates, but
they failed to create a new Mexican agriculture. May it be that
instinct can destroy but that it cannot create? Enough time has
passed for us to judge the men of the Revolution with certainty:
they were magnificent destroyers, but nothing that they created to
replace what they destroyed has turned out to be indisputably
better. This is not to say that the Revolution created *nothing*, absolutely nothing. During its time new institutions were born, as well as
an important web of highways, impressive irrigation works, thou-

sands of schools, a good number of public services, industries, and agricultural areas hitherto unknown. But none of these things, in spite of their undoubted importance, has succeeded tangibly in changing the country, in making it happier. Thus the achievements of the Revolution have always remained in a most vulnerable posture: exposed to the fury of their enemies, they have not engendered in their supporters the burning conviction that comes with the knowledge that the task has been well done. For the justification of the Mexican Revolution, as of all revolutions, of all movements which subvert established orders, cannot be other than the conviction of its necessity, of the fact that without it the country would be in a worse condition.

To create in Mexico a democracy with some aspects of authenticity is of course a task that would discourage any sensitive man. It is so complex, so arduous, and so slow that it should be conceived as the consequence or end of many other changes and not as a task in itself, to be met head on, let us say. A country whose scanty population is scattered into an infinity of tiny settlements in which civic life is at present impossible, settlements which live isolated from each other, out of the reach of knowledge and of wealth—such a country cannot suddenly create a favorable environment for conscientious and responsible civic life. It would be necessary beforehand to increase the population, for which end our soil would have to be made more productive; to complete our physical communications, increasing our railway system fivefold, our highways tenfold, our airways one hundredfold; to create, as nearly as possible, a system for the communication of ideas as well, with complete postal and telegraphic services and all the means of expression, making these both honest and accessible (books, newspapers, radio); to inaugurate gigantic projects in hygiene, educational propaganda, and economic production aimed at saving from death so many children who today die in their first years. In short, what would be necessary is educative action—slow, consistent, and extremely costly—to give all Mexicans a common consciousness of their past, of their interests, and of their problems. Such a task could have begun only once before in the history of Mexico: in 1867, when the victory of the Liberal Party was achieved; when the country, though it had less resources, had fewer necessities; and when the country was led by a group of men without equal in our history, men with the virile optimism of those who feel a nation being born from their own hands, and for whom liberalism was a new religious faith. Juárez and Lerdo in fact attempted it, as did Iglesias, Zarco, and Zamacona, with great energy and consistency; but in the end they succumbed to the blows of a militarism which the country's agony of intervention and empire could not purify.

Of course the Mexican Revolution did not intend to take on this Cyclopean task, much less in a systematic way. Its first act was to attack a regime which not only had clung to political power long beyond its time but which with inhuman obstinacy rejected the opportunity of renewing itself by admitting fresh vitality, new blood. The Revolution, consequently, set out only to ventilate, to change the political atmosphere of the country; and, on the positive side, to create public opinion, and to make easier its expression; to provoke opposite views as well and at all events to respect them; to assure periodic and peaceful renewal of the men in power, giving admittance to new talents. The idea itself that the principal task of the Revolution was to alleviate the economic, social, political, and cultural condition of the great masses led to the hope that in these masses there would eventually awaken a genuine interest in government, and a necessity to participate in it in order to defend their new rights and interests.

It is difficult to judge the civic progress of Mexico since 1910 with a certainty free of prejudice or passion. Justo Sierra would not have thought it small, had he assayed it with that superior and distant kindness with which he wrote all our history. One needs but a touch of the moralist, however, to label it as of little worth.

It was no mean feat to replace the principal government leaders at short intervals, and many times in spite of their wishes and their efforts. Thus was dictatorship avoided, and even the dominant and prolonged influence of any one man. But one cannot forget that this renewal in office has sometimes been brought about at the price of violence and even of crime; nor that the process has had a flavor of dynastic rule and palace intrigue rather than of popular choice, so narrow and so uniform has been the group from which the "elect" have come! Nor can one forget that the process has been truly fissiparous, reproducing itself after the manner of inferior biological organisms.

More significant yet is the fact that these changes in office have not undergone to date the only test that could give them a genuinely democratic character—victory at the polls of a party or group which is alien or, better yet, opposed to the government. This last perhaps was not a matter of distressing urgency while the Revolution had sufficient prestige and moral authority to suppose that the people were with it, and that consequently it did not matter very much who was its physical embodiment. But now that the Revolution has lost this prestige and moral authority, when even its aims are confounded, now it should be necessary to submit to the people the actual naming of its leaders, for the question is no longer a matter of persons but of what is known esoterically as "the system." Then one might see whether Mexico's civic progress has been if not complete at least genuine. Moreover, let us not be deceived if this test should occur when it is too late: in six years, for example, the differences between the Mexican Revolution and the conservative parties may be so insubstantial that the latter may slip into the government, no longer as opponents but as near relations. Very much the same thing would happen if the revolutionary government made slight electoral concessions to the opposition parties, concessions which, while sufficient for the government to sprinkle itself with the rosewater of democracy, would prevent the opposition from participating in any effective way in the government, but which nevertheless would give full satisfaction to the interests of those parties, especially their economic interests, by means of a "constructive" government program. In such a case, not only would there be no democratic advance but the Revolution would reach the extremes of sterility, for all of its efforts would be expended in retaining power, with no other motive but political and economic greed.

The blackest of omens is the role played by the Congress in the revolutionary era. All congressional bodies have ceased to be organs of government in a technical sense, to the point that for some time there has not originated in a congress anywhere in the world a revenue law or a budget for public expenditures; that is to say, they no longer accomplish the ends which are supposed to be the very essence of a parliament. But in any democratic country the congress continues to discharge equally important functions, acting as censor to the executive, as an organ expressing public opinion, and as final judge in acts of such great national importance as a declaration of war. If we judge our own according to this model, so modest from an intellectual and a technical point of view, so fertile from a civic, our judgment cannot be other than the most vehement and absolute condemnation. In the revolutionary legislatures there never has occurred a single debate that deserves to be remembered, as do those of the legislatures of 1856 to 1876; and, if there were any doubt about the matter, it would only be necessary to consider the way in which the recent amendment of Article 3 of the Constitution was made or, on the other hand, how its extremist wording was approved years ago. The revolutionary congresses have been as servile as those of the Díaz regime, with the difference that the latter was by definition a tyranny, and that the Revolution is, also by definition, rebellion, independence. In the eyes of the nation, without consideration of classes or groups, there is nothing so despicable as a congressman or a senator. They have become the yardstick of all human misery. That is why the civic progress that Mexico has achieved in these last years seems so vulnerable, because to expect the restoration of the Congress in its full prestige as a governmental organ essential to a democracy is hopeless.

We have said that the task of making Mexico into a great democracy could not have been attempted except in 1867. This can be seen by considering the character of the periodical press of the time —the great instrument in shaping public opinion and with it democracy itself—and the character which the press assumed after 1896, partly as consequence of an unfortunate contagion from abroad. Of the sixty Mexico City dailies in the Juárez and Lerdo era, only two or three remained; in place of the partisan periodical written by the best pens of the country—the best in literary quality, moral authority, and strength and honesty of political convictions—there appears the informative newspaper, a "mere assembly plant of news," the major part of which is manufactured abroad; to replace the motives of political and social faith came the appetite for money. Mexican democracy will never cease to lament that unhappy transformation of the periodical press, a transformation which on the other hand has been general throughout the world. But even so, the case of Mexico's modern press is pathetic because in any European or Yankee capital, and in several of South America, there is always some newspaper which is honest and effective, to which one may turn in search of an informed and just opinion, a newspaper which not only records the facts truthfully but which comments and evaluates. That is why the press of this country must carry upon its shoulders an immense responsibility: it has exchanged the superior and lasting satisfaction of enlightening the public for the fugitive and worldly pleasure of enriching itself; it has denied to the people of Mexico, in sum, all guidance and all light.

Extreme class distinctions are a very old phenomenon in Mexico; it could be said in fact that all our history has been one long and distressing effort to diminish them. There were social inequalities among the Indian communities before the Conquest; they existed during the colonial period and during the era of the war for Independence. The Porfirio Díaz regime, therefore, cannot be saddled with responsibility for all of them; and yet, its long duration, its very stability, made these differences more apparent and more rigid, incarnate in actual persons, with that irritating ostentation which resides in the palpable.

The Mexican Revolution was in fact a revolt of the impoverished many against the wealthy few. And since the wealth of the country was agricultural, revolution was directed perforce against the great landowners. For that reason too agrarian reform took in large measure the oversimplified character of a mere distribution of the great riches of the few to alleviate the poverty of the many. Once it had triumphed, the Revolution made some efforts—few, weak, and almost always foolish—to justify agrarian reform on other grounds: those of jurisprudence, economics, and even agricultural technology. But the reason which made reform irresistible came from the purest Christian source: a feeling of obvious social injustice.

Unfortunately, in order to endure, even a measure justified by the best moral and social reasons needs some success to sustain it; in the case of economic activity success can be measured only in terms of profits made. These in turn depend—as economists proclaim to no avail—on the good use of factors of production. Now then, agriculture during the Díaz regime was weak in leadership and initiative since it became in large measure an extractive industry owned by absentees; it also was weak in respect to the soil because of natural limitations and lack of technology. On the other hand it was strong in regard to capital because whether much or little it all belonged to the landowner, and because the labor involved, moderate and somewhat mechanical, received an extremely low wage.

From this point of view—and it is of course the most important one—it could be said at first that agrarian reform was socially justified because it gave the peasant the satisfaction of being a landowner. But as time went on it could maintain itself only if the peasant-owner received more from his work than he had as a peasant-hired man. For such an improvement it was necessary that the new agriculture be more profitable than the old, and this required in turn that the elements of production be employed in a better fashion. It was necessary that the leadership be wiser, that a new capital advantageously replace that of the landowner, and that capital and technology be used to overcome some of our more serious natural limitations, which since times long past had been strangling Mexican agriculture.

This was a problem that required vision and initiative, technology, consistency, and honesty; and in every way the Revolution was quite inadequate to these needs. It lacked the vision necessary to grasp the panorama of our agriculture and to draw from it what might justly be called the strategy of agrarian reform. Reform should have begun in the zones where industrial crops were cultivated (sugar, coffee, cotton), the most prosperous and advanced, and not—as really took place—in the cereal zones, on the plateau, where the natural conditions of soil and climate are decidedly unfavorable. Initiative was lacking also, for the Revolution awakened too late to the idea that agrarian reform involved more than partitioning the great estates and giving the pieces to the peasants. This fact is evident: the first credit institution for the new agriculture and the initial attempt to reform teaching of agricultural methods date from 1925, that is ten years after the first agrarian law, the famous one of January 6, 1915.

Technology was lacking; from the beginning it was not understood that merely shifting the title to the land could not produce the miracle of greater profits from labor which operated under exactly the same physical, economic, and technological conditions. No serious effort was made to discover what changes in methods and in crops could best overcome the unfavorable conditions in which our agriculture has always existed. It is said, for example, that Russian geneticists have developed, from Mexican varieties, a hybrid corn which by shortening the growing period of the plant escapes both early and late frosts, so frequent an occurrence in Mexico. But because of a lack of technological institutions and technical spirit, not only has the experiment originated abroad but its advantages have not been proved or applied in Mexico to date.

There was also a lack of consistency, of arduous and sustained effort, the only kind which could lead to tangible and enduring results. It is sufficient to examine the consistency not of the obscure work of some agricultural experiment station, which depends above all on accumulating data year after year, but of the ordinary yet more significant procedure by which the *ejidos* have been parceled out. It will be seen then that there was no consistency and that furthermore the grants of land have not always been dictated by prudence or necessity, but rather by the desire of each particular person in power to appear as the bravest dispenser of lands. Consistency in the form of logic and thoroughness also was lacking; the lands were given to the peasants but not the means to process the products which they derived from them. The flour, rice, and sugar mills, the equipment for drying and roasting coffee beans, the cotton gins, and the oil presses remained the property of the former owners of the land, that is to say of the enemies of the new owners under the agrarian law. Furthermore, many of the great projects of the Revolution should have been inspired by the firm belief that agrarian reform must be successful at all costs. A great part of the educational and sanitation work should have been developed in relation to the agrarian colonies; highways should never have been built merely to attract tourists until the *ejidos* had the roads necessary for their social and economic ends. The same is true of irrigation projects, public health, and social improvement.

As for honesty—is it necessary to give details?

This is not to say, nevertheless, that agrarian reform did not produce some favorable results; only that its success has not been great enough to command a favorable public opinion. The truth is that the program is in the worst condition possible. Its destructive work was harsh enough to bring down upon it all the hate and resentment of those who suffered thereby, and of those whose interests are opposed to the principles which inspired it; but in its constructive aspects its success has not been sufficiently clear to maintain the unshakeable faith of those who expected of it terrestrial bliss for ten or twelve million Mexicans.

In its beginnings the Mexican Revolution was more a revolution of farmers than of industrial workers, but since it always had a popular character it soon made of labor one of its most useful supports. In its turn the Revolution gave the worker such personality and strength that already in 1917, in Article 123 of the Revolutionary Constitution, the labor question was given equal importance with that received, in Article 27, by the problems of agrarian reform, of mining policy, especially the petroleum question, and in general by the problems of all the "modifications of private property" that occasioned such great alarm among the Mexican and foreign *bourgeoisie*. Labor legislation in time has become more prolix than even the legislation on agrarian reform; the activities and size of the tribunals charged with its application are in no way inferior to those of the administrative organs required by the agrarian laws. The labor movement soon became stronger and more solidly based than the agrarian. Some Mexican government leaders made "socialist" experiments in the labor field which have no parallel in that of agriculture. Such for example was the administration by the workers of the National Railways and the railways of Yucatán, of the sugar mill of Zacatepec, of various mining operations, and of some industrial plants. In sum, the Mexican Revolution became, if you will, more industrial than agricultural, more urban than rural. At the same time, the Revolution has encountered few sources of embarrassment and disrepute like those which the labor movement has given it. Why? Because labor at its best has been confused; at its worst it has been irresponsible, dishonest, lacking in superior vision, and even in great initiative or simple political drive. But this, in turn, has its explanation.

The labor movement, emerging as a new economic and political force, disrupted an established equilibrium in all parts of the world, incurring by this sole act the necessary displeasure of those sections of society which represented the old forces, usufructuaries of the stability which every equilibrium presupposes. The state in the beginning opposed the organization of labor because it persisted in maintaining the equilibrium; but convinced at length that its efforts were in vain, it discovered that this new force could either make it all-powerful or destroy it. This gave rise to one of the most serious problems of our time. And it was not long before three main solutions to the problem appeared. Fascism and communism each suppressed one of the disputants: fascism the worker, communism the capitalist. Democracy, on its part, declared itself alien to the dispute and announced that its role would be merely that of a "referee," that is, one who arbitrates a contest but neither prevents nor suppresses it. For this purpose it devised industrial legislation which, in spite of the great complexity introduced into it by the jurists, is not different in its conception, its methods, and its ends from the rules of the Marquis of Queensberry, which govern pugilistic encounters.

The Mexican Revolution did not have sufficient genius to devise a juridical system which, without impeding the spontaneous birth and development of labor disputes, would permit their efficacious solution in the superior interests of the community. Furthermore, in its simple role as "referee," it has been so constantly and unnecessarily partial that it has "ganged up" on labor's opponents. All the risk and dignity of a contest between two honest rivals has disappeared. All labor legislation was conceived to favor the worker. It could not and should not be otherwise, since by definition the worker is the weaker party, facing the almost invincible power of wealth. But in administering this legislation, the revolutionary governments, without even condescending to play the friendly conciliator or impartial judge, have ruled almost always in favor of the worker, no matter how notoriously unjust or grotesquely puerile may have been the specific cause defended at the moment by the worker.

Not only have the courts in the majority of cases decided in favor of the worker, but they have always made the employer pay him back wages. In this manner the worker has lost the sense of danger, of risk or adventure inherent in all struggles, which he needs to strengthen him so that he may stand alone and win his own victories. The employer has lost his faith in justice; and once over his first reaction of vengeful resentment, he has set himself to corrupting the labor leaders as the only means of preventing his conflicts with the workers from reaching the courts.

The harm done to the cause of labor—which being the best of causes has a permanent value—has been illimitable and to a certain extent irreparable. In the first place an opposition has been created, so bitter that nowadays labor hardly has a defender who is sincere and disinterested: to capitalists and reactionaries all ills come from the irresponsible and excessive power of the workers; as for honest liberals, they do not want to defend labor's cause without first trying to cleanse it of all the excrescences produced by a blind governmental policy. In the second place, the government has wasted all of its many opportunities to gradually develop in the organization of labor not only a conscience and a sense of responsibility, but also a feeling of independence from official favor and of dependence on its own resources, the latter being as important as the former. The Mexican labor movement has come to depend so completely on protection and support from official sources that it has been transformed into a mere appendage to the government, whose every step it follows: good, doubtful, or frankly censurable. In fact, it is nothing but a governmental instrument and has no other role but to serve the government as a claque. This marriage has been harmful to both spouses. It has prevented the government from resolving problems of great importance to the general economy, such as those of the railroads and the oil fields, problems whose solution would have given it the prestige and authority which it so badly needs. Labor has been degraded and dishonored, and, even worse, it has been condemned to disappear or be pulverized the instant it ceases to hold official favor, leaving no trace except a memory of the sad figure it cut in life, that of the bully.

Nonetheless, the achievements of the Mexican Revolution in pursuing its three major objectives: political liberty, agrarian reform, and labor organization, have been neither slight nor meager. They would have been enough to maintain for a long time the moral authority of revolutionary governments, if in the eyes of the nation the efforts made to achieve these goals had possessed an immaculate probity. What was humanly impossible was to have faith in mediocre and dishonest officials. Thus a general administrative corruption—ostentatious and offensive, always cloaked under a mantle of impunity to which only the most refined virtue should aspire—has spoiled the whole program of the Revolution, with its attempts and its successes, to the point that the country no longer cares to know what the original program was, what efforts were made to achieve it, and whether there were any results. Mexico's sole aspiration is sweeping renewal, true purification, which can be satisfied only by a fire that will raze even the soil itself in which so much evil flourished.

It must be remembered that the Revolution was a most violent movement, whose destructive visage is gradually being forgotten. It exterminated an entire generation of men, many groups, and whole institutions: it wiped out the army and the bureaucracy of Porfirio Díaz' time; it put an end to the most powerful and richest class, that of the great and middle-sized landowners, causing most of the higher and a good part of the petty middle class to disappear; it caused many of the best sources of national wealth—transportation, the sugar industry, all raising of livestock—to languish to the point of extinction. Even some great professional groups—university teachers, for example—saw their ranks so reduced that even their cadres properly ceased to exist. The Mexican Revolution, in sum, created an enormous vacuum of wealth and unmade the social and economic hierarchy that had been fashioned in the course of almost half a century.

This nearly complete devastation of the national wealth was received by some with jubilation, by others as a happy omen that in the future Mexico's resources, though limited, would be equally distributed. At some time in our revolutionary history, the inspiring statement that in Mexico there was not a single millionaire and that large social groups were bettering their economic conditions could have been true. But sad realities soon asserted themselves in the necessity of recreating the wealth which had been destroyed. No greater burden fell on the shoulders of the men of the Revolution; it was the most severe proof of their rectitude, fortitude, and creative capacity. The failure of the Revolution in this great moral test was the most flagrant of its shortcomings. Instead of being distributed equally among the most numerous groups and among those in greatest need of moving up the social scale, the new wealth was allowed to fall into the hands of a few, who of course had no special merit of any kind. Wherefore the bloody paradox in which the government, while waving the revindicatory flag of an impoverished people, by prevarication and by theft and embezzlement, created a new high and low middle class which in the end dragged the Revolution and the country itself once more to the brink of social and economic inequality.

With the Revolution the previous hierarchy disappeared, and that fact also contributed to the general dishonesty: the whirlwind carried the rubbish skywards; men suddenly found themselves making salaries of a thousand pesos, which they tried to preserve forever by stealing a million while the whirlwind lasted. Not among the least causes for dishonesty in government is the constant insecurity of man and woman in this land, because to the state's omnipotence we must add an arbitrariness which has all the marks of a Biblical curse. Victim of it the Mexican falls and rises, again and again, during the whole span of his life until death permanently ends his struggle. And the man who lives insecurely tries to protect himself, not caring whether in doing so he violates a law or sets aside a moral precept.

Administrative dishonesty in Mexico has its causes, which we have barely outlined. They do not mitigate its social monstrosity by a single jot or lessen in any way its deadly political effects, for the dishonesty of revolutionary leaders more than any other factor has split the very heart of the Mexican Revolution.

In its first attack upon the old regime the Revolution did not even mention the vices of Díaz' educational system, which was very vulnerable to criticism in spite of the fact that it enjoyed the support of such a monumental figure as that of Don Justo Sierra. Already during the life of the regime men like Antonio Caso, Pedro Henríquez Ureña, and Alfonso Reyes had pointed out the limitations of the higher philosophy on which it was based. But this was not by far its principal fault. With all its weaknesses, higher education was not bad, either for the country or for the times; more than that, it embodied a seriousness and dignity which it soon lost and which it has not recovered. On the other hand, popular schooling, the primary and rural schools, and the most necessary technological training—in agriculture, for example—were limited in the extreme, both as to ideas and as to number and efficacy. In this the Díaz regime gave a true and correct picture of itself: the educative effort of the government was exercised exclusively among the middle classes of the great urban centers, with the vain pretension of creating an elite from whom at a later date would pour forth the light of redemption to illumine all the Mexican people. To the small, populated places—that is to say, to the country as a whole—would some day trickle, with the "necessary" passing of time, the waters from that distant spring.

José Vasconcelos in 1921 personified the educative aspirations of the Revolution as no man ever embodied, let us say, agrarian reform or the labor movement. In the first place, Vasconcelos was what is known as an "intellectual," that is to say a man of books and intelligent preoccupations. In the second place, he had attained sufficient maturity to see the faults of the Díaz philosophy, but was young enough not only to rebel against it but to have faith in the transforming powers of education. In the third place, Vasconcelos was the only intellectual of first rank in whom a Revolutionary regime had confidence enough to give authority and means to work. The conjunction of such unheard-of circumstances produced unexpected results. There appeared in Mexico a brilliant aurora borealis heralding a new day. Education was understood no longer as education for an urban middle class but in the only way that it can be understood in Mexico —as a religious mission, an apostolic mission which rushes into all corners of the country carrying the good news that the nation has wakened from its lethargy, that it rises and goes forth. At that time there really was the evangelical impulse to teach one's neighbor to read and write; then there really existed in the heart of every Mexican a feeling that the need for education was as great and as human as the need to slake thirst or to kill hunger. It was then that the first great mural paintings appeared, monuments which aspired to fix for centuries the sufferings of the land, its problems, and its hopes. Then one did feel faith in books, in books of perennial quality; and books were printed by the thousands, and by the thousands were given away. To establish a library in a small and remote town had as much significance as building a church and putting on its cupola brilliant mosaics announcing to the traveler the proximity of a home where he could rest and find shelter. Then the festivals of popular dance and song were not curiosities for the tourist's sheeplike eyes, but were presented for Mexicans, for our own encouragement and our own delight. Then was the theater a popular form, for free political satire, and above all, the mirror of custom, vice, virtue, and aspirations.

Had Vasconcelos died in 1923, he would have gained immortality, for his name would have been indissolubly associated with that era of magnificent spiritual renaissance in Mexico. But Vasconcelos continued to personify, and still personifies, all the vicissitudes of education in Mexico. In 1923 he was fighting his best friends and supporters: Antonio Caso and Pedro Henríquez Ureña, Vicente Lombardo Toledano and Alfonso Caso. The places which they vacated were occupied by bards who had learned the arts of flattery from their adolescence. By 1924 the apostle of education, the teacher of youth, the Quiroga, the Motolinía, the Las Casas of the twentieth century, turned out to be a modest but ambitious politician, who inevitably was swept away, drowned, and effaced in the vortex of politics. And he not only left his work unfinished—the most important and urgent task in the country—but he brought into disrepute the name, the profession, and the intentions of the intellectual to the point that the Revolution never relied upon another.

Vasconcelos exiled himself, first to fail as a university professor, then to shut himself up for long years in France, Spain, and Argentina, neglecting to read, to study, to see things, not dealing with or meeting anyone, blinded and obstinate—all in a sterile sacrifice which could benefit neither him nor his country. And there he is, the symbol of the educative aspirations of the Revolution: ailing, disoriented, arbitrary, inconsistent, converted to Catholicism shamefully and tardily, thus losing the respect of the liberals without gaining that of the Catholics.

It could be said that it is unjust to identify the glory and the misery of one man with a work which was collective and for that reason enduring. It is in truth, but only in one sense: the educative effort of the Revolution did not end with Vasconcelos' abandonment of his ministry; its momentum lasted perhaps ten or twelve years more. During those last years, once the evangelical tension was relaxed, the work already begun was amplified, polished, and rounded in many important aspects. But its trajectory was identical with that of the man who personified it in its moment of glory: in the end it became chaotically inconsistent, its accomplishments much more apparent than real; and above all it failed in its attempt to win over the youth of the country. Today youth is reactionary, an enemy to the Revolution, just as Vasconcelos has been and still is.

If we judge the present situation of Mexico with any degree of severity, it is difficult to avoid the conclusion that the country is passing through a most serious crisis. The magnitude of this crisis leads us to think that if it is underestimated or ignored, if the best efforts are not immediately employed to lead the country out of it, Mexico will drift aimlessly, without a definite course, losing time that cannot be lost by a land so far behind in its progress; and it will end by entrusting its major problems to inspiration, or to imitation of and submission to the United States, not only because the United

States is a rich and powerful neighbor but because it has been successful in a way that we have not been able to imitate. We would call on that country for money, for technical training, for patterns in culture and art, for political advice; and we would end by adopting unchanged its whole scale of values, so alien to our history, our interests, and our taste. To the North American influence, of itself overpowering, would be added the dissembled conviction of some, the frank interests of others, the indifference or the pessimism of the majority, making possible the sacrifice of our nationality and, more important still, of the security, authority, and happiness we may gain by forging our own destinies. Many of Mexico's problems would then be resolved; the country might even enjoy an unaccustomed material prosperity. But are we sure that our people, ourselves even, would in truth be happier? Our Indian, for example. Would he gain by passing into the unredeemed status now occupied by the Negro in the United States?

What could the country do to recover its course, to attain along with material progress a better political, social, and human organization?

One solution immediately comes to mind: to hand over the government to the Right. Since the Left has worn itself out carrying its program as far as it could, an effort which after all has taken it thirty years, since the Left has become corrupted and no longer counts with the moral or even the political authority necessary to create an efficient and acceptable government, then let the Right have its turn, for it has not led the country since 1910.

It takes a heart-rending effort not to recommend this solution, at least out of the simple but human desire for purification, for making a clean slate of everything. Undoubtedly the Left would have to cleanse itself or die. Labor would lose its mentor and supporter, but it would become independent; it would have to close ranks, expelling its venal leaders, creating resistance funds, and husbanding its power to make use of it only for just and important causes. All workers would perceive from bitter daily experience that their interests are theirs and theirs alone. The workers would not be the only ones who would need to purify and strengthen themselves; the farmers also, though they have fewer means to accomplish it. Among them too are dishonest leaders, and a submission to the government that borders on the old feudal servitude from which they hoped to liberate themselves. Likewise, they already have the psychology of those who receive without merit and without effort—the same that their ancestors have had since colonial times.

The liberals would have to undergo a like process. With the Right in power, the hairy, clawlike hand of the Church would show itself bare, with all its greed for power, all its incurable obscurantism toward the problems of the country and its best men. The Church would persecute the liberals, it would eject them from their posts, from their university chairs; it would deny education to their children. The liberals would quickly become victims of a general ostracism. They would also feel in full force the unleashed persecution of an intolerant and uncomprehending press, blind and devoted servant of the most transitory and petty interests. The rich would cast aside all subterfuge and would show themselves: ostentatious, haughty, despotic, big-bellied, and encrusted with jewels and furs, as they already begin to appear in press photographs. The liberal would be caught by surprise and belittled; then he would feel the anxiety of the man who is no longer master of his destiny; finally he would be despised and persecuted. And he would have to react, to reunite with others like himself, to fight back militantly and together. In such manner the liberal would again take up the task which he has now abandoned: to lead the country wisely along cleaner and less obstructed paths, first regaining political power in a struggle which no doubt would be risky and hard, but in which he would temper his body and his spirit. In theory this solution even would have the advantage of giving the United States a moral and political lesson, since the United States has shown so little interest in the true and healthy progress of its neighbor and friend, and so much in Mexico's cheap and silent submission.

Only two considerations prevent our recommending that solution: its dangers, surely, and even more the fear that we would obtain no other benefit than to become the theater of a new and sterile struggle. For Mexico can expect very little from the Right.

The Mexican Right, as is true of right-wing parties throughout the world, extends no cordial hand; it lacks the understanding and the generosity that is so greatly needed by our unfortunate country. Furthermore, it offers us nothing that is new or better than what we now have. It seems then that Mexico could not find itself in a more desperate and distressing position, for it cannot hope to better itself by appealing to the very simple formula of changing its government and political label. Such a course could attain nothing but the eventual purification of the Left.

Let us turn our thoughts away from the Sinarquistas, a party with an intellectual vulgarity proper to the deserts, and from the right-wing parties which arose from dissension among Revolutionary factions. Let us consider Acción Nacional. It seems clear to me that Acción Nacional counts solely on three sources of support: the Catholic Church, the new plutocracy, and those who have lost confidence in the Revolutionary governments; but Acción Nacional reveals its ultimate weakness in the fact that it depends much more on the third source than on the other two, and this in spite of the traditional generosity of the Catholic Church, which is quick to suckle any retrograde party. This means that Acción Nacional would collapse after forming a government. That moment reached, what would keep it alive and help it guide the country? It does not have today either men or principles and, consequently, could improvise neither the one nor the other. In its long years of existence, its scanty and intermittent activity has been devoted to a labor of denunciation; but it has said little or nothing about the way it would organize the institutions of the land. I seem to remember that once it did maintain that the "base" of education is the family, something that can mean either very little or too much, more probably the former than the latter.

And who are the men of Acción Nacional? They have no "sex appeal" for the Mexican public. None of their leaders come from the people, or even from the country or the village. They are from the upper middle class; their interests and experience are confined to the walls of the office or the twilight of the church. They know no other air than the fumes which rise from the asphalted streets of the great cities. They are those who in Porfirio Díaz' time were known as the "decent" people, which meant from the point of view of form a distant reminiscence of the English mode of dress, and at bottom a Little Lord Fauntleroy mentality. And, to repeat, much of the value that these men of Acción Nacional seem to have today comes from the disrepute suffered by the men of the Revolution. The press and the Church have made of Manuel Gómez Morín, head of Acción Nacional, an almost-saint, and of Vicente Lombardo Toledano, the major figure in the labor movement, an almost-villain. But Manuel

Gómez Morín knows better than anyone else in this world that he is not Lombardo's superior, either mentally or morally. The fact that so many young Mexicans voted in favor of Dr. Mario Torroella for senator from the Federal District has only one explanation; they voted against Fidel Velázquez, secretary of the Workers' Confederation, for one cannot seriously suppose that the former can be objectively viewed as a better legislator or government official. There is one undoubted merit that the men in Acción Nacional do possess, Manuel Gómez Morín more than any of the rest, of course. They were the first to shake off the political apathy so characteristic of Mexicans; they were the first to preoccupy themselves as a group with some of the problems facing the land, and to propose solutions different from the official formulas. In sum, they have sacrificed part of their well-being (be it large or small) in opposition to the government. But their defects are much greater than their merits; they represent, they are instruments of, not Catholicism but an ecclesiastic hierarchy which has no moral superiority of any sort; they represent or they play up to questionable plutocratic interests.

Mexico may and should have a well-founded mistrust for a party, for any party, which has not known how to forge a clear program during its fasting period as the opposition, a program truly of national action, not one that merely gives the comforting impression of moving toward a new day instead of toward the dead and silent night.

That same distrust, but in extreme degree, should we feel toward a military party, something that unfortunately we cannot lightly discount. Most of the leaders of the Revolution were military men; yet no sensible Mexican saw a major obstacle in that fact, because they came from the people and not from a caste, and because they themselves had made the Revolution. The same thing may not be said today. For one thing, those leaders have suffered the same relaxing process which the Revolution has suffered; for another, some of them are dead and others have lost their influence. We do not know well enough those who have taken their places; but it would not be at all strange if they believed, as every professional soldier does, that they represent order and the national dignity. As long as they are the only ones who believe it, so much the better; but the danger will be acute if civilians begin to share this opinion. Then we would have order, much order, but very little dignity, either national or personal.

What remedy, then, is there for Mexico's crisis? We have said that it is grave. On the one hand, the cause of the Revolution has ceased to inspire that faith which all navigation charts must inspire if the pilot is to remain at his post; to that must be added the fact that the men of the Revolution have exhausted their moral and political leadership. On the other hand, there is no clear basis on which to found the hope that redemption may come from the Right, because of the interests which it represents, because of its antipopular spirit, and because of its lack of preparation.

The only ray of hope—quite pale and distant to be sure—is that from the Revolution itself there may come a reaffirmation of principles and a purification of men. It may not be worth the trouble to speculate on miracles; but at least I would like to be clearly understood: to reaffirm means to affirm anew, and to purify would mean to use only those men who are unsullied and honest. If principles are not reaffirmed but merely juggled about, if men are not purified but merely dressed up in their Sunday best and decorated with titles (of lawyers!), then there will be no autoregeneration in Mexico; and consequently regeneration will come from the outside. The country will lose much of its national identity, and in no long period of time.

MEXICO AND THE UNITED STATES*

RELATIONS BETWEEN MEXICO and the United States present a problem that is extremely complex. For that reason, it can be set forth usefully and appropriately, with each of its many elements given just value, only after sustained meditation. Otherwise the picture, instead of being carefully considered, will turn out to be partial and even grotesque. These pages merely attempt a preliminary approximation to the more solid and detailed statement of the problem which someone with better qualifications may sometime essay.

Official relations between the two countries today are excellent. With the exception of Canada, it is doubtful that the United States has had better at any time with any other country, especially with any of its neighbors. In fact, aside from the old problem of the Chamizal† (where lack of agreement damages the United States in

---

* First published in *Cuadernos Americanos*, Año VI, 6, November 1947, Vol. XXXVI.

† It was announced on July 18, 1963 that the problem of the Chamizal has been resolved by turning over to Mexico this 437 acre area—an area which, until the formal convention is signed, is still a part of the city of El Paso. The United States will receive approximately one-third of Cordova Island, another piece of land the sovereignty of which was brought into question by changes in the main channel of the Rio Grande. Reimbursement for property and for

Mexican eyes) there is no important matter pending between the two countries that requires settlement. Mexico has completed payment of the debt incurred in the expropriation of the foreign oil company holdings. Other debts resulting from government and railroad loans and from decisions of the Mexican-United States Claims Commission for personal and property damages to United States citizens during the Revolution (mainly during the decade 1910–1920) are being amortized. Although the North American government did not in fact pay the Mexican claims, these, having been deducted from the larger total owed by Mexico, are no longer pending. To the settlement of great problems between the two countries we must add the visits of President Truman to Mexico and President Alemán to the United States. For the first time they have given to good relations a certain air of popular sympathy or, at least, popular tolerance.

And yet I believe that Mexico and the United States are so far from resolving their problems that, in truth, it can be said that the process of understanding has not yet even begun. The abundance of past issues, the persistence and magnitude of present ones, could ruin official relations or convert them into a meaningless farce. And not, of course, because the leaders of either country lack goodwill or even intelligence, but because the forces working against good relations are numerous and persistent, exceptionally vigorous, and, to make matters worse, irrational in nature.

I suppose that most foreigners—and certainly the majority of North Americans—seeking an explanation would think first of this historic fact: Mexico and the United States fought a war a century ago, which ended not only with the complete victory of North American arms but with the loss by Mexico of more than half its territory. And then, in 1914 and in 1917, first United States naval and then United States land forces occupied part of the soil which had been left to the Mexicans.

Nevertheless I am convinced that those events, painful and unjustifiable as they undoubtedly were, have left in the Mexican neither a desire for revenge, nor a feeling of enduring rancor. It was

the cost of relocating some 3,500 persons living in El Chamizal will be paid for in part by a payment of $4,676,000 from Mexico to the United States. [publisher] to be expected, of course, that they should create in him feelings of distrust and skepticism. We are not able to suppress a slight smile before avowals (and worse if they are repeated too often) that from today on, let us say, we are the greatest of friends. If there ever is true friendship between the United States and Mexico, it will not be the instantaneous result of a declaration by a North American politician, even though his name be Roosevelt and the name of his declaration the Good Neighbor Policy.

The animosity of the Mexican toward the North American arises in part from the memory of those painful events. But in a much greater measure it is of recent origin, and is made up of reactions that are purely irrational; more than anything else it is born of the fact that the two countries follow different paths which, notwithstanding, fatally converge.

These reactions, causing much of the Mexican hostility toward the United States, are dangerous because their irrational character makes them all the more difficult to explain and to control. Some arise from points that are childish but real. The Mexican, for example, is irritated by the noisy haste of the North American, and annoyed by his weakness for rubbish, one of his most lamentable characteristics. At other times these irrational reactions are born from more serious matters, humanly speaking. The Mexican, who endures the continuous presence of the Yankee tourist, comes to consider him a new Croesus, a conscienceless wastrel in a poverty-stricken country. And the fact that the *peladito,* through necessity or slyness, wheedles a few coins out of the tourist cannot but exasperate the Mexican.

The North American of course has preconceptions of his own about the Mexican. There is not the least doubt, for example, that he considers the Mexican his inferior physically, intellectually, and morally. The Mexican is viewed as inconstant and irresolute, as having limited vitality, as being inclined to laxness, ready to take on obligations which later he is neither able nor willing to meet, as being endowed with small imagination and quick to understand a problem but slow in finding its solution—not to mention the fact that the problems which the Mexican *sees* are not tangible problems, the physical or chemical, but those which are vaguely and grandiloquently called "transcendental." At best the North American finds the Mexican unnecessarily courteous and "colorful," that is to say, picturesque; and when he is very, very discerning, he comes to the obvious but negative conclusion that the Mexican is complicated in the extreme.

The truth is that the Mexican and the North American are two radically different beings; they have different attitudes toward life and the world in general, and they have different scales of values.

The North American, fabulously rich, is accustomed to count up what he has, what he makes, and what he loses; hence his tendency to base many of his value judgments on magnitude, on quantity. The Mexican, thoroughly poor as he usually is, has very little or absolutely nothing to reckon up, and consequently the notion of magnitude or quantity is somewhat strange to him; for this reason he bases, or endeavors to base, his judgments on the notion of quality. The North American, who in his country has natural resources that no other country has known until now (perhaps Russia may have them), has found through experience that he can do things, and that their accomplishment requires only determination and effort. This makes him naturally active and confident. Mexico is poor in physical resources; for that reason the Mexican believes that his determination and his effort are not enough, that before and above man there are given conditions—providential, he would call them—which are very difficult or impossible to set aside. This makes him a skeptic, distrustful of action, a believer in forces superior to himself, more likely to cavil than to act. He leaves for tomorrow many of his enterprises, not from laziness or mere indecision, but because the insufficiency of his resources has taught him over and over again that you can't make the day dawn any sooner no matter how early you get up in the morning.

This same disparity of means has produced another important difference in the attitudes of the Mexican and the Yankee. Mexico's natural resources, as has been said, are limited; for that reason a good part of the wealth of the country has been built in one form or another on human exploitation, to the point that the Mexican Indian has been called the country's greatest natural resource. All native civilizations anterior to the Conquest were based on great masses of serfs, the sole work-producing element of the population, who were governed and exploited by two small castes, the military and the priestly. During three long centuries of Spanish domination, the exploiters were different but the exploited remained the same. And all the century and a half of Independence has been nothing but a painful effort to base our wealth more on nature and technology and less on man himself. To the Mexican, therefore, liberty and equality have not come naturally; he has fought for them and has barely and partially won them. That is why he is ever in fear of losing them, and why he guards them with exaggerated suspicion and zeal. He is covetous of a treasure that he has barely glimpsed.

The colonizers of North America were men who, dissatisfied with a limited liberty which they enjoyed in the country of their origin, fled from it to the northern part of the American continent, and found there a rich and uninhabited land. It was almost totally lacking in men to be enslaved and exploited. The few that were found could be neither enemies nor slaves because they had no roots in the soil; they possessed the land without owning it, for they had fashioned nothing enduring upon it. The immensity of the land and the scarcity of its population gave the colonizers the feeling of complete liberty, of unlimited space where one might fill his lungs to the bursting point. This historical experience, almost unique in the world, gave the North American the idea that liberty and equality are part of his nature; but it also gave him (alas!) two other ideas: first, the belief in his own superiority; second, the idea that since he always has been and is completely free in his country, he may also be as free in other countries and may do in them whatever he pleases. At all events, it has made him completely incapable of understanding why liberty in Mexico has made its way so slowly and at the cost of so much blood; why Mexico has had such a troubled history; why the Mexican distrusts the North American, whose country he has long called, not without reason, the "Colossus of the North." The Mexican considers the North American the greatest danger to his own liberty, both individual and national.

His general environment of poverty has made the Mexican into a lusterless figure, modest and retiring in manner; but at heart he used to feel secure in his world and even proud, arrogant about his poverty. He was a being not quite belonging to the actual world, not very twentieth-century or very Western. He did not believe that wealth was an unequivocal sign of intelligence and virtue; in it he saw a great deal of good luck and a little of fate. Because of this fact, I firmly believe that until, let us say, fifty years ago the Mexican did

not covet wealth in any major way, nor did he see in it the best goal
for his efforts, either individual or collective. He did not seek
wealth as eagerly as he sought the liberty and the necessary calm
to find his chosen way, the physical leisure to pursue it, and the solitude to enjoy it. And he believed in God precisely because before
Him nothing seemed to count in a decisive way except virtue and
honor, and because He undoubtedly would know how to appreciate
withdrawal more than ostentation. That poverty, that solitude, that
dreariness in which the Mexican lived did not fail to offer some
compensations: his very ignorance never was an obstacle to his being born with a wisdom coming from the earth, the wisdom of the
man untouched by primers or newspapers. A sensitive man in spite
of his chapped feet, cracked open from so much walking barefoot
over rocks and mire, the Mexican possesses an artistic feeling and
capacity which I doubt has its equal in many countries on earth. He
rejoices before a landscape; he is entranced in studying a human
face or contemplating a religious image; colors move him; the most
distant musical note finds in him a sympathetic echo. The world in
which he has lived, to say it once and for all, has not been a material
world but more, much more, a spiritual and religious one. That has
been the sole reason for his existence, the floating plank to which he
fastened himself while all the world, especially the United States,
went a different way, preferring the fugitive and external pleasure
of the material to the permanent and interior gladness of the
spiritual.

The North American on the other hand has lived in wealth; but
wealth shapes or deforms the human being much more than he
thinks. The Yankee, for example, never is more sensitive than when
he perceives a quantitative difference, a most and a least; and he
who is less rich wants to be richer and richer still, until he loses the
concept of limit or end, or that of repose or leisure, which is worse.
What has kept North American society from exploding until now,
subject as it has been to this tenacious and oppressive force, this in-
satiable appetite, has not been the equality of wealth, since this of
course has never existed, but the "equality of opportunity" for everyone to become rich. And until now the repeated experience of North
American society has been that in effect some have succeeded in becoming wealthy; consequently anyone can do the same if only he is a
rugged fighter. The day will come—and it is not far off—when this

experience, already so restricted, will become rarer and rarer or completely impossible, or it will be attainable only at the price of violence and of crime. Then the scale of human values that rules in the United States will change, but then it will be too late for the Mexican's salvation. Meanwhile, it is understood that wealth is not to be enjoyed in silence, but that it must be made manifest, it must be displayed, to glitter and shout until it blinds and deafens. Hence the loud colors, the speed, the noise, and the airs; hence the necessity that the crowd applaud, that it imitate, that it admire and envy. Not that the North American is a hardened materialist without any hope of spiritual salvation; he has never maintained that wealth is an end in itself but that it is merely a means. But the trouble is that he has been so preoccupied with means and spends so much time in obtaining them that they not only have become ends but also the only end in existence, so that it no longer makes any difference whether we call them one thing or the other.

Because of this fact the Mexican sees the North American as an intruder: a giant who breaks into his poor and calm solitude to be admired and envied. And the Mexican has begun to admire; he envies already, but not without rancor, for he feels that he has been forced to abandon his placid nook in order to dig feverishly in the earth, seeking a treasure to make himself worthy of a world in which the watchword is no longer virtue and meekness but the sound of a gold coin slapped on the bar of a cheap saloon. From this point of view I know of no greater historical aberration than that of the Catholic Church in allying itself with the United States against Mexico. It sacrifices one of the best types of religious man on the altars of those who perhaps will never be truly religious.

Obviously I do not attempt to draw a general or complete picture of the psychological differences—let us call them that—between the Mexican and the North American. I merely outline some of them in order that we may turn to the conclusion that relations between the two operate against a background of limited concord. The principal factor that keeps these people apart is the different paths that they pursue, paths which differ and nevertheless converge because, among other reasons, they are so close to each other.

At the end of the eighteenth century or the very first years of the nineteenth, Mexico seemed to be the country with the best and the surest future among all those of this continent, including of course the United States. Its territory then was greater than that of the United States or of Brazil; its population was more numerous and more permanently settled on the soil. Urban concentration, a characteristic of the Modern Age, was already apparent; around 1800 Mexico City was the most populous center in America. Our foreign trade reached important proportions, a good part of it consisting of silver, a precious metal then as coveted as gold, and raw materials such as dyewoods, of great industrial possibilities as shown later by their use in aniline dyes. Mexico also enjoyed the prestige of having been the seat of the most brilliant Indian civilizations and the most solid, extensive, and experienced colonial organization in modern history.

The United States possessed a territory which was little more than a narrow strip parallel to the Atlantic coast, on which its scanty population had incrusted itself, as if fearful or incapable of advancing into the interior, into a land which seemed endless, whose wealth was precisely not in the settled part but in that which lay to the west. The United States in fact did not exist: there were thirteen colonies, practically independent from each other and with weak ties to the metropolis. This was, then, a country which we would now call alluvial, without any roots in the past, made up of fragments and unfused materials. It is true that it obtained its independence before Mexico did, with greater dispatch, defeating a power whose star already was beginning to shine brightly in the sky of international affairs; and it also is true that the Constitution of Virginia, the Articles of Confederation, and the Federal Constitution were political documents which had no parallel in Mexico, and which should have been a vivid sign that here a people was being born with an original mind for politics and an uncommon capacity for social cooperation.

But even those facts, whose significance today is as great as it is undeniable, had at that time their negative counterparts. The quick North American victory seemed less due to the power of the United States than to the weakness of England, whose navy—already the most important one in the world—was unable to maintain numerous and well-provisioned armies on the scene of action. Also, there was an undeniable air of miracle about the victory, since it was achieved by thirteen independent colonies, precariously united solely for military struggle; their origins, their governments, their interests, and their aspirations seemed then irreconcilable. The very fact that the new country chose the name "United States" reveals the degree to which its origin began in disunion.

Though the origins of the two countries were so different, and though the signs were so clearly favorable to Mexico, time soon marked out the paths of each: continuous ascent for the United States, until it now occupies the highest peak in history; for Mexico open descent at first, and later an ascent that is barely perceptible.

The United States possesses a territory which with well-founded arrogance the North Americans call a "continent," because of its magnitude, bordering on the two great oceans of the world, and because it contains whatever one may wish for the building of a great modern civilization. And in addition the United States is a well-balanced country, as little vulnerable as may be possible in a civilization so complex and necessarily universal as is civilization today. The country lacks nothing necessary to feed a great population well and abundantly, with great surpluses which make it an extremely important exporter of foodstuffs. It has abundant raw materials, for the most part of good quality and very often located as if by a providential hand; hence the presence of capital, of technical aptitudes, and of a domestic market without parallel in history.

Mexico, on the other hand, in time lost territory instead of gaining it; it was deprived of very good agricultural lands and of mineral, hydraulic, and petroleum resources, some of which were extraordinary. The territory it had left—in clear and stubborn contradiction to the legend—is in good part mediocre or, for the present, difficult to exploit. Cut into fragments by the high mountains that crisscross it, its narrow valleys barely permit an unstable agriculture on lands which are exposed to an age-old process of erosion and which are badly watered by a capricious rainfall; and when, as on the coast, the soil is good and rainfall is abundant, then man finds himself in an unfavorable situation because of the heat, the dampness, sickness, and pests. Mexico's population eats barely enough to get along. Construction of communications systems has been painful and costly, and consequently such systems are scarce. Thus material and spiritual intercourse, that is to say the formation of nationality itself, has been difficult. Mexico's mineral resources—varied, of medium quality, and to be found almost always in moderate quantities —have fallen into foreign hands for lack of capital, of technical

aptitude, and of a favorable nearby market. One hundred years—
and Mexico was an economically backward country; not the most
important on the continent, nor the second most important, nor the
third, nor the fourth; in nothing would it merit the rating of excellent. Its modest economy is barely sufficient for it to live; it exports
as much as it can, always fearful of the price its articles may bring,
buying abroad some consumer and almost all capital goods.

Not only in its economy but in its history is the United States a
miracle. Posthaste, noisily, in a cloud of dust it galloped from the
Atlantic to the Pacific, at the same time doing two things in themselves difficult of accomplishment: exploring and dominating an
immense, unknown territory and creating a nationality—and this
last, we should add, with human elements which were not always
affinitive and which sometimes seemed incompatible. The United
States accomplished two other things, and these also simultaneously:
it became not simply one nation more but a model political community, which boldly and firmly experimented with the greatest institutions and best forms of democratic life that have been known until
now. And all of this, one might say, beginning with nothing—free-
hand, bareback.

Mexico, on the contrary, achieved its independence under the
worst historical conditions. The long struggle to attain it destroyed
part of the national wealth; another part, persecuted, fled to Spain;
and the major part of what was left belonged to the Catholic
Church, enemy of the new nation. Thus at its very birth our country
faced a conflict that would swell into its most violent forms for the
next half century, and for which even today there is in fact no appropriate, stable, and just solution.

Furthermore, Mexico was the child of a powerless power. Not
only had Spain's vital energies diminished almost to the point of extinction but, no longer capable of creating, it had fallen perforce into
the habit of hiding, in order to preserve, the many things it had
given the world and those things which the world had given it.
Mexico, like all Spanish colonies in America, lived thus under the
star of conservation and reaction, not moved by the great creative
forces of modern society, as was the country that would later be the
United States, except in the most tortuous and tardy way. This could
have been a historical accident easily overcome in the seventeenth
century; but the fact that Spain did not take part in the drama from

which came the political, economic, and philosophical revolution of liberalism was fatal to the new nations of Spanish America. They were born in the midst of a whirlwind of ideas and acts to which they were foreign and whose true scope they were unable to gauge. To understand and appraise them, to profit from them—that took time, effort, and so much grief! Far from growing and developing throughout the nineteenth century, Mexico exhausted itself trying to catch up with the world; it had not finished digesting Spain when it began to swallow the modern world.

For those two main reasons— and for many other secondary ones —Mexico also is in a certain way a miracle of history, not a miracle of fecundity but one of survival. It is in truth a miracle that the country should still be on its feet, and even more that it still believes in its own destiny.

So Mexico and the United States are different countries, and their paths differ also. Nevertheless, they have not been able to go their own ways; they are neighbors, whether their interests coincide or clash. There is a conflict between them, latent at times, at other times acute; a conflict that perhaps will not again lead to war, but which is not any less real or less painful because of that fact. It is now exactly a century since the first stage of the conflict began. Mexico crossed the path of the "manifest destiny" of the United States; its territory was in the way. The avalanche came and demolished it. This was the first adjustment Mexico had to make in the crushing process to which it has been subjected, to which it still is subjected because of its "good-neighborhood" with the United States. But though this blow was so spectacular, so deeply painful; even though it covered our whole history with a thick black pall, its very memory sinking the Mexican into a silent gloom; in spite of all this, that experience has not been the worst nor the deepest one. Mexico, even today a very imperfect nationality, was even more imperfect a century ago; it could thus survive the amputation, as may an unformed or new organism, whereas a mature or integrated one could not.

The second adjustment was worse, even if it did arrive silently, when in 1890 the colonizing wave sweeping impetuously from the Atlantic finally reached the Pacific. Then the United States found itself between two oceans, with the imperious necessity of communicating quickly between one and the other. To secure such communication it needed to cut the continent in two at the nearest narrow place, and before Nicaragua or Panama the United States thought of Tehuantepec. Even though the incision was not made in our territory, we could not prevent our country from becoming an appendage to the geographic mass of continental United States. It was then that we became part of the "North American system." Then it became clear that Mexico not only could not put up a struggle—it had learned the impossibility of that by painful experience—but that it could not even flee. To the north was the United States; to the west a barren ocean which seemed to lead nowhere; to the east the Atlantic, rich and populous but an ocean to which we did not even have direct access. Our Gulf of Mexico is not part of the Atlantic Ocean any more than is the Mediterranean; it is like the latter an inland sea, a lake bottled up by the peninsula of Florida and the closed arc of the Antillean archipelago. No exit was left but to the south: Guatemala and the rest of Central America—also part of the "North American system." Where could Mexico go?

After all, this second adjustment of Mexican life to that of the United States was but a consequence of the internal development of the latter. What would happen when its external development began? It was not necessary to wait very long for this eventuality. In 1917 the United States resolved to enter the European war; it decided the outcome and emerged from the venture richer than ever and with universal consent that its immediate zone of influence would be Latin America, and Mexico first of all.

There are historical events that operate providentially, performing an anesthetic function without which societies could not adjust to some situations, well-rooted in the past but suddenly consummated and appearing as something new, imperatively, incisively new. Thus, when in 1914 the first World War began, the Mexican Revolution entered its violent phase, leading to a final and complete victory. Mexico came out of the Revolution a new country: hard-fisted, dynamic, aggressive, with a nationalistic tone that it had lost in the vain and lengthy process of Europeanization during the Díaz regime. Mexico seemed to care little that the United States had become a power of the first class, that the war had made it lord and master of the Americas. Mexico defied it with agrarian reform, beneath whose axe North American properties and persons fell; and with legislation and policy concerning the oil fields, which limited and hurt Yankee

interests until they were finally dispossessed in 1938. In 1917 Mexico
initiated a vigorous policy of *rapprochement* with other Latin American countries, with the end of defending itself from the United
States and disputing its influence and prestige. Mexico was banished
from the League of Nations. As mute protest against a North American policy of persecution, it declined to attend the Inter-American
Conference in Chile, and on one occasion Secretary of State Kellogg
declared publicly that Mexico was in the prisoner's dock because of
its great international crimes. Mexico intervened more than once in
Central American politics, opposing Yankee designs. It recalled its
diplomatic representative when North American marines invaded
Nicaragua, making a hero of Sandino, and it permitted expeditions
against Juan Vicente Gómez to be organized in its territory, thus disturbing the peace of America in the name of democracy. The United
States, vexed and almost inclined to end it all by force, changed its
tactics instead and sent Ambassador Morrow, the genius of the new
diplomacy. This did not prevent Mexico from continuing its international policy of Olympian independence. It established diplomatic
relations with the Soviet Union before any other country on the continent, long before the United States of course. It placed itself on the
side of the Spanish Republican government; it opposed Italian imperialism in Africa; it censured the passive attitude toward the Japa-
nese invasion of China.

In a series of ups and downs relations between Mexico and the
United States were disagreeable and at times violent until 1938,
when dissension seemed to culminate in the expropriation of the
North American and British oil companies. But in truth Mexico
fought so tenaciously against its new situation of dependence only
to gain time in order to adjust itself to it. A short time later Mexico
became an ally of the United States in the second World War.

The century-old crushing process undergone by Mexico has now
entered its final stage. It is taking place in all fields, since the pertinacious, the unassailable North American influence is felt everywhere:
in customs pertaining to food and dress; in the language, in thought,
in the ideals of life; in the economy, in society, in religious policy, in
education and the arts; in all interior and exterior acts. This influence is exercised, furthermore, in a world in which distances no
longer protect, a world in which the press obfuscates, radio deafens,
cinema fascinates, in which an airplane shoots out like a magic

arrow from Washington to Mexico City today in ten hours, tomorrow in six, the day after in four. That is why North American influence on Mexico is now like the God of the Christians: omnipotent and omnipresent. And to all of this we must add still another detail: the United States is not simply a great power but the only one; all the money in the universe is there, almost all the power and the technology, much of the civilization of the present and of the future; and also the United Nations, that is to say the government of the world.

What will happen? What will be left of Mexico after this last stage of crushing? Will it be able to resist, and in such event, what will be its principal means of defense? Is the North American influence as overpowering as it appears to be?

Our territory does offer some defense, not because it is ours but because it is what it is: poor, mountainous, and outside the temperate zone—circumstances which do not lend themselves to the repetition of the North American "experiment," an experiment that was based essentially on an abundance which permitted waste and on stretches of level land which facilitated physical effort to the utmost.

Our population will be an even greater obstacle. The Yankee way could be pleasing to our middle class, and they may consequently prefer it; but even among them there is an evident repugnance toward uniformity, and too great a pride to obey any master. The North American can be an individualist in the sense that he prefers to take the initiative rather than leave it up to the group; but he is not an individualist in wanting to be different from the rest; the Mexican, on the other hand, enjoys being different and tries to be so. In the Yankee submission does not lead to rancor, perhaps because he has always considered it transitory. The Mexican, rebellious and undisciplined, accepts a master and obeys him, but he never respects him.

The Indian will present even greater resistance. Naturally, composing as he does a great inert mass on which small aristocratic groups have rested, he could again be a slave, this time of the North American as he once was of the Spaniard and of the Creole. But only with difficulty could he ever manage to perform the role of the North American mass, which is gregarious, fluid, impetuous, sensible to the stimulus of wealth. The Indian's indifference, his absorption in himself, his profound distrust, his slow rhythm, and his stubborn silences will make it difficult for him to participate joyfully and voluntarily in a civilization of noise, violence, and tenacious struggle—though one can never be sure about the fascination of money or the influence of the confessor.

Formerly it was customary to count on the Catholic Church as one of the decisive powers of resistance against Yankee penetration. Perhaps that belief was based on an oversimplification: since the United States was a predominantly Protestant country, the Catholic Church feared that its predominance would be religious as well as political and economic. Our belief was also based on the fact that the Catholic Church, severest of bigots, looked with repugnance on a life as "free" as that of the North American: in which woman is a libertine, without scruples in her sexual relations; in which divorce is universal; the cinema a seedbed of licentious habits; dress, a call to sin; the perennial contortions of the dance, a pretext for the rubbing of bodies. But it is quite clear that those Mexican patriots who counted on the help of the Catholic Church were mistaken, though this disillusionment has not yet reached the country's public opinion.

The Catholic Church, which so ardently denounces the supranational character of Communism, also is an international power, rarely allied with and almost always adverse to the purely national forces of any country; and, like Communism, it obeys with blind fidelity the dictates of a central organization whose sole incentive is the possession of power for the realization of its ends all over the globe, without caring or ever having cared about the problems or goals of any state or nation—these nations she considers in most cases as cannon fodder in the great, continuous battle for wider and wider dominion and subjugation.

The international picture has changed a great deal in the past few years, not only for Mexico but for everyone, and perhaps most of all for the Vatican. For one thing, it is quite clear that the Vatican came out of the last war with its prestige and power much diminished. Its intimate, manifest alliance with fascism and falangism in Italy, Spain, and Portugal placed it within the conquered party, nor were its intermittent clashes with National Socialism sufficient to change the results.

International life, however, has many alternatives, so that even the most hopeless of the conquered often have been able to rise and to climb to great heights, merely by awaiting the propitious moment to play a good card. And the division among the victors—precisely the same thing which Hitler had depended on for victory or salvation—has given the Catholic Church a new opportunity, perhaps the best of those which have come to it: the possibility of being the additional weight which will incline the balance either to the side of Russia or of the United States. It is true that in a sense the Vatican's choice was inevitable, not only because an understanding with the United States is safer and more proper but because it is a rule of international politics to support the second best in order to achieve first place. And on this point anyone else might have made a mistake, but not the Catholic Church. She knows that as a corrosive power, permanent and universal, Communism is much more fearsome than anything else in the world because it alone, by its very nature and scope, can be a match for the Catholic Church. The latter, furthermore, is as ambitious as Communism itself can be; in the same way that Communism does not despair of triumphing in the United States, the capitalist paradise, the Catholic Church sees as a goal within its reach Catholic predominance in the old Protestant Eden.

If the Church is engaged in an international game of this incredible magnitude, will it care anything at all about the Mexican nationality? If the Catholic Church now aspires to destroy Communism by allying itself with the United States, asking as reward for its services that it be allowed to expand there until it has attained predominance, is it conceivable that it would wish to compromise itself by defending Mexico?

Someone wishing to make a long list of the forces which Mexico could count upon to resist the crushing out of its nationality could very well deceive himself by counting Mexican capitalism among them, thinking that since North American industry may cut off its very life Mexican capital would see its worst enemy in that industry and in the country that protects it. Again time—and more quickly than seemed possible—has pulled the blindfold from deluded eyes: for some time now Mexican capitalism has been living from the crumbs of Yankee capitalism; and with the invention of enterprises of mixed capital, the rich Mexican has reached the peak of his vanity and ambition; he is rubbing elbows in an administrative committee with his powerful North American colleague.

Another way to gauge Mexico's capacity for resistance is to ascertain what kind of pressure we are being subjected to and what its source may be, as well as to discover if opposing forces can be created to contain it. One of these pressures, it seems to me, is the vague, disorganized influence exercised by a country that becomes a "model" because of its power, resources, and prestige; another is true penetration or deliberate and organized influence, which is brought to bear by some parts or groups of the model country, typically its government, its capitalistic groups, and the leaders of its religious or its laboring classes. As to the first kind of pressure, it is no less deep and pertinacious, nor less difficult to combat, because it is vague and disorganized. Nor will all its results be unfavorable: it has caused a great deal of the progress and renovation occurring in the countries where it has been felt. And let us remember that the second pressure is not always a sinister influence merely because it is deliberate and organized.

How could one combat or at least counterbalance the first type of influence? In general there would be just one means, working in two ways: on the one hand we could fight against this influence; on the other we could strengthen our own national character. Both of these approaches would require the creation of a cohesive, ardent, and sensitive public opinion. But who are those who create and channel a national public opinion? It is evident that government organizations should have much of the initiative. These would be followed in degree of efficacy by those enterprises which manage public media most successfully in expressing thought: the dailies and journals, radio, the cinema, and books. Finally there are all the men who think and feel, above all, those whom we call intellectuals.

If the problem of North American influence on Mexico is as deep and serious as it appears to be, if one of the unmistakable means of attacking it is the creation of a national public opinion, if there exist in Mexico groups capable of creating it, then why have the days and years passed without our seeing even the glimmer of such a public opinion? There are only two explanations; there may be a third but it would be merely a combination of the first two. Either there is no consciousness of the problem and its magnitude or there is a fear of creating a public opinion that might be offensive to the United States or that could become embarrassing to that country at any given moment. In either case these explanations could not be thought discouraging, for if they were, that would mean only that the work of rectification should have begun much sooner.

Deliberate and organized influence or penetration is exercised for the most part by the government of the United States, or by the agencies and organizations influenced by it. Such penetration neither can nor may be limited or lacking in persuasion, because, to the uncontrollable impulse toward mere domination which every imperialist nation feels, one must add the present situation of the United States, its genuine, acute necessity of counting on the submission of neighboring countries, or on their sympathy and support, if the euphemism is necessary.

In spite of any number of arguments that could be made to the contrary, another solution to the problem of deliberate penetration seems more feasible. It is feasible in theory of course; failure could be quite possible for the man framing the theory or putting it into practice. An agreement reconciling the economic interests of both countries is not impossible nor even difficult to conceive in broad outline, nor would an agreement be impossible on international policies. Mexico cannot and perhaps should not leave the middle road which is followed by the United States; but there is one right which it cannot renounce and another which it must obtain and safeguard: first, it must continue to think about and evaluate for itself the problems and situations facing it; and second, it must secure a formal commitment by the United States not to make any important international decision without hearing and heeding Mexico's opinion. And for all of this, to repeat, we need a national public opinion. The broad foreign policy of the country and specifically the extremely grave problem of relations between Mexico and the United States cannot and should not be completely entrusted to the individual and consequently transitory and fickle actions of a minister of foreign affairs or even of a president. The actions and judgments of both should receive their inspiration from the public opinion of the whole country, and they should be judged by it.

We must take a quick look at the United States from within in order to complete this schematic balance of forces favorable and unfavorable to Mexico in its hours of trial. We must do it keeping in mind an elemental fact: the United States is more than just its government or its capitalists; there is in that country as in few others

on earth a citizenry whose opinion is independent of its government
and of its captains of industry. There are countless examples which
show that North American public opinion carries weight with the
government of the United States, but I will point out only two, both
referring to our international relations with that country. The recent
struggle with the Catholic Church in Mexico was sometimes understood and appreciated by North American diplomats and by high
officials in the Department of State, some of them going so far as to
believe that our governments were in the right. Notwithstanding,
they could not even conceal the significance of the struggle, precisely because the North American people traditionally have seen
with great repugnance all quarrels with or persecutions against any
church or religious creed. On the other hand, this same public opinion was an efficacious curb on North American administrations when
the first disagreements arose with the oil companies during the last
days of the Obregón regime and the beginnings of that of Calles, and
even in 1938, when the dispute culminated in the expropriation of
the holdings of foreign oil companies.

What may be expected then of Yankee public opinion in Mexico's
favor? Some years ago I would have ventured to say without hesitation that we could expect much; today—the hesitation has increased.
And there are reasons. Before the second World War the United
States was powerful of course but not omnipotent; in this respect one
might call on the well-known thought of Lord Acton's: "Power corrupts and absolute power corrupts absolutely." I mean that twenty-
five years ago the North American people were more capable than
they are now of having doubts about their government and their rich
men, and existing circumstances allowed them greater freedom for
doing so. In fact, they would go so far then as to admit that all of
them were to blame for the mistakes of their government. This feeling was almost unanimous in the case of the intervention in Mexico
in 1926, as it was about the occupation of Nicaragua. Since the second World War the North American people have become victims of
an almost hysterical impatience against all complaints, petitions, or
differences of opinion, not to mention criticism or censure. Such is
the weight of the obligations which they think they bear; so well has
this mistaken sentiment been cultivated by the government, the
press, the radio, and big business: no other people in history, they

feel, has voluntarily assumed so much responsibility for other nations, nor has any other been as generous as the North American
people; every want and every obstacle faced by the world must be
met by the poor taxpayer of the United States. It is amusing to see
the painful confusion of graduate students from the best Yankee
universities when they are assured that the loans made to Mexico for
the Altos Hornos project or for the termination of the Pan American
Highway, for example, are true loans and not gifts pure and simple;
that is that Mexico will have to return the principal and to pay an
interest equal to that prevailing on the money markets. And, naturally, ignoring the true nature of these operations, North American
public opinion believes that it is a veritable felony for Mexico to
want these loans free of conditions or demands of a political nature.

But more than anything else, North American public opinion is
passing through a crisis because unfortunately its leaders, or the organizations and institutions which maintain it, have assumed such an
intransigent, reactionary tone, while those few who have kept a liberal course have been so clumsy or so unfortunate that they are
cornered and proscribed. It is no irreverence, simply a historical
truth, to state that since the Roosevelt era the conservative tone of
the government and of its principal associates has become more and
more apparent, even though Roosevelt, because of his own political
genius and superiority in respect to his allies and opponents, was
able to give that tendency a transitory air and keep alive the liberal
hopes. Truman, a simple politician and no statesman, decided to
tear from the Republican Party's grasp the succulent anti-Russian
banner, easy lure for domestic and foreign demagoguery. With that
act he inevitably gave a conservative tone to his own party, and in
the end to the country as a whole. Wallace, the most outstanding
dissenter after Willkie's death, turned out to be such a poor politician that, besides letting himself be tagged with the indelible label of
Communist, he has provoked an adverse reaction that has blackened
the general tone of North American politics. Add to all of this the
incessant work of the press and the radio, ably manipulated now by
this group now by that; and the behavior of Russia, perhaps skillful
in the long run for the attainment of its own ends, but uncouth and
heedless of public opinion, which it has alienated day by day, apparently in an already irreparable manner.

Through the working of all these and of some other minor but con-
current factors, public opinion in the United States for the first time
in a great many years seems uniform, closed, even regimented, although without apparent violence or persecution. Is it possible to fit
into this picture any understanding of the problems of Mexico, problems of life and death to us but of very little importance to the
United States? In spite of the inevitably somber tone of this picture,
some reaction is to be expected because, among other reasons, were
it not to occur one might well fear that the great Yankee democracy
had ceased to exist.

Many people, North Americans especially, would put forward the
process of mutual understanding as a force from which may come a
better comprehension between the two peoples and, therefore, a
solution to common problems without detriment to either and even
without friction. And, in support of their hopes, they would point to
the growing number of tourists who freely come and go from one
country to the other; to the larger and larger number of professors
and students who spend their time elucidating the past or the present of the two nations; to the books which pass from hand to hand in
their original languages or in translations, carrying information and
opinions back and forth and laying bit by bit the firm foundations of
a conscientious and informed friendship; to radio and television,
which make it possible for us to hear and see today the stars of
sports, the screen, and the theater; tomorrow the politician, the general, or the university professor; day after tomorrow the hero and
perhaps the saint.

The benefits of this process of mutual understanding are indubitable; there is no doubt that in the long run it will be the only permanent solution to the major problems arising between the two
countries. This does not mean, however, that it may not have its
limitations, some of them unavoidable, nor that these are unworthy
of our attention now.

In the first place the effects are slow; the results are much more
uncertain than might appear at first sight. Suffice it to recall the relations between England and the United States to have a concrete
idea of this slowness and incertitude. It would be hard to imagine two
other countries in which everything could be so propitious to mutual

understanding and profound friendship; the bonds of a single language, of a common tradition, and a like spirit were tightened and
sealed by a long series of great common interests which became
clearer and clearer as the nineteenth century ran its course, forging
for the two peoples a parallel destiny in addition to their common
past. And yet, let us not forget that as late as the last world war an
anguished North American editor asked Professor Brogan to write a
book interpreting present-day England for the people of his country.
Nor that a professor from the United States on a visit to Oxford
University was told confidentially by an English colleague how
much he lamented the lack of great historians in the United States.
Nor should we forget that "only 20 years ago, Big Bill Thompson
won election campaigns by promising that 'if King George comes to
Chicago we'll warm his backside for him'"; nor that Hearst's great
newspaper chain and the picturesque Colonel McCormick's influential Chicago Tribune have always fanned an anglophobia which has
become chronic.

Secondly, I am afraid that tourism will in our case encourage misunderstanding, making it frequent, actual, and visible for everyone
instead of silencing or combatting it. One important reason, which it
would be worthwhile to follow up, is that few things set the North
American and the Mexican farther apart than the impression each of
them makes when he is outside his country. The Mexican improves,
the North American worsens. In both cases the impression is false
because it corresponds only in a distant way to the national reality
of each. The strength of the United States is in the community, not
in the individual; the best of Mexico is in the individual person, not
in the social being. That is the reason why the North American appears in an unfavorable light when he is detached from his group
and seen as an individual, as he must be seen, perforce, abroad.
Rarely will he seem distinguished, that is to say different; almost always he appears vulgar. The Mexican, on the other hand, will appear distinguished, different, or individual, not only in the color of
his skin but in the tone of his voice and his calm, deliberate manner.
The North American (and the Argentine too, for example) is like the
hydrangea, which looks well in a flower bed. The Mexican (and the
Chinese, to cite another case) resembles the orchid, a flower to be
displayed like a jewel, alone on the breast. It is not strange then that

the Mexican who has traveled in the United States and brought home a favorable impression of the Yankee girl's physical beauty, there frequently corroborated, should on seeing her in Mexico alone or in small groups ask himself in perplexity where such a woman could have come from, so colorless, homely to such a remarkable degree. Nor is it strange that the Mexican should be able to make conquests in the United States that he would not even dream of in his own country. It is quite possible that time may gradually reverse this situation, that with age and misfortune the North American may gain in individuality, while the Mexican, rejuvenated by a better diet and healthier because of efficient sanitary installations, may lose in individual distinction and gain in collective cohesiveness. But then, little or nothing will have been gained in understanding.

Research by professors and students into the present-day life or the history of the two countries is perhaps the surest way to understanding. In this all the praise must go to the North American, the reproach to the Mexican. There is an equal necessity and urgency for them to know each other's problems, and if one of the two has the greater need it is without a doubt the Mexican. The efforts made by the latter to know the history and literature of North America are extremely recent and practically nonexistent, while those of the North American have been astonishingly effective. At any rate, the small groups of intellectuals of each country who devote themselves to the problems of the other nation are in truth the only ones working on solid ground, even though as is to be expected their labor is slow, limited, and sometimes ineffective before the urgency and the magnitude of present-day problems.

Few and quite uncertain appear to be the forces—actual, appropriate, and at hand—with which Mexico could maintain its nationality and sustain it to the end. Everything in Mexico seems to be weakness, and everything in the United States strength. Is it really so? There may be no universal law compensating inequalities, but in this case such a law does function; for the vulnerability of the United States is equal only to its incredible strength.

In the first place, the general situation of the United States in the world is nothing enviable. At no time in history, it is true, has any country been so absolutely predominant and able to bring together so much power and so much wealth. The United States is today what the lion is among the animals, indisputably the king; except that the lion is king of the forest, that is to say of a living world, while the United States is king of the desert, the sole inhabitants of which are the wind of desolation and the cold of hunger and death. To have company, to bring together living things who will give it some warmth, who will listen to it at least, the United States must literally feed and maintain its allies—England, France, Belgium, Holland, Norway—and revive its former enemies—Germany, Italy, and Japan. It will have to convert into reality the fiction that China is a first-rate power. It will have to win Italy and Spain, and dispute all of Eastern Europe with Russia. And above all, it must contend with the Soviet Union, which is fanatically convinced of the goodness of its own cause, intransigently disbelieving the goodness of others.

This is no small task, even for a great country like the United States. It may demand more talent, more experience, and greater means than the United States possesses. And this is granting the possibility that North American public opinion might one day accept the idea that high fame presupposes some responsibilities. Even if done well, it means that the United States would be less wealthy and less powerful when it concluded the task than when the task was begun.

On the other hand, the power of the United States will cause a commensurate reaction. Until now the majority of the Mexican people have not felt the naked force of this power; perhaps only the government has felt it, and governments are discreet. They give in easily, so eager are they to make their peoples think that life can be lived happily and securely if it is merely surrendered without reservations to the governmental magic. But Mexican public opinion is capable of a clear reaction in matters like these, as can be seen from the defeat at the polls of Ezequiel Padilla, the Foreign Minister who was a "friend" of the United States, and the immense popularity garnered by President Alemán during his trip to the United States merely by saying that Mexico would continue to watch over her independence.

In sum, so great is the power of the United States that the decisions it makes in its international policy will necessarily have their repercussions in Mexican public opinion, as they will in that of other countries, so that with each decision the United States will gain some friends and lose others. Even when it abstains from action—as in Spain and Santo Domingo, for example—the abstention has its consequences. But undoubtedly the most transcendental decision made by the United States seems to be the decision to contend with Russia. If such is the case, then the United States has failed to see the problem, for it wastes all its breath in trying to demonstrate what some of us already know too well, that the Soviet Union is imperialistic. As long as the United States does not demonstrate that it is not imperialistic itself and that it opposes the Soviet Union because it is not, for that reason and that reason alone, it can not count on the support and the sympathies of Mexican liberals. And an undoubted motive for the alienations of these sympathies is the fact that the United States should call up in its defense the most retrograde of forces: the Catholic Church and all those groups which with a suspicious promptness are gladly disposed to take part in the anti-Communist crusade. If such is to be the permanent international policy of the United States, that country may count on the support of the great captains Franco, Somoza, and Trujillo, and on all blinded Catholics, but not on the liberal elements of Mexico and Spanish America.

And here we have one of the most vulnerable sides of the United States; it is a country that has not simply lived in liberalism and democracy; it has contributed to liberalism and democracy many of their fundamental theories and the best institutions and ways of life they have produced. The United States is their child and has drawn from both much of its moral and material strength. Is it possible that —not to survive but merely to aggrandize itself—the United States will find it necessary to create a retrograde, reactionary world made of antiliberal and antidemocratic forces? The United States can be sure of one thing as far as Mexico is concerned. This country, poor and sluggish if you will, lives for one reason alone, with one sole end: to achieve, to practice, and to live liberty and democracy. All our history is but one long effort to achieve this end. And if there is one way of definitely alienating the friendship and admiration of Mexico, it is by convincing it that only here, in Mexico, may a Mexican live as he likes. Fortunately, the Mexican liberals will not be entirely alone; they will have the company of North American liberals, who are not few; and of those Yankees who, without being manifestly liberals, are honest and understanding. And these last are even more plentiful in the United States. From North American public opinion we may expect great aberrations, it is true; but we may also expect the strictest justice.

RUSSIA, THE UNITED STATES, AND LATIN AMERICA*

ALL OF YOU are without a doubt well versed in the art of giving and listening to lectures, an art which fortunately works both ways. On hundreds of occasions you may have heard the lecturer begin with the prudent admonition that he was not going to give a *lecture*. Sometimes, after this remark he offers us words like *talk* or *discussion* as substitutes for the other term, which seems more formal and exacting; and on some few occasions he will adduce reasons to justify one name or another.

In my case I have a genuine interest in establishing that this is neither a *lecture* nor a *discussion* nor a *talk*, for all these words imply a teaching or a lesson which the speaker wishes to impart to his audience. And I do not seek to teach anything, not this time at least.

The only reason I find myself in the uncomfortable situation in which you now see me is my desire to perform an elementary civic duty. Every day one sees that, while the Latin American countries have got themselves up to their necks in the whirlpool of a real and active international life and its immense risks, there does not exist

* First published in *Cuadernos Americanos*, Año VII, 1, January 1948, Vol. XXXVII.

among them a public opinion concerning the problems, advantages, and dangers of such a life. Nor have they even developed the habit of reflecting upon these things in purely friendly conversations. If we do not initiate that public opinion, shall we have the right on some other occasion to complain that our governments were unable to understand and defend the true interests of our peoples? And if those in power should hit on the right course, would it not be better for us to have the privilege of sharing with them the ensuing satisfaction, the glory even?

I believe that we should begin our analysis with a very evident fact: the present-day world has two centers of gravity, Washington and Moscow; and because these are new and unique, and perhaps because their powers of attraction are greater than those of others before them, the world is undergoing at present a process of adjustment and readjustment. The Latin American countries cannot withdraw from this readjustment, but this does not mean that they cannot observe and study its different phases and attempt to avoid some of its gravest dangers.

In any case, it is plain that the future international orbit of our countries will be determined in part by our will and our real power in making our own way, and in another part, the major one doubtless, by the results of the clash between the United States and Russia. For that reason one may attempt a preliminary approach to this intricate problem by essaying brief replies to the following questions. First, what degree of real union exists today and may exist in the near future among the countries of Latin America? Second, what may these countries expect, respectively, from Russia and the United States? Third, what attitude could our countries assume in case of an armed conflict between the United States and Russia, an attitude that would obviously be determined as much by the best interests of Latin America as by the authentic possibility of asserting those interests?

In the first place, we must admit that there does not exist among the Latin American peoples any consciousness of the ideal or the convenience of uniting. Even more, none of them has the political education sufficient to play at least the negative role of censor a posteriori of the conduct adopted by its rulers, with the sole exception, perhaps, that they would condemn too exuberant a friendship for the United States and would applaud on the other hand an attitude of opposition, or at the least a differing and distant one. The sentiment and even the idea of union is found in but a few men in each country, men whose position most often does not help them to translate their ideas into action (as would be the case if they were politicians or members of the government) or to propagate them in an effective way (as they might if they were directors of newspapers or magazines of large circulation).

Fortunately there are historic factors more powerful than the ideas and sentiments of men, which are working in favor of such a union and which will in the end impose it in spite of the Latin American peoples and their rulers. On the one hand there is the common origin of our countries, and the similar kind of lives which they have led. On the other there is the decisive fact that none of them has the economic or human resources to stand on its own, or to be reckoned with alone as highly as when its actions are in concert with those of the rest. Then there is the evident tendency in present-day international affairs toward an interplay of great blocs of nations rather than single ones, no matter how rich or powerful these may be. Lastly there is the geographic accident through which our countries occupy the same continent with a foreign people, the most powerful and most gifted in history.

The union of the Latin American countries is in a way fated; the real problem is whether this union will take place in time to preserve liberty and independence or inopportunely, when it will have no other use than to console us in our unhappy hours of servitude. The problem of union, then, is that of precipitating it so that it does not take place too late.

Understanding among the Hispanic peoples has been growing over a period of many years, although its most notable advances date only from the last thirty or fifty. In no other field are they greater, perhaps, than in that of intellectual relations. Martí, Rodó, or Darío; Pedro Henríquez Ureña, Alfonso Reyes, or Gabriela Mistral have accomplished in this field what only Bello, Bolívar, or San Martín accomplished in their own time. Books and magazines of all Latin American countries circulate in the others with an amplitude and regularity hitherto unheard of; and there are publishing houses that have embarked on editorial projects in which the Latin American writer occupies a place that is not only important but exclusive. Congresses and conferences are now frequent and are being held periodically; in them the friendship and camaraderie of men and women are born and confirmed.

Though the economic histories of each of the Latin American countries have been so diverse, the fact seems to have been established that in all countries the deeper and graver the problem, the greater the similarity among the positions of the various countries towards it, and the easier it should be, therefore, to essay a common solution. The degree of affinity in ideas and objectives that the Latin American delegates to the Bretton Woods Conference discovered in each other, for example, was surprising and pleasing to all of them.

It is true that in the economic field this affinity has had up to the present only negative origins and therefore has not been as fruitful as it should be. What has drawn the Latin American countries closer to each other has been the fear of great pressures from the outside, the oppressive sensation of their own weakness, the subordination of their interests to the truly or fictitiously more urgent interests of Europe, and above all the unequivocal impression that our countries travel not in the main stream of international life but laterally to it, as though drifting off course. It is also true that the discovery of an affinity of interests generally occurs too late, leading to improvisation or to the concentration of the common effort on questions of small or deceptive import. And it is still further true that at times the union thus formed is weakened or broken upon the appearance of nationalistic prejudices which are most often unfounded or irrelevant. The most serious failure, however, lies in the fact that to the *rapprochement* attained on one occasion there is not added that of another, because of the inexplicable incapacity of Latin Americans to store away and to study acquired experience, to sustain an effort, to stitch the past onto the present while leaving a loose thread with which to tie in the future. Thus it is as if the task of unification were begun each day at the zero point, and not at the stage which was reached the day before.

In the field of politics what progress exists is contemptible. In the present century there has not been a single president in Latin America who can be remembered as a champion of the Latin American cause. The same may be said about the foreign ministers and in general about all political figures of any importance. In this there has been no marked difference between tyrannical regimes, such as those of Gómez, Leguía, Vargas, or Perón, and those that are more or less democratic or revolutionary. This phenomenon is so general and so uninterrupted that it is cause for surprise and demands some kind of explanation. Without a doubt, no little influence is exerted by the intellectual and moral mediocrity of Latin American rulers: uncultured, of narrow vision, *arrivistes* in general, when they are not out-and-out power grabbers, their governmental actions serve the petty and fugitive interests of their henchmen and their pals. The rulers are not completely to blame, of course. The magnitude, the number, and urgency of the problems which the Latin American countries have always faced lead to a kind of action very much like that of the fireman. In the middle of an alarm that confuses and distracts, he must fly, most often clamoring for the right of way, from one end to another to prevent a conflagration that threatens all with ruin or extinction. Thus, only rarely does the Latin American spirit have the serenity to see beyond tomorrow and to attempt enterprises that, because they are of fundamental significance, yield their fruits only in the long run.

The lack of politico-governmental action to channel, invigorate, and hasten the union of the Latin American peoples will be remedied only if there awakens in them a current of public opinion which will make the accomplishment of this union the undoubted, necessary, and permanent objective of all governments involved. In the arousing of this public opinion the intellectual can assume a decisive role and certainly the greatest of responsibilities. He is a professor, a newspaperman, sometimes an adviser to representatives of governments; and above all things he is one who discourses and convinces.

These and many other great tasks that logically fall on the shoulders of the intellectual are not easy ones, for often his position within the society in which he lives could not be more helpless or precarious. This is particularly true because he rarely has free access to the means of expression which create public opinion or influence it: the dailies, the radio, or the cinema. These three, in general, are of a low intellectual and moral level; they serve the short-sighted interests of shareholders or of sectarian groups; they have no feeling of public responsibility and tend to lack even a feeling of courtesy, which should make them seek and accept with respect the free opinion of others.

That is why I think that the major obstacles to union are the apathy of the good men of America, the stupidity of our rulers, and the corruption or levity of the press, the radio, and the moving picture industry. I know, of course, that other obstacles have been given more attention: geographic barriers, lack of means of transport to reach across the immense distances separating us; our fragile social organization; but these have always sounded to me like explanations whose true end is to justify man's incapacity to undertake great enterprises.

Only one other obstacle to union may be considered independently: the will of the United States; that is, whether it would favor such a union as propitious to its interests, or whether on the contrary it would combat it, believing it to be prejudicial. I am firmly convinced that the United States would in no way be harmed by the establishment of closer relations among the Latin American countries; but I doubt very much that this conviction is shared by the average North American citizen, and even less by the Yankee leaders, no matter how great we suppose their enlightenment and their good will to be. My fear is founded, it is true, on a very oversimplified consideration. The United States up to the present has given no evidence that it will make use in international relations of that wonderful pragmatic spirit of continuous experimentation and innovation, which in technology has led it to marvelous inventions. Instead, it follows with a fidelity worthy of a better cause the well-traveled roads used by the other great powers which have preceded it in ruling the world—in spite of the fact, of course, that these roads have led other powers first to disaster and then to destruction. If I judge correctly, the United States would be an empire; and it is well known that all empires have followed the rule of opposing the maintenance of relations among their colonies, while allowing and encouraging separate ties between the metropolis and each one of the colonies.

This would mean that the unification of the Latin American countries could only be obtained in spite of the United States. Would such a union be viable under these conditions? I believe that it could, even though it would be necessary then to engrave quite deeply in the heads and hearts of all Latin Americans these simple words: "Union will be attained in the exact measure that you work for it."

I have stated that this union is extremely necessary, and at the same time that it has not been achieved, and that it is difficult of attainment. It is logical then to ask how it could be attempted. I do not deny the necessity and the interest of this particular question, although I will not refer to it on this occasion for I only wish at this time to make a general analysis. I will limit myself to the observation that in this great task the intellectual, the writer, the professor, and the artist must take a prominent part. Our America can be the source of inspiration for any imaginative work, and it is an almost virgin field for all kinds of scientific studies. I have already said something about the sphere of action of the intellectual: to create and to channel a public opinion that will help to attain and to hasten this union.

Many times have I asked the question both of myself and of others, "What may we expect of the Soviet Union?" Unfortunately I do not believe that one can give any sincere answer other than a flat "Nothing." I say "unfortunately" because it seems to me that the isolated condition in which Russia so persistently lives denies the world, and particularly us Latin Americans—so given to nourishing ourselves from abroad—some of the very few possibilities left in the world for spiritually renewing and enriching ourselves.

In the first place, Russia has, I suspect, few things to offer us; and in the second, it seems to have no desire to give the things it has. What may one suppose that Russia could give us? Money, for example? I doubt that it has money in such extreme abundance, for we must not forget that the Soviet Union is a country whose economic, political, and social modernization had barely begun when the war irreparably destroyed much of what it had achieved. To this, one must add that Russia apparently believes that another world war is inevitable, and for this reason preparations for war are one of its principal labors. Therefore, if it is going to invest some money abroad, it will without a doubt do so in those countries that can protect and aid it by reason of geography or affinity.

Would Russia give us political support if we needed it? It is perfectly conceivable that Latin America could obtain the favorable votes of Russia and its satellites if in some international conference Latin America should ask them to support some proposition of its own, especially if that proposition were inimical to the United States. One should not discard a priori such a possibility, nor is there any reason to belittle its value or efficacy in the abstract. But one must frankly agree that political support which does not arise from decisive geographic conditions, which is not nourished by permanent economic interests, and which cannot at some future date lead to military action is perforce precarious or incidental.

Can we profit from Russia's technical advances, from its artistic and educational innovations, that is to say from its culture? We could undoubtedly derive immense profit from it; but undoubtedly also there does not seem to exist at present any real possibility that such a thing might occur. The Soviet Union broadcasts the idea that it is a hotbed of art, science, and technology; but it does little to show and less to prove it.

In reality, what Russia signifies today for Latin Americans is something very different, something which has nothing to do with geography or politics but with history. This something is often forgotten; but here, in an analysis which attempts to be as just and as well-balanced as humanly possible, this point will be considered and given all the enormous importance which it deserves. Russia today bears the banner of social and economic progress for the Latin American peoples, as England, the United States, and France did in the nineteenth century. It was not chance that took Miranda to England and Torres to the United States in search of support for our independence; nor was it chance that Nariño should translate the Declaration of the Rights of Man, which became an essential part of all our political constitutions; nor is it chance either that the name of my country is the United Mexican States. England, the United States, and France gave to our peoples, as they gave to all Western civilization, the political philosophy by which we have lived for something more than a century. This philosophy has had great success in the countries of its origin, and a very mediocre one in ours. Furthermore, for reasons we cannot go into now, the majority feel that this political philosophy has stagnated; and, at all events, it is a fact that it has not cured all our ills, not even the major ones— poverty and inequality, for example. And even though it is just, from a rational viewpoint, to condemn as foolish the belief that a political philosophy is a panacea, it is a fact—irrational but nonetheless a fact —that peoples, the great human conglomerates, want to find such a remedy; and that to find it they will drive themselves until they fall exhausted. If someone will walk a mile for a Camel cigarette, may not a people go a league, ten or a hundred, to find the philosopher's stone?

But as happens with many problems related to the Soviet Union, the positive definition is as important as the negative; to say that there is nothing we may hope from Russia does not mean many other things whose true extent must be clarified.

In the first place, it does not mean either of these two things: that there is a strong reason why Communists should be persecuted in our countries; or that the Communist thesis and Communist action lose in theoretical validity or possible political efficacy: both theory and action antedate the Soviet Union and can exist without it. Communism is an economic and social, rather than a political, thesis; its partisans offer it as the final solution to all the problems of the organization of human groups, and there is, therefore, no theoretical reason to reject the possibility of its being tested in isolation within the limits of a country.

It is natural that in the confused times in which we live these two statements will provoke angry retorts, suspicion, or skepticism, especially since they are presented in such a schematic form. Important and aggressive interests are involved, deep and inextinguishable prejudices; and dominating the picture is a huge ignorance.

Recognizing how inhospitable is the medium and the time for the calm reception of these two statements, I will merely refer to the only doubtful point which they raise. Will the security of a state and of a government be justification enough to eliminate, persecute, and even destroy the Communist Party and its members? The question arises, first, because to a Communist there is no national loyalty, only a supranational one; second, because the Communist theory accepts violence as the only possible method of "storming" into power and establishing the "dictatorship" of the proletariat. There is no doubt that every government has the right for legitimate security reasons to exclude those who do not accept national loyalty as a principle from offices where true, authentic state secrets are handled; but on the one hand it would not have the right to exclude them from all offices (the purely technical ones, let us say) and on the other, since possession of a right is as important as the manner in which it is exercised, it would be necessary to exclude not only the Communists but all those who put partisan interests above those of their country, and to do it in the most honest and open manner. A government loses this right—and soils itself in mire and ignominy besides— when it acts as did the United States in discharging seven State Department employees against whom no better charges could be made than that they were considered "potential security risks"—and this after months of harassment by public opinion—and discharging them, furthermore, without giving them an opportunity to defend or justify themselves even against such a vague accusation.

As for the political action of Communist Parties, a clear distinction should be made between cases where it is developed openly, within existing institutions and laws, and those other cases where it assumes the air and the methods of a true conspiracy against the state. In spite of what certain interests may assert and what ignorance may believe, the truth is that the Communist Parties of Latin American countries have worked much more in the first than in the second manner, though one cannot say the same for those of Europe and Asia. Every genuine liberal therefore should condemn the anti-Communist acts of the present governments of Brazil and Chile, not only because they are antidemocratic and have become even criminal but because of their true and twofold origin: the specific and reiterated pressure of the United States (where then is the national loyalty of these governments?) and the fact that the Communist Parties had begun to influence decisively the national life in Brazil and Chile, especially by taking advantage of the division, often the dissolution, of the liberal and conservative groups. For we should not forget that if there are many who think that the liberal political philosophy at its best has stagnated, what will they think of it when it is enunciated and practiced by our Creole politicians? Political power has belonged to liberals and conservatives for a full century, and even though undisputed advances have taken place in every country, the problems still to be resolved are so many and so enormous that our peoples must feel like the lame and drooping mule at the well. They have taken an infinite number of turns around the same spot without slaking their thirst or seeing the water of their efforts irrigate the fields. If the liberal or the conservative is some day to regain the authority and prestige he once had, it will not be for sure by denouncing the Communist as a traitor but by being himself an exemplary servant of his country.

In the second place, this does not mean that the Latin American countries should ignore Russia completely, and much less that it is a just, pleasant, or noble task to insult it with the impunity that distance gives us. Even in the United States at the beginning of the year of our Lord 1947, a university professor still had liberty and moral authority enough to label any international policy accepting a mortal hostility towards Russia as a cardinal principle as being not only foolish but criminal as well.[1] And the converse is also true. Few acts in recent international life (in spite of the fact that all of it has been so inharmonious) have been so gratuitous and so self-defeating as the insulting comments of the Russian press about President Dutra; insults are poor weapons of offense, especially when they are used against Latin Americans. To begin with, public opinion about Dutra in Brazil and in Latin America generally had already been formed some time before; and it was in no way changed by the remarks of the Soviet press; in sum, Russia gave to the Brazilian government a longed-for pretext to break diplomatic relations and to give to the persecution of the Brazilian Communists the character of a national crusade, a pretext which it previously lacked. But in spite of this, let us not forget that if Russia does not take us very seriously it is due in part to the arrogance and the lack of understanding of the powerful, but also because Russia takes us for nothing more than tools of the United States.

In sum, this does not mean that those of us who have not shared and cannot share, be it for physical or organic reasons even, either the faith or the theories or the methods of the Communists, do not recognize that the Soviet Union is a unique case in modern history, a country which has undertaken and realized material and spiritual tasks of great proportions, approaching them in a determined and intelligent way and resolving them with dreadful but deliberate sacrifices.

In contrast to Russia, from whom we can expect little or nothing, the United States can give us everything or almost everything: money, technical aid, political and military protection. From the point of view of pure gain, there cannot be the slightest room for doubt by any responsible person about the extraordinary degree of attraction that the United States has for us. But there is something more than the attraction of gain, though that in itself is powerful enough. There is also our geographic destiny and what we might call historical coincidence. The first resides in the obvious fact that we

[1] Joseph W. Ballantine, in *A Foreign Policy for the United States*, edited by Quincy Wright (Chicago: University of Chicago Press, 1947), p. 35.

live on the same continent, that since the year when the **Panama Canal** began to operate, thirteen of the nineteen Latin American countries have been a part of what has been so aptly called "the North American system," not to mention the fact that distances daily become shorter, and therefore the same fate is being extended to the six Latin American countries south of the Colombia-Brazil line. By "historical coincidence" I mean simply that like the United States we are branches—no matter how deteriorated or secondary—of the great trunk of Western civilization. Our general way of life, therefore, resembles the North American more than the Russian, let us say. This is a much stronger bond than is commonly supposed; to me it seems as strong as economic ties, and scarcely weaker than geographical ones, especially if the comparison with geography is made for a relatively short historical period.

I believe that, in spite of the frequent and sometimes prolonged dictatorial or personal regimes, in our countries the individual man always has had a wide field in which to move according to his tastes, his opinions, or his mere personal caprice. Rarely has he been subjected to the iron discipline of the state; and when his lot has been to support for a long time the discipline of some ruler—a thing, unfortunately not completely unheard of—he has in the end always shaken it off in an explosion which is all the more violent and complete, the deeper and more robust the roots of dictatorship have seemed to be. From this point of view our peoples have lived a democratic life: free and individualistic, even though it has not been peaceful nor always contained within institutions that are clearly outlined and respected. And this is, in essence, the same life that the North American people have lived: democratic, free, and not exempt either from great explosions or fierce civil war.

The United States, then, can give us everything or almost everything; but is *give* the appropriate word? Most people would say that *sell* is more accurate even though it is inadequate on three counts. Latin American countries have not always paid for what they claimed to have bought, and since it is possible that in the future this may occur again, with greater frequency, I am not sure whether it is worth the trouble to insist on the use of a word and a concept to which history may give the lie. Then, many transactions which formerly were simple contracts of bargain and sale have attached to them nowadays not only a price in money but in something more, which is "hard to tell," as the old song puts it. The scarcity of machinery for example has made the United States the sole supplier, and when the buyer faces a seller who has no competitor, he has to offer something more than money. Finally, there are things that have no price, that cannot be paid for in money. Such for example are political security and military protection. These two, as is the case with many of a purely economic nature, are paid for with subjection.

This is the true way of looking at the problem before us: the United States in fact can give Latin America everything or almost everything, but at the price of money and subjection. And we should not forget, if we are to see the picture whole, that the geographical circumstance of our living on the same continent and the historical coincidence of having similar ways of life both work in favor of our subjection.

The fact that our nineteen countries are subject to the United States is deplorable; one would give anything to change that fact. But it is not entirely unusual, nor does it have the irremediable and extreme character that one might see in it at first sight.

This last statement is the only one, I suppose, that requires some commentary. In the first place, all coins have two sides, both heads and tails. And if it is true that necessity, geography, and history tie us to the United States, it is no less true that the United States is tied to us by exactly these same circumstances, although economic necessity might seem in this case to operate with less urgency and intensity. There is a great factor, nevertheless, favoring us in a perfect and exclusive way: the strength of our insignificance would permit us to be happy without the United States, even happier than otherwise, if you will. But the United States cannot be the same without us because of the weakness of its greatness. We are its Achilles' heel —and woe if a poisoned arrow should find the vulnerable spot!

I know that it is extremely important, and fascinating besides, to explore this situation, which appears like a prophetic curse on the head of the North American colossus. In fact, I have essayed an exploration of the subject in a recent article.[2] As examples only, I will note some of the many arguments to show that if Latin America is tied to the United States, the United States is also fastened to Latin America.

[2] "Sobre Estados Unidos," in *Revista de America*, I, 3 (March, 1945), pp. 361–365.

The United States is capable of committing grave errors in its international affairs, so precipitately has it come into world power; but it would take extraordinary effort to imagine pride and vanity so blinding the United States that it would forget such an obvious fact as this: in all of Latin America one may find evidences of outrage and violence on the part of the United States—of its government, its capitalistic enterprises, and even its private citizens. And what has hurt one country directly and immediately is a sinister menace to the rest. In Latin America, consequently, there lies a thick layer of mistrust, quietly asleep like stagnant water, of rancor against the United States. If some day no more than four or five agitators, protected by official tolerance, embark on a campaign of defamation and hate against the United States, on that day all Latin America will seethe with unrest, and it will be ready for anything. Moved by a definite discouragement, by burning hate, these countries, though apparently submissive to the point of abjectness, would be capable of anything: of sheltering and encouraging the adversaries of the United States, of becoming themselves the bitterest kind of enemies possible. And then there would be no way to subdue them, or even to threaten them.[3]

An even graver error would be for the United States to believe that it could silence such a popular revolt with physical force. The very military weakness of Latin America would give to North American armed intervention such a clearly criminal stamp that the United States would not dare attempt it. Furthermore, I am not thinking of a military movement in Latin America, but of a species of general civil disobedience, which while being deadly effective would avoid or give no occasion for physical repression. But even if the occasion for military action should arise, what would the United States do? Sterilize the whole continent with its atomic bombs, the continent which it inhabits itself, the continent from which it draws a good part of its physical wealth and from which it could obtain even greater human riches? Would the United States occupy all the ports and capital cities of Latin America? But what about the rest of it, where there would also be men resolved to civil disobedience in the face of military intervention? Not to mention the fact that to maintain even a modicum of order would require the diversion of mili-

[3] The recent refusal of Panama to approve the treaty leasing military bases to the United States is a case in point.

tary forces and supplies so large that the United States, by the fact
of its occupation of Latin America, would become an easy prey to
any aggressor.

It is true that the sword is the ultima ratio in all conflicts, human
or divine; but it is not nor can it be a reasonable argument. It is the
ultimate one because it is appealed to as a last resort. Long before
reaching this point the United States would attempt by all possible
and imaginable means to obtain from Latin America as full and as
spontaneous a cooperation as possible. In fact, all the efforts of the
former to dominate the latter have no other explanation or end except to secure this cooperation, precisely because it is not as perfect
or as voluntary as the United States might wish. In the field, then,
not of violence and conflict but of cooperation, the United States
needs Latin America today, and will need it tomorrow and always.

To this add the fact that our ever-closer association, the ostentatious omnipresence of the United States, and its facile reproaches
against all things Latin American have begun to give Latin America
the function of censor and judge. It will perform the task impec-
cably, of that we may be sure. From this point of view, the United
States again appears before Latin America in an extremely weak and
vulnerable position. The North American, for example, has boasted
of the justice and efficacy of his social philosophy; equal opportunity
for all. Why not give it then to Latin Americans? Or is it that this
social philosophy has been made only for them and not for us? The
wealth of the United States and this social philosophy of theirs have
excited a covetousness that will not be satisfied without North
American economic and technical and moral aid. Not to give it, not
to share the wealth in some way with Latin America will arouse
the feeling of repugnance and contempt that a miser excites—worse,
because a miser traditionally is a fiercely solitary being, who
meddles with no one, who flees from everyone, while the United
States would be a miser turned ruler, that is to say a miser with a
cudgel. Well then, Latin Americans would be beggars, but also with
cudgels.

The frame of reference is not essentially changed if we admit that
our subjection is greater still, for what is important is to recognize
that there are different kinds of subjection. The slave is subject, but
so is man before the forces of nature, and nothing, in short, has im-
peded the former from freeing himself or the latter from counter-

balancing and dominating the forces of nature. What I mean, in sum, is that it will depend on men rather than on circumstances whether our subjection will be great or little, tolerable or intolerable; it is important to recognize that the ultimate course our lives will take must depend much more on us than on the United States. As always the greater load falls on the shoulders of the weak, who nevertheless have the greater necessity of using their strength.

Let us agree to begin with that the present is far from reassuring. On one side there is all the strength (colossal, hence almost uncontrollable) of the economic and political interests of the United States, in the world and in Latin America. For some time now the North American has suffered the giddiness of high altitudes; but now he has assumed the rough impatience of one who feels the unaccustomed weight of world responsibility upon his shoulders. This makes it easy for him to believe that the great end of saving humanity justifies any means and consequently may carry everything in its path. In this hair-raising process of shock one must take into account the extremely complex and irritable sensibilities of the Latin American; the time could come when his mind may close against all feelings except those of rancor and of hate, when he may have no other desire than that of vengeance.

The rein upon that overpowering impetus can only be imposed by North American public opinion and the North American government, and by our public opinion and our governments. I believe that the North American people have not formed an opinion about us; the occasion has not arisen, or they have not had the necessity to do so; but insofar as they do have an opinion, it is rather favorable than unfavorable. On the other hand, few, very few Yankee businessmen or officials look on us sympathetically after having dealt with us over a long period of time. This fact, a quite painful one, is in no way surprising. To understand the Latin American countries requires an infinite patience, and to esteem them an inexhaustible store of sympathy. And if it is unusual for one of these two virtues to spring forth, how much more to find them in flower side by side.

Let us accept without any more scrutiny what was presented previously in summary form: public opinion and the leaders of our countries are not precisely the best bulwarks needed by our independence and by the difficult and complicated game in which our countries will be engaged in coming years. Nevertheless, we can count only on that, and on nothing more. That is why I have said that directing the ultimate course of our relations with the United States will be more our task than theirs; and that this direction will be neither easy nor pleasant.

And now let us jump to the last point in our subject: the attitude of Latin America towards a possible armed conflict between the United States and Russia. But first let us point out that conflicts of this sort rarely occur without being preceded by a clash of interests, of ideas, by a whole process during which the opponents begin first by taking preparatory positions, then positions of defense, and finally positions of attack. All of us in fact (the North Americans first of all) admit that the struggle has reached its preparatory stage. Would Latin America gain anything by entering into a war on the side of one of these two factions? On what side may it and should it be? On the side of the United States, to whom it is tied by material interests, by history and geography, or on that of Russia, physically, economically, and spiritually so distant?

For us to be against the United States in such a conflict seems to me not only impossible but unjustifiable, unless the United States offends us in an irreparable way or adopts political ideas which deny our own concerning liberty and democracy. But I think that the solutions we should investigate are those which assume that no conflict will occur, or that if it occurs that we may be neither against the United States nor for it. These two solutions really are a single one, for among the very few ways in which war could be avoided would be for Latin America (and China and India as well) to declare unequivocally, and promptly first, that it does not think the war between the United States and Russia is necessary or justified; second, that if war occurs it will not take part in the conflict.

From what point of view do we wish to examine the necessity for, or justification of, such a conflict? Let us look first at the thesis of the unbelievers, of those who think they have the answer to everything. They tell us that the conflict is fundamentally one of interests and that consequently it shall be settled by war, as such conflicts always have been. It is true that history seems to support this thesis with crushing weight, for in fact the great conflicts of interests have always been settled through war. Always? Perhaps not; compare those that ended in peaceful solution with those that led to war, and you will see that the former are not few. But here, as in anything that is truly meaningful, statistics would not be decisive. What is important, strictly speaking, is to consider whether any interest, no matter how great, is greater—is more important—than the danger which the next war will cause, not to the vanquished alone but to the victor as well. It is no longer a matter of lamenting the destruction of some districts in a few cities, or the loss of a few hundred ships or some thousands of airplanes, or even of a few insignificant millions of men, women, and children—the twenty million that Russia lost in the last war, for example. It is now a matter of the literal destruction of the human species and of all its works, the good and the bad; it is a matter, moreover, of making the earth barren for generations, so that even if there should be a couple who would escape death, there would be no apple, no original sin. There would be no possibility, in sum, to repeat the history of humanity. Before this perspective what is the value of all interests: petroleum, the markets, dominion over the seas? And it still is a valid thesis that if man has discovered effective means to resolve conflicts between individuals, there is no reason to give up hope that he may discover means to resolve conflicts between nations.

Let us examine now the thesis offered by the ideologists, who are astute as well as profound. They say that the conflict is only secondarily one of interests and primarily one of ideologies; the United States cannot look with approval upon the aggrandizement of a country which is organized according to economic, political, and social principles different from its own. Some maintain that we have democracy and liberty on the one side and on the other tyranny and totalitarianism. Others assert that there is on the one hand a Communistic imperialism and on the other a capitalistic imperialism. A third group holds that in one camp are ranged those who believe that the individual is the best moving force in social, economic, and political life, and in the other camp are those who exalt the state, the collectivity, to the detriment of the individual. In sum, that the light is on the right hand and darkness on the left, that the sky is above and hell below.

Let us not set ourselves to investigate whether these antinomies are correctly defined or not; let us limit ourselves to an investigation of whether the existence of one presupposes the necessary exclusion of its opposite. And let us begin by noting that heaven and hell have coexisted for centuries, and that light and darkness have done so for an even greater time, not to speak of democracy and tyranny, of republic and monarchy. Could North American democracy have the vanity to believe that it has resolved all the problems of human relationships? Whoever should believe that, let him travel without a blindfold over his eyes through the South of the United States and see how the Negro and the Mexican live there. Does not Russia have a similar vanity? To support it, let Russia throw open its borders and permit a coming and going of people without restrictions, to see whether all of us will want to live in Russia or whether Russia itself will be depopulated.

In my country, gentlemen, bus drivers are very honest men. When all seats are taken they shout at the top of their voices to those trying to get aboard "There's plenty of room—standing room, that is!" Now then, in the matter of systems and forms of political, social, and economic organization there is plenty of sitting room. That is why it seems to me that Latin America should act with the calm of one who travels sitting down, though with the energy and tenacity of him who strikes blow after blow. Latin America has but one true and authentic road before it: to continue its efforts to achieve liberty and equality, which it has partially obtained with so many hardships. Only in this way shall it be faithful to the blood that stains so many pages of its history!

THE PROBLEMS OF AMERICA*

A SLIGHT WARNING to begin with: I will not deal with all of America, only with ours, this which we call at times Latin America, at other times Ibero-America or Hispanic America. The name is used here without a modifier merely for convenience, and to be frank, for the pleasure of committing a verbal theft, since real theft is forbidden.

Another warning of greater importance but one which should also be made before we begin: to speak of somebody's problems presupposes the existence of that somebody. Are there among the various countries of America sufficient similarities for them to have common problems? I do not deny that the question may lack interest and in the present case should be taken for granted, but, aside from the fact that it has been the subject of a number of essays and even books,[1] I shall assume that the similarities exist. I shall attempt to make my remarks about the problems of America valid for all of it, though I will try to make the proper distinctions whenever they seem necessary.

* First published in *Cuadernos Americanos,* Año VIII, 2, March 1949, Vol. XLIV.

[1] See, for example, Luis Alberto Sánches, *Existe América Latina?* (Mexico: Fondo de Cultura Económica, 1944).

A useful point of departure might be the assertion that Latin America has not made as much progress as it should and could. *To progress* means *to go forward*, presupposing the existence of a goal, a goal that can indicate at any given moment whether we are advancing, standing still, or going backwards.

According to what goal could we judge our America? The Yankees, who are victims of the counting mania as well as of a persecution complex, on several occasions have attempted to "measure" the progress of Latin America,[2] and naturally have concluded that it is slow and scant. They have counted the population, for example, or they have appraised the volume and value of production, exports, imports, and other factors to measure economic progress. Social progress has been estimated by counting the school population, or more boldly the number of inhabitants per hospital bed, per washing machine, per telephone, or per automobile.

In spite of the infinite fondness that I have developed for things North American in my old and persistent effort to understand them, I believe that these are mistaken measures, for the following two reasons, among many others. First, because if they are applied to a relatively recent period a just conclusion would be that Latin America has progressed to an incredible degree. Mexico, for example, has created 25,000 rural schools in twenty-five years, beginning in 1922, and in the last seven years has built an average of 10 hospitals per year. It could be asserted, therefore, that our countries have advanced in the last thirty years at the same feverish pace in which the North American Middle West developed a century ago. Second, though the day may be near when we must accept the North American man as the measure of all things, up to the present the standard is simply *man*, which means that the progress of one community must be measured according to its own patterns and not against those of another.

To me these criteria are not yardsticks of progress, or at least not of the progress which I have in mind, which is not simply material or economic or even what is called social progress, but human progress in general. And I do not believe that there is any other way to measure this kind of progress except by the degree to which a man learns

[2] See, for example, Russell H. Fitzgibbon and Claud C. Wooten, *Latin America Past and Present* (Boston: D. C. Heath, 1946).

to live together with his fellows. This ability for social cooperation depends in part (and in great part if you will) on the material well-being which a people enjoy; but it does not always depend on that material well-being, as can be proved if proof were needed, by present-day Argentina.

There is one thing that has always claimed my attention in Latin America: the indifference, the aloofness in which man lives in respect to his fellows. "Love thy neighbor as thyself," says the Christian precept. Well then, among us our neighbor is not really our neighbor, for the resemblance is small and the distances are great.

In fact, American man has always felt the vastness of the land that is America. "Broad and alien is the earth," the Peruvian novelist has said. Ours is an "empty continent," says a Mexican writer. And in Argentina the expression "populated desert" seems to have lost its original meaning by force of repetition.

The truth is that geographers [3] speak of the common demographic unit in Latin America as the very primitive one of the "closed cloister": a spot of humanity here, another there, and between them emptiness, the no man's land in which man does not exist at all, much less coexist. It is not only that there is nothing between one human blob and the next, but also that each of these blobs—whatever its size or situation—is dense at the center, thinning out as one approaches its periphery. This means that, for the present and for many long years to come, there is no hope that one human patch may spread until it touches on its closest neighbor, both merging into one and thus enlarging the area in which men may live together. That is why geographers assert that in all of Latin America there are just three regions having a "healthy" demographic growth, areas in which the center grows without sacrificing the population density of the periphery: the highlands of Costa Rica and Colombia and the southern states of Brazil.

Many curious consequences derive from this claustral demographic unit. The first of these has been noted—the low degree or total lack of social relationship between the men of one cloister and those of others. The second is the fact that the country or nation is an entity in good part fictitious, or if you will a reality which is scarcely

[3] See, for example, Preston E. James' excellent geography, *Latin America* (New York: The Odyssey Press, 1942).

half real. For in addition to the territorial continuity which most
writers on international law establish as a characteristic of the state,
one would expect of the nation that its population also be continuous
and without a break. The third is the necessity that there be created
in each populated patch—with a manifest waste of time and effort—
all kinds of institutions and services, since by definition a cloister is
a self-sufficient entity in economic, political, social, and even spiritual affairs. Finally, the largest patch seeks to govern the lesser
ones; but since each one is a cloister, the inhabitants of one do not
know why those of another seek to impose upon them general laws
and customs. These are imposed, but through violence which may be
grave or slight, passing or permanent. Such lack of understanding is
easily explained. If the human body recognizes the primacy of the
heart, it is because the heart serves the whole body; to each part of
the latter it sends pure blood, the red, and from each part it takes
away the poisoned blood, the blue. The heart governs the body because it fills two general functions—sacred functions one might call
them: it nourishes and it purifies. But why should a distant and isolated cloister seek to govern other cloisters, distant and isolated too?
Why, if their peoples do not live together—simply because one is
greater and stronger, or because it is located in a dominant position
on the plateau or the coast? The truth is that communications, authority, and power are all concentrated in the largest cloister, and it
seeks to use its power and authority for its own benefit, and not for
that of all the cloisters.

It is scarcely necessary to say that if our demographic unit is the
primitive one of the cloister there do exist very serious reasons for it.
Almost all the land in America is inhospitable, so that with the possible exception of Uruguay there is no country in which the progressive occupation and development of the land can be an easy task,
one that can be accomplished so to speak with the simple passing of
time.

In Mexico, for example, the north-central part is a wasteland with
little or no hope of redemption, even disregarding the cost of possible artificial solutions. The great central plateau depends on scanty
and irregular rains; the Gulf Coast region and the part to the south,
toward Guatemala, is completely tropical: hot, wet, aggressively
prolific, unhealthy. The country in truth can depend only on small

isolated valleys in the great central plateau and on fertile expanses in the northwest. In addition there is the tangle of mountains and mountain ranges that slice across the country, literally cutting it up into bits. This geographic description of Mexico is essentially valid for Central America and the Caribbean. Colombia, Ecuador, Peru, and Chile are victims of the colossal Andean barrier, theme of repeated literary flights. And though the Colombian may count on excellent highlands and hillsides which he occupies and works with pleasing success, in order to move men and their wealth from one place to another he has to struggle against the mountains which devour his time and efforts; in the northwest his land contains a jungle so dense that one is seized by the idea that it could become a trap for men. Brazil has the jungle too, nor does it lack the desert, and in addition, right in the center there is the justly named Amazonian "hole" or basin. Ecuador and Peru also have their untamable tropic and desolate desert regions. Half of the territory of Chile is barren. Not all of Argentina is pampas, much less wet pampas; it also has its deserts, and a Patagonia which suffers habitation only when the human wolf dresses in sheep's clothing.

And the tragic thing is that in these inhospitable lands is found a good part of the wealth that man in America needs to live; the Peruvian and the Bolivian Indians have to climb up to a height of 4,000 meters to tear from the earth the tin or the copper which they sell in order to buy corn and wheat for their sustenance. Thus the inhospitable areas force the population to concentrate in the less inhospitable ones, isolating one populated area from another.

As is always the case, not everything is disadvantageous in this demographic growth of the claustral type; as pleasant and as useful as human intercourse may be, it should not be as close as it is in Europe. There man feels it imposed upon him; he is compelled to live with his fellows, elbow rubbing elbow, as if they were all on a chain gang, on their way to prison or to exile. One of the reasons which make the human climate of America decidedly healthier is that up to the present there has existed between man and man enough land to work and pure air to breathe. Unfortunately the separation between men is at present so great that it becomes sterile like the desert; and like the desert it engenders solitude and abandonment.

Of course there has been an enormous advance in the process of occupying and taming the land. It is impressive for example to reconstruct a map of the areas populated by the early Americans at the time of the Discovery and the Conquest. Three-fourths of them lived in the extremely restricted strips where flourished the great Maya, Aztec, and Inca civilizations, and the less advanced one of the Chibchas. The rest of our enormous territory was not inhabited at all, or it was sparsely populated by disorganized tribes. Today the population is much greater and concentrated in denser groups; the distances and the obstacles which separate some demographic nuclei from others have been reduced. In spite of this, neither Latin America as a whole, nor any individual country in it has been able to imitate the North American feat of populating and taming a territory of great magnitude in a bare century and a half. Not only that, but all the Latin American countries are still very far from achieving that goal, and in some cases one cannot say when or how it could be done.

The stubbornness of the soil [4] explains in good measure its incomplete mastery and occupation; the partial occupation and mastery of the soil explain the primitive demographic unit of the cloister; and this explains in part what interests us most: the limited degree to which men have been able to live together in our America. But this does not explain why our capacity for social cooperation should continue to be limited and defective within a cloister, whether we call it a nation, province, or settlement. Here deep and obvious reasons

---

[4] It is common even today, in the mid-twentieth century and not in the sixteenth or the seventeenth, for some to see the wealth of the American continent as unlimited, especially as compared with Europe. As long as this opinion is maintained (or the opposite one, which I have adopted in this and other works) merely on the capricious ground of extreme affirmation or denial, either one or the other may be argued with equal brilliance and spirit. Perhaps there is a sane compromise between both extremes, and it would be this: there is not the slightest doubt that the natural economic possibilities of Europe have been explored and exhausted. The natural economic possibilities of Latin America, on the other hand, seem to be very great, limitless if you will; but only on the condition that the technology and the capital put to the task of exploitation of natural resources be limitless too. At all events, up to the present it is undeniable that man in America has been put to great pains merely to obtain a frugal livelihood.

come into play, but they are of a much different kind. It is no longer nature which separates man from man; it is man himself. Latin Americans must not be very wise, if they have not been able to get along with each other in spite of being condemned to live together in closed cloisters. It is evident that the monk, secluded in truth within a cloister—physically and materially shut up—makes the greatest effort imaginable to live congenially with the persons who must share the whole of his life. And yet, the Latin American has not attempted to do the same with all due determination; and even when he has done so, he has failed for the most part.

It is enough to take a look at the social structure of any of our countries; and on this point unfortunately there seem to be no exceptions, even in degree. None of them has a middle class (or at least it is not numerous and compact) whose existence may mitigate the trenchant and painful contrast between an excessively poor low class and a disproportionately rich high class. Perhaps the only thing that these two classes have in common is their dense ignorance. For the rest, they could not be more different or more distant. And I insist that we should not dissemble the abominable indifference that separates our low from our high classes. The superficial observer tends to see the straw in his neighbor's eye but not the beam in his own, so that those who come from countries where European dress is general, very frequently believe that social distances are smaller in their countries and greater in countries with Indian populations, simply because in the latter case there is added to social separation the colorful note of a picturesque costume.

There is no modern society of course in which social differences do not exist in clearly visible form; but ours seem to be greater than in others, more offensive, poisoning to a greater degree the entire social body and leading to violent convulsions from time to time. The reason among others is that one expects that in our America there should be a great deal of space, of air, of light; and sufficient food and shelter for all. And when we talk of social classes let us not forget that phenomenon to which sociologists give so much importance: social capillarity, the greater or lesser facility or difficulty with which a man of lower social rank may detach himself from his class and climb to a higher one.

As to our clear and profound class divisions, I suppose that it is not necessary to speculate a great deal to admit them and to feel their magnitude. It is enough to think of a Bolivian or Peruvian Indian at one extreme and a *señorito* from La Paz or Lima on the other; a Negro from Colombia's Caribbean coast and a rich industrialist from Antioquia; a Chilean *roto* and the dandy from the Union Club of Santiago; a Mexican businessman with summer houses at Cuernavaca, Taxco, and Acapulco and a nomadic Lancandon Indian. It is possible for some ingenuous Latin American to think that though social differences are great in our America they are not so great as in Western Europe or in the United States, because among us there is no true aristocracy nor any genuine industrial proletariat: the first a truly supercilious class; the second not simply low but subterranean.

It may be that our high classes are in fact not as high as the traditional European aristocracy or the improbably rich of the United States, though one cannot believe that there is anything in the world as low as an Indian from the Bolivian plateau. But even if this were true, it would be of no help to us. For one thing, European aristocracy is less aristocratic than it is commonly supposed, and consequently not as high as it pretends to be. For another, it contributes extremely little or nothing to the life of the community; it ceased to be a measure of social comparison or a source of envy or resentment a long time ago. In fact, it is a confined social group. In any event, up to the point that it is a true aristocracy, it has had the time to polish and refine itself. Ours, on the contrary, is so recent, it has been created so close to our own eyes, it has been so crudely mixed, with money as its sole ingredient, its fortunes derive so directly from plunder, from official favors or pure luck, that it cannot be the object of admiration; and at times one might be inclined even to deny it the right to oblivion. To these limitations we should add its general lack of good taste and refinement. Many of the heroes of our Independence were wealthy gentlemen; in all the countries of America the high middle class which developed during the second half of the nineteenth century on occasion became enlightened, generous, and progressive. But the rich man of this century is beyond God's grace, from whatever side you look at him. Thus, we should keep in mind that our aristocracy governs or has governed our countries, directly or indirectly; and even in those countries where it has been cast down, it does not accept a purely ornamental role but awaits the opportunity to return to power. That is the reason why, at best, it is seen with distrust; at worst, it is considered an enemy.

Our economic structure is another formidable obstacle preventing men from effective social cooperation in our America. If we agree that the social structure is characterized by profound class divisions, we must suppose that a good part of these divisions have their origins in the disparity of means and economic opportunities. On one extreme we have great wealth invested in lands, in estates, and now in industry, which permits an easy life, one of idleness and indifference; on the other, a miserly and uncertain wage; on the one hand the palace with its private racetrack, according to what one hears about Buenos Aires; on the other, the famous *conventillo* or tenement. And let us not forget that the vices created by this economic organization produce effects which every day become more generalized and more greatly felt. In no way was it the same to be poor in the twelfth century as it is to be poor in the twentieth, for modern industry has awakened man's cupidity by unfolding before his eyes in store after store an infinite variety of commodities, of services, of satisfactions and pleasures—things that man in other ages could not even imagine, and consequently could not covet. And man himself has changed, of his own doing and as a result of external actions; it is certain that the human being of this century is not content to keep on being poor, nor to tolerate the fact that the decisive difference between men should be that of wealth. For many centuries, the Christian religion succeeded in being a rein to the material appetites of man, or a compensation for his poverty. Today Christianity has forever lost that function, retaining the more modest one of giving an innocent air of pure good luck to riches acquired perhaps by devious means.

But there is a factor which is often forgotten in analyzing the peculiarities of the economic structure of our countries, something which impedes as well a fuller capability for social cooperation in the men of America: the coexistence of primitive economic forms and institutions with others that are extremely advanced. All of us know of the brilliant Panagra poster: a monster of the air crossing the skies of Peru or Bolivia at a speed of 500 kilometers per hour and at a height of 6,000 meters, while below in the burning desert some Indians with their herd of llamas look up at it in astonishment. And in truth Panagra, that old procuress of imperialism, has been kind to us Latin Americans, for without doing violence to the truth it has substituted the llama for another, more primitive but no less generalized means of transportation—the backs of the Indians themselves, on which both goods and persons have been carried for centuries, and still are being carried today.

Not only in transportation but in all of the economic life of our America do we see proof of the coexistence of primitive forms with those which are extremely modern. Beside the celebrated factory of Carretones, in which glass is blown by pure lung power to make that unique Mexican glassware, we have the modern plate glass factories of Monterrey; beside the sarape and the poncho, woven by hand on primitive looms, are the great textile mills of Antioquia, San Pablo, Santiago, or Orizaba; and in Buenos Aires, beside the great department store where one may buy, according to the old formula, "anything from a pin to a locomotive," one sees the carts pulled by beasts of burden daily going to offer vegetables to housewives and housemaids throughout the city.

It is not easy for men to live harmoniously together when they exist in economic worlds which are radically different. Is understanding an easy thing between the man who carries his corn to market on his back and the man who receives by air some spare part for the machinery of his factory? In fact, one very frequently finds in Latin American countries human groups that live on a strict barter economy, while others operate on an economy which is the child of the most advanced capitalism. Steinbeck presents no other problem in his dramatic novel *The Pearl*.

Social and economic differences among our peoples are so great and so deep-rooted that they cannot be lessened or readjusted in a normal way, in a tranquil, daily, and mechanical manner, let us say. "Social capillarity" also is lacking or weak, since the means to move from one class or group to another do not exist or are inefficacious.

The means and opportunities to acquire an education which will compensate somewhat for a person's humble social origins or economic poverty are tragically limited in our countries. Schools are scarce; those that exist are concentrated in the great urban centers. In the small towns and the rural communities they either are totally lacking or they are rapidly decreasing. The efficacy of their teaching is quite limited, because of their changeable philosophy, their routine methods, and the poverty of their resources; because they do not serve the vocations and the varied interests of modern man; and because they lack a superior and evangelistic inspiration that may raise them to the level of the saving task that they must undertake. Their economic means are perhaps even more restricted, for not only are they controlled by a few individuals but they suffer from the poverty of our countries as countries. The accumulation of capital in our countries is quite small and, consequently, credit is restricted; it does not serve the whole country, but only the principal cities, and in these it is granted to him who already has a fortune, not to him who begins one.

Not only are the means for social mobility scanty; the same is true of the opportunities. Societies as rigid, as static as ours scarely give a chance to the individual who wants to change his status. Compare, for example, the normal opportunities offered by countries like the United States and Canada with those that exist in the South American countries that are the most like them—Argentina and Brazil. The daily history of the United States is full of the shoeshine or newspaper boy who becomes a magnate; in our countries the most similar cases would be that of the demagogue or outlaw who overnight becomes the ruler of a country.

Let us summarize what we have said up to this point, since there is no harm in bringing order into chaos once in a while. The stubbornness of the soil in America concentrates the population in the less inhospitable zones, isolating it from the populations living in other zones, thus giving rise to a demographic growth of the closed-cloister type which makes it difficult for men of one cloister to cooperate on a social plane with those of other cloisters. Within each cloister the human ability for social cooperation is feeble because the social and economic structure profoundly divides men into classes or groups. The division persists because sufficient means and opportunities are lacking for men of a lower class to rise easily to higher classes or groups.

Let us note this last conclusion: in a society deeply divided into classes or groups, and in which in addition there is a lack of normal means and opportunities to change one's social position, men in the lower groups meet with great resistance in their efforts to rise into the higher groups. Does this mean that the man of the lower class bends before this resistance and is resigned not to climb on the social ladder? This has occurred to some extent in societies far removed from modern times, but not in those of today, even those as modest as ours.

What really occurs is something quite different and quite lamentable. Since social change does not occur fluidly and normally, in a daily and mechanical way, it occurs instead from time to time, once every twenty or thirty years, let us say. But then the change is a radical one, it is total and profound; it comes violently and sweeps away laws, institutions, habits, and customs, leading to civil war on the greater number of occasions. In sum, social change becomes revolution, and at times attains the proportions of a veritable cataclysm. During the Mexican Revolution beginning in 1910, for example, Mexico failed to increase in population for the first time in its long history, so that the census of 1920 registered a net population loss of 826,000 inhabitants. The land-owning class disappeared as a whole; in it had been concentrated from 60 to 70 percent of all the country's wealth. Great professional groups, the make-up of governmental and political classes, the army, the faculties of the universities—all were thoroughly made over, or very nearly so. New social classes emerged, with decisive political power: the brand-new collectivist owner of the land, the working class, a popular army, and a new high middle class, so new, so young, so delicate that of the thousand millionaires that Mexico boasts today not one of them has been a millionaire for more than ten or fifteen years. He who knows first-hand this kind of change, occurring from time to time in our countries, will not think the expression "cataclysm" an exaggerated one.

We still must introduce, even though in a hurried and schematic form, the other great problem of America: the continual disturbances and adjustments which the action of external factors imposes on our countries.

Though few would deny that American societies suffer disturbances as deep as those of other peoples, many would doubt that these disturbances are deeper, or that most of them—all the significant ones at least—are due to forces originating in lands foreign to our America. Such a position lacks all sense of ethics or responsibility. It does not make us believe for an instant that outsiders are the cause of our ills. On the other hand it is based on a fact as irremediable as this: once "discovered" by Europe our America remained clinging to but not entirely within Western civilization. Since then our life has been above all a sustained effort to find out what Europe first and now the United States have invented, so we may adapt it to our own living conditions.[5]

It can be said that it took us three centuries to assimilate the forms of political, economic, and social organization we received from Spain—its art, its religion, and its language. The task was overwhelming because Spain was America's first contact with Europe and the contact was complete, involving each and every phase of a civilization then the most complex and dynamic in the world. But Spain, in the very act of the Conquest, or soon after, lost the initiative in Europe, ceased to be the source of Western civilization. The Dutch from the middle of the seventeenth century, the French in the first part of the eighteenth, and the English from that time onwards through the nineteenth, left Spain farther and farther in the rear, until it became typically a country with a Golden Age behind it, a country in which yesterday in all respects had been better than today. For that reason Spain, instead of originating changes and reforms, received them from Western Europe and transplanted them later to America, but tardily and incompletely, and, at times, in quite spurious versions.

Partly because of this, it can be said that the process of adjustment and dislocation to which America has been subjected since its first contact with Europe was more tolerable during the epoch of our dependence on Spain than it was later, though other circumstances contributed in making this so. On the one hand, Europe of the seventeenth and eighteenth centuries was indisputably a society of continuous and sometimes profound change, but this was neither

[5] It is a different problem to explain why one part of the American continent, the United States, not only remained in the very current of Western civilization but finally became its principal source, at least in things material and political. Perhaps the principal factors—none of which came fully into play in Spanish America—were the existence of a great territory, empty of men and full of great wealth; and more than that, although that already is a great deal, the happy historical accident by which the United States was founded and directed by England, the country that set the tone of contemporary Western life. To that one would have to add an incredibly good fortune which has made North American history happy as few histories have been.

swift nor revolutionary. In the field of political organization, for example, the English revolution of 1685, mother of the modern parliament, did not spread into the rest of Europe, as happened with the three other great revolutions, which did reach almost universal proportions: the independence of the United States, the French Revolution, and the Industrial Revolution. But these three, in spite of their dates, in reality open the nineteenth century and belong in the contemporary period. The difficulty in communications, furthermore, obstructed the propagation of changes, large or small. Thought was transmitted only in printed form, and in America only on a very limited scale. It is estimated that in Mexico, where Spanish colonial culture flowered as in no other place, there were printed in the three centuries of Spanish dominion some thirty thousand publications, or barely one hundred per year. Besides, overland transportation was extremely limited, and that on the seas was scarcely better. The time which the caravels of Columbus took in their voyage to America would be appreciably shortened only after the nineteenth century was well on its way, when the famous North American sailing vessel, the Clipper, crossed the North Atlantic.

The two circumstances which made less urgent our necessity to adjust to new conditions lost their validity with the progress of the nineteenth century, the first of our independent life. For one thing, known means of communication reached countries which had heretofore been without them. And new means were devised, which perfected or completed those already existing, all of them tending toward the instantaneous and incessant transmission of ideas and news. For another, European society set itself determinedly on the road of technological and scientific progress, taking material well-being as the goal of personal and collective life. In this field, change began to be a daily occurrence and of a significance which became more and more abstruse and revolutionary.

In addition two new circumstances soon made themselves felt. If there was one field in which Spain's legacy was of no consequence at all, it was in science and technology; that is, precisely the one in which the more dynamic and better gifted countries labored with the most ardor and success. Furthermore, Europe itself, and even more strangely the Catholic Church, failed to see until it was too late that a world as advanced as the one being created by the new

science and technology could not be contained in the molds of existing political, social, and moral organization. Thus it was that
Europe—and even more the United States—began to be for our
America on the one hand the source of the most amazing technical
advances and on the other a source of the most lamentable moral
and political regression. It is not surprising, therefore, that though
the necessity to adjust to changes in European society became more
urgent in the nineteenth century, our capacity to adjust was ex-
panded only after much delay, and with grave and irreparable
damage.

Thus did we pass all of the nineteenth century, musing on economic and political liberalism, not with the sorrowful though tranquil attitude of the muser but in the midst of clamor, dismay, anxiety, and violence. In no country of our America was the triumph of
liberalism complete, and its partial dominance was not obtained
without war and bloodshed. There will come a time when some intelligent man will study the history of liberalism in our America;
then shall we see how painful has been its progress, the incredible
contortions it has had to make to work out its course, the extremely
comic deviations it has suffered on being transplanted to our environment, so different from that of Western Europe, where it was
born. And I have a feeling that the student will not be able to escape
this conclusion: we inherited from Spain a central political organization, somewhat authoritarian, in which initiative and the ultima
ratio resided in the state; we abandoned our inherited ideas, institutions, and experience to embrace the liberal philosophy, in which
the state abstains from action and the individual is the sole mover
and regulator; only to discover that scarcely had we turned the last
century when there began a return towards a political organization
similar to that which we had received from Spain, and which was
rejected by the best men in America to put us in step with modern
Europe. We cannot say that we have lost a century of our existence;
but we can say that we were victims of the illusion that a politico-
economic philosophy had universal validity solely because it was
illuminated and brought to flower by countries which we looked up
to as models. We certainly were victims of that illusion; first because
we associated the liberal philosophy with our desire to liberate ourselves from the domination of Spain and the Catholic Church, and

second, in a more general way, because the human tendency to attribute universality to what man invents or experiences seems to be incurable.

This lack of perspicacity on the part of the American countries in evaluating the great changes which have their origins in the creative countries of the Western world, in discerning their true significance, their final course, their transitory nature or relative permanence, is revealed in a fact which could be observed in Mexico after 1920, and which in these very days of our Lord can be seen in other American countries—in Argentina, Brazil, Colombia, Peru, Chile, and Venezuela.

In none of these countries was the arrival of the Industrial Revolution noticed in time—though perhaps it came in carnival disguise. Here was an economic-social revolution that presupposed the loss of power by the land-owning oligarchy, and consequently the desperate efforts of the latter to retain that power; the birth of a financial and industrial oligarchy, destined first to thrive at the expense of the old one and finally to replace it; and even more important, the transformation of a rural proletariat—disorganized and meek—into an urban and industrial proletariat—aggressive and organized. These profound changes are the essence of every contemporary history of Western Europe; they have been studied step by step, in all their details and vicissitudes, and they have been studied accurately besides. Notwithstanding this fact, no statesman in Latin America, not one of its thinkers that I know of, took the step or said the word that the situation required.

Our poor America always marches at the rear, and it does not even have the advantage of avoiding the precipice into which those who went before have fallen so tragically and spectacularly. To me, the political phenomenon of greatest recent interest in Latin America is the one that years ago, at the end of the other World War, appeared first in Italy, then in Germany and Portugal, soon after in Spain, then in France and in Poland, though it did not reach its final consequences in these last two countries because the second World War came down upon them. Similarity may not be identity; consequently it is only as a similarity that it is pointed out.

Certainly in our America this phenomenon appears like this: the leading groups most capable of administration become the most blind politically, for they have not been able to take note in time (and some still do not even have a suspicion) of the changes that have taken place in their countries during the past few years. These changes are two above all, and one of them is older than the other. The first is a gradual disillusionment with the liberal and democratic formulas and methods of government; the second is the birth and proliferation of an industrial proletariat, and in some countries of a new juvenile mass. This has created great popular groups, sunk in dissatisfaction and in the most complete political disorientation, easy prey consequently to the first adventurer who winks at them. There is a formula which though grotesque still is illustrative: the liberal leaders have ceased to attract the masses.

This phenomenon has been seen with great clarity in Argentina, and it seems to me, with no less clarity in Colombia. The radicals in Argentina (who represented liberal opinion for many years) ceased to exercise the seduction they possessed at their peak during the first government of Irigoyen, to such a point that it was useless to seek a man or a name that could bring radicalism out of its gloomy indifference. The Tamborinis sounded like the Moscas, and the Moscas flew very much like the Tamborinis.† In Colombia what new thing could the name of Señor Turbay tell us? At best he was the dark horse of liberalism; at worst not the dark horse but the black omen. In a long career of political depreciation, he raced from extreme to traditional liberalism; that is to say he became the type of man who expresses definite opinions on the problems of the rich but is silent, or cautious at least, about the problems of the poor.

But one must agree that the masses which carried Perón to power, that followed Gaitán until the defeat of the liberal party, did not and do not move toward the right. On the contrary, they fell in the tragic trap because they sought and wished for their own betterment, for change, for progress; in sum, they followed the "leftist" sign of life, which they could not find in the other camp, that of tradition and deterioration. And—as in romantic novels—they also fell—because of a man; because of a physical, tangible man, to whom the masses give their greatest confidence when institutions become dehumanized and depersonalized.

And since no one noticed in time, this same fault cost Mexico a long and cruel revolution which fortunately brought it "up to date,"

† Puns on these two men's names with *tambor* (drum) and *mosca* (fly). [translator]

at least for a day. To Brazil the cost was an apathy and confusion of which its own jungles can give one an idea. Argentina fell into the trap of a demagoguery as vulgar as it was false, and which perhaps has cost it its future for the next fifty years. To Peru the cost was a plunge once more into the darkness in which it has lived for a whole half century; to Venezuela the loss of a chance to accelerate its progress, a chance to continue it by peaceful ways, as it had begun to do so courageously. To Colombia the necessity of resorting to the assassination of its demagogue to obtain a breathing space which (one cannot yet tell) may lead to genuine and modern democratic progress or may be just another bloody mark in the history of our oligarchic governments.

To my way of thinking America is faced with many problems, but especially with two great ones, on whose solution depends in great part the tempo of its progress. One is the slight degree of social cooperation that one finds; the other is the problem of discerning and profiting from the course of Western history and civilization, in order to shorten the road that we must travel.

I would not be at all surprised should the readers of these comments object in whole or in part to what I say, tired without a doubt of the somber and for the most part insincere tone which life has been taking these days; and they may ask angrily, "And what is the remedy for all of this?"

Overcoming my natural timidity, I will confess it has always seemed to me that the division of labor makes some men feel surer of themselves in the analysis of ills than in the giving of advice as to their cure. But if I must venture this time into the field of the herb-doctor and the medicine man, I would risk a couple of conclusions and two remedies.

Government is the major force in all modern societies; our personal and collective lives depend on it to an already incredible extent, which in the future will be greater still. Consequently, the quality of their governments is today the major problem of all countries, and in order to assure that his government is the best one possible, no citizen may refuse to participate in the "public thing."

The American countries belong in the sphere of Western civilization, but more in its material and political fields than in the cultural, this being a situation that is emphasized by the present preponderance of North America. Since our bond with Western civilization is more passive than active, we tend to imitate without reflecting, as well as to reject "the lessons of history." It is truly a necessity for Latin America to believe in its own creative genius and to screen very carefully all foreign innovations.

BACKGROUND OF TYRANNY*

ONE CANNOT CALL the political situation of our countries either democratic or tyrannical without first defining what we understand by democracy, for the concepts and institutions of the Western world suffer unsuspected deviations when transplanted to Latin American soil. A democracy in the English, North American, Scandinavian, or even the French style has never existed in any country of our America. Of this we can be sure because among other reasons in a truly genuine democratic society tyranny by definition is inconceivable: tyranny is always imposed and never consented to, while the very essence of democracy is that the form of government is consented to by a majority of the society affected by it. It is almost unnecessary to mention that in each and every one of the Latin American countries there have been tyrannies from time to time. Even more, they are occurring again today with a facility which points to the existence of old habits, and perhaps of a morbid pleasure which must be periodically satisfied.

Democracy in Latin America, more than anything else, must insure at least a minimum of personal freedom and of public freedom; the lack of one or both of these freedoms justifies the application of the term "tyranny" if not that of "dictatorship." (The first being the abuse of or the imposition in extraordinary degree of any power or

---

* First published in *Cuadernos Americanos*, Año IX, 4, July 1950, Vol. LII.

force; the second occurring when a government, invoking the public interest, exercises its powers outside the constitutional laws of the country.)

We must keep in mind this condition for Spanish American democracy—the existence of personal and public freedom—since honestly or dishonestly the custom often is to take as a criterion for the success of a democracy the fidelity with which electoral results reflect the will of the voter. To admit this as a valid criterion would be to fall into the evident absurdity of saying that while Argentina and Colombia are today perfect democracies, Mexico lives under a tyranny. In present-day Colombia, for example, the Conservative Party recently obtained a unanimous election in favor of its truculent candidate. But who voted? Solely and exclusively the conservatives, for the liberals, who form the majority party, stayed away from the polls. This action was agreed upon by the liberal leaders, as a means of withholding their approval from an immoral and illegal election.

Aside from this fact, the present government of Colombia, at the head of which is Sr. Ospina Pérez—polite, rich, university-trained, good-looking, a man whose snowy head suggests the kindness, tolerance, and comprehension of the father—conducted during the long months before the elections a terrorist campaign that was positively criminal, murdering liberals and burning their homes and political clubs. Such persecution frightens and nauseates: the appearance of the police in public places, cafes, or cinemas to beat the liberals they found there until they left them bloody and lifeless, merely because they were liberals.

In Mexico, on the other hand, complete personal freedom has existed for the past thirty years, and a public freedom almost equally free. And yet, the results of municipal, provincial, and federal elections continue to give overwhelming majorities to the government candidates, though Mexicans are convinced that those candidates have long since lost the sympathy and support of the whole country.

The failure of personal and public freedom to find an outlet in political action engenders first discouragement and then desperation. Electoral fraud should have the same results, in even greater degree. This is not the case, however, as Mexico shows, perhaps for two principal reasons. First, it seems that man shows greater resentment against his inability to attempt a thing than toward the final barrenness of an effort freely made. Thus electoral fraud creates skepticism rather than desperation. The second reason is the difficulty or impossibility of proving such a fraud convincingly and mathematically. That is why the existence of those two freedoms is what counts for the present in drawing a dividing line between democracy and tyranny. The judgment could not be more liberal, for what this line divides is the hope of democracy from the brutal reality of tyranny.

All well-born men and women must have a sense of physical anguish when they contemplate the present political scene in Latin America. Of the twenty countries that make it up, seven (Nicaragua, Venezuela, Brazil, Argentina, Peru, Colombia, and the Dominican Republic) live under indubitably tyrannical regimes; nine (El Salvador, Honduras, Costa Rica, Panama, Paraguay, Bolivia, Chile, Ecuador, and Haiti) are in such a precarious political situation that any grave occurrence—a presidential election or an economic crisis, for example—may precipitate them into unmasked tyranny; and no one would walk through fire to prove that the remaining four (Mexico, Guatemala, Cuba, and Uruguay) are yet immune from tyranny, nor even that they have made encouraging political progress in the last few years.

It is disturbing that sixteen of our countries either live under a tyranny or may soon come under one. Even more disturbing is the relative magnitude or importance of this fact because in political matters, as in many others, man is more inclined to imitate the bad if it is great than the good if it is small. Of the three largest countries of Hispanic America, Brazil and Argentina now live under tyrannies, while only Mexico enjoys liberty. Of the five medium-sized countries, Venezuela, Peru, and Colombia have fallen under dictatorship; Chile may suffer the same fate; only Cuba lives in a democracy, and that democracy is far from ideal.

One may also judge the situation by noting which countries have progressed politically in the last fifteen or twenty years and which may be said to have regressed. Mexico, Cuba, and Uruguay have remained democracies during this period, making small or disputable advances. Nicaragua, Brazil, and the Dominican Republic were and still are tyrannies; Venezuela, Peru, Colombia, and Argentina abandoned democracy, the first three becoming dictatorships, the fourth a tyranny. In Costa Rica, Panama, Paraguay, Chile, and Haiti the political situation has worsened. Lastly, El Salvador, Honduras, Bolivia, Ecuador, and Guatemala have improved so recently that a new regression would surprise no one. The situation could be summarized in the following chart:

Still in a bad situation	3 countries
Decidedly worse	4 countries
Considerably worse	5 countries
Still in satisfactory condition	3 countries
Slightly better	5 countries

This is to say that not only are twelve countries in a bad political situation, but nine have worsened while only five have bettered themselves. It may be concluded that dictatorship and tyranny are the predominant phenomenon in Latin America, and that in the past few years tyranny has progressed while democracy has lost ground. To complete the picture it should be repeated that democracy has not made tangible progress in the countries which have lived in freedom during the past twenty-five years. On the contrary, of the three democracies thought, at one time, to be the most successful in Spanish America—Uruguay, Colombia, and Costa Rica—the first remains stationary, the second has fallen under the worst type of dictatorship imaginable, while the third is entering a crisis from which there is no telling how it will emerge.

The question inevitably looms before us: what forces condemn or seem to condemn Latin America to fall time and again under tyranny, to remain sunk in it up to the neck like an animal in a bog?

Latin Americans think they know their own history more or less, and the bold ones say they have a quick answer to all problems, even to one of such exasperating complexity. But, would not North Americans and Europeans feel perhaps that questions of this sort would tax their capacity for investigation and even for understanding? A fine surprise would be theirs if one suddenly told them that it is in their own world that this deplorable Latin American spectacle has its remote inspiration.

Though recognizing that it is very difficult to make valid generalizations from numerous and infinitely varied facts, I believe that the phenomenon of Latin American tyranny, like so many others in the history of our countries, is founded on a general cause. It results from the process of violent adaptation by the Spanish American countries

to a Western civilization which was not theirs and for whose as-
similation they were not even moderately prepared. We need not go
back too far, to the native societies anterior to the Conquest, because
then the phenomenon is obvious. Those societies resembled European society in nothing; their concept of the world and their scale of
values were entirely different. However, let us begin with the end of
the eighteenth century or the beginning of the nineteenth, when the
Spanish American countries were preparing or obtaining their political independence, while Western Europe and the United States
were definitely turning toward the contemporary stage of their
history. What were the dominant traits of this contemporary Western
society?

One of them was the liberation of the individual in relation to the
state, the attempt being made to reduce the state to the mere function of police vigilance; the other an eagerness for material progress,
an appetite for wealth as the major preoccupation of the individual
and the loftiest goal of the state. That is to say, Western Europe
turned toward political liberty and material progress and with these
two goals constructed a philosophy that was unrivaled in the world
during all of the nineteenth century and the first years of the
twentieth.

Now then, for nothing were the Spanish American countries as
poorly prepared as for obtaining political liberty and material
wealth, for they had never been either free or rich, nor had they
made of liberty and wealth a major or minor preoccupation. The native peoples found on the continent by Spanish and Portuguese conquistadors lacked any sort of social organization, or they had developed an extremely rigid form of military theocracy. At all events,
the mass of people never counted for anything, except for labor of a
slavish or servile nature. Spanish and Portuguese rule confirmed and
prolonged for three centuries more an organization in which an improbably small group dominated the immense majority. There was
scarcely a change in the governing group, composed now of an
ecclesiastic hierarchy and the bureaucracy. As is logical to suppose,
in such societies individual freedom was almost totally unknown, and
wealth could not have been an incentive to the individual nor a goal
which the state would set for itself for the benefit of all the governed.

Let us remember that this rule lasted for three long centuries, and that it was a colonial rule. This must be understood, in the first place, as a government exercised in the interests of the metropolis rather than of the colony, a government whose original and supreme authority resided outside, there being within the colony only a secondary authority. Finally, Spain and Portugal imposed upon our countries a centralized and authoritarian government. The Creoles, mestizos, and Indians never elected a colonial official; all were designated by the King, who never named Indians or mestizos and only rarely Creoles. That is to say that the Mexicans or the Peruvians for three hundred years were ignorant of a government of their own and of the means to exercise and choose it.

If the Spanish American peoples lacked the preparation to quickly attain individual freedom and even national independence, they were not better armed to attain in a relatively short time a national wealth abundant enough and distributed adequately enough to reach the majority, making them feel that in truth there was material progress for them and for everyone.

Again, let us not go all the way back to the peoples before the Conquest, but let us see what colonialism may have bequeathed to our countries. Little or nothing, in truth. In the first place, the goal of material well-being appeared in the Western world when Spanish and Portuguese colonial rule was about to end, so that our peoples were not even acquainted with the philosophy of immediate ends. Second, we did not learn from Spain and Portugal how to manage our economies. Since our lands were colonies they were exploited not for their own benefit but for that of the metropolis. All attempts at industry were suppressed in order to make us consume Spanish manufactures, and since Spain was interested above all in precious metals, our agriculture, commerce, and industry were sacrificed to the search for ores and their extraction. The capital that was accumulated during the three centuries of domination did not belong to native Americans. A good part went to the Crown, which spent it to maintain its imperial policy; the Catholic Church received another part, also spent on imperial policy; and something remained as private capital in the hands of the Creoles.

When independence was achieved, the Crown lost its revenues, which fell on the new independent states; the capital of the Creoles fled to Spain in search of security, and the seizing of Church wealth was a task that took more than half a century. While this was taking place, it was necessary for the new states to appeal to foreign credit, which was granted at usurious interests, with irritating guarantees attached, and perhaps with the intention of getting our countries in debt in order to seize them later. Partly with the disentailed properties of the Church, partly through foreign loans, and partly through the profits of an international commerce that at last began to be organized, the Spanish American peoples attempted to develop their wealth and to distribute it better, but not before the last quarter of the century. Progress has been incredible but it is recent; and there is so much still to be done that on viewing the situation today one is discouraged.

Even though most historians consider the end of the eighteenth century and the French political and the English economic revolutions as the step from the early modern to the contemporary eras in Europe, all of them agree that the transformation was gradual, so that to speak of "revolution" is nothing but a way of underlining the importance of the change, in no way suggesting instantaneousness or speed. The individual liberty which liberalism presupposes had as its antecedents the end of slavery (occurring in Western Europe centuries before), the end of serfdom (also occurring centuries before), the breaking up of the corporations or guilds (which was completely consummated in England before the beginning of the Industrial Revolution), and the appearance of the middle class, a class whose maturing also took a great many years.

In Hispanic America, on the contrary, slavery existed as a general phenomenon until the first years of the nineteenth century: serfdom in fact persisted in Mexico until 1910, and it can be found even today in other Latin American countries. The existence of a middle class could not be clearly seen until the last third of the past century.

For these and other reasons one may contend that the Spanish American peoples embarked into nineteenth-century life when their own political, economic, and social evolution would have placed them only in the fifteenth century of European history. This assertion is without a doubt mistaken on many points, but aside from the fact that it is true in as many others it helps us understand the substance of the problem of American tyranny: our peoples cannot develop in a normal way, and will not be able to do so for some time, because they live in a century which is not their own—for which they are not prepared—so that they feel compelled to achieve in a century or a century and a half what others did in four or five.

Let us remember that even the major countries of Latin America did not complete the skeletal structure of their railroad and telegraphic communications until the period between 1890 and 1900, and that to date not one of these communications systems can compare—in size, speed or volume of traffic—with those of the United States or the Western European countries. One should remember too that the first great modern dailies of Latin America date from this same period. Can anyone believe perhaps that a democracy could exist without the railroad, the telegraph, and the modern daily newspaper? And even if these means of communication had existed earlier, their influence would have encountered insurmountable barriers in an extremely poor system of education. If today, in spite of a sustained and almost gigantic effort of thirty years, Mexico still is 51 percent illiterate, what were the prospects with which it began its life as a free nation in 1821, the year in which its political independence from Spain was consummated?

And it is not only a matter of spiritual and material communication; we must also take into account the work methods, the limited natural resources, the difficulty of their exploitation, low productivity, low wages. These are factors which keep 80 percent of the population of Latin America in poverty, a poverty which creates in all these men and women a moral and mental attitude of dependence, of veritable slavery, completely at odds with the psychology, the judgment, and the actions of an independent people whose way of life is individually their own as that of citizens of a democracy must be.

There is of course a historical ambiguity in the word "democracy," since the nature of democracy has changed radically in the countries which invented it—England, the United States, and France—during the period from the nineteenth to the twentieth centuries. First came what one might call a drawing-room democracy, confined to the circle of those who governed, a small circle of cultivated people who did wish to govern in a new sense, in a popular or democratic sense. This is government for the people. This form of democracy was soon followed by a democracy of the public square, of the great masses, which draws its existence and character from the compact demographic density of the urban centers created by modern industry. This is democracy for and by the people. The success of the first depends essentially on the goodness of the man who governs, be his name Jefferson, Juárez, or Sarmiento. The success of the second depends not so much on Harry Truman as on the American people.

While all Spanish American countries have been able to produce great democrats of the first kind, none of them has even approached the national conditions for a contemporary democracy. Wealth and culture, which like health and security are among the highest goods of man, still are the patrimony of a few; and for that reason Spanish America, in spite of its great advances, has not been able to go beyond a type of oligarchic government, tyrannical or not, dictatorial or not, cultivated or illiterate. This is how one can explain, for example, the apparent paradox of Mexico. From 1867 to 1876 it lived in a democracy of the nineteenth-century type that was close to exemplary; it attempted a contemporary democracy with the best intentions, and the result was nothing but demagoguery, democracy's horrible excrescence.

Here, too, has history been cruel with Spanish America. After it had managed to introduce the forms of a liberal political organization and created the enlightened type of executive which such government demanded, the content of democracy changed, and Spanish America was invaded by foreign capitalism, which created the modern mass mentality but not the conditions of general well-being.

Though it was late in discovering this transformation of democracy, Latin America might have attempted it, with its amazing adaptability, were it not for another unfortunate circumstance. The inventors of democracy themselves began to lose faith in it after the first World War. To the enormous difficulty of creating and maintaining the social conditions that would make possible a real and authentic democracy was added the doubt whether it was worth the trouble to spend so much effort in attaining a form of government whose excellence Englishmen, Frenchmen, and Americans were beginning to doubt.

It seems certain to me that no country on earth—and Latin America could be no exception—has been able to achieve simultaneously the two great goals which Western Europe set for itself—individual freedom and general wealth—except as the result of a long process which, though acquiring greater momentum in the last century, nevertheless had extremely old antecedents in an evolution that seemed more geological than social, precisely because of its age-old slowness.

Into this crude and rapidly drawn picture there enters the obstinate and sad figure of the Latin American tyrant. He is an impatient man, consequently a violent and arbitrary one, who attempts to force the political march of his people when it seems to him that it is not on a level with material progress, and who suppresses liberty when he thinks it is choking off economic progress.

Between 1800 and 1810 the Spanish American countries clearly showed their desire to become political entities independent from Spain or Portugal. The first task that faced them, apart from the obvious one of creating a physical force capable of making their desire respected, was to give themselves governmental institutions of their own. But this did not necessarily mean that their institutions should assume a different—much less a radically different—character. Thus, the Spanish American peoples could have chosen to go on living within the general framework of the political organization inherited from Spain, the only one with which they were familiar and the only one which corresponded to their social realities, with the intention of course of modifying this framework in the direction of others which were more advanced, more humane, and more in keeping with the Western world in which they would have to live in the future.

Instead of simply choosing their own way, they elected what was different, with the very understandable desire—no less unfortunate because understandable—to put as much distance as possible between themselves and the mother country; and because they wanted besides—also with good reason—to overcome what they considered a shameful backwardness. Naturally, the "different" political institutions, those found in the liberal philosophy then in vogue, were foreign to them; and while it was extremely simple to borrow the form of these institutions, it was impossible suddenly to create their content: the social, economic, and even moral conditions which a genuine democracy demands. The problem was, then, to force the political development of these countries, and to attempt this task there arose the tyrant, the impatient and arbitrary man who is embodied in O'Higgins for Chile, in Artigas for Uruguay, and in Bolívar for Greater Colombia, Peru, and Bolivia.

After forty or fifty years the initial goal was achieved with the mastering of the most apparent forms of political liberty: separation from the mother country; the framing of liberal and democratic constitutions; the conquering of the oppressive and reactionary power of the Catholic Church; the repulse, sometimes by force of arms, of European and North American imperialism. Then our countries discovered that this political progress, indubitable and magnificent though it was, had been attained with great, with immense sacrifices of time, of effort, of human life, and above all of wealth— of wealth, that is to say of the new and coveted goal. Political progress, attained almost always by force of arms in long, interminable civil struggles, had been gained only at the expense of material progress. Liberty, in its desperate desire to spring forth and grow, had destroyed wealth; and without wealth, liberty itself seemed precarious. The Spanish American peoples then felt a keen desire to end the struggle for liberty in order to move peacefully toward wealth. There was an attempt to force material progress, and to attain this end the tyrant arose again, the impatient, violent, and arbitrary man who for the new goal proposed was typically embodied in the Argentine Rosas or in the Mexican Porfirio Díaz.

It seems to me that this is an extremely broad and general explanation, but one which can be given for this strange and somber phenomenon of the appearance, disappearance, and reappearance of the Latin American tyrant. There surely are other explanations, for there always is a general and distant view of things and other views which deal more in particulars and are closer to the subject. In any case, mine should not surprise the European or the North American, for both have pointed out on more than one occasion the major weakness of contemporary Western civilization, the lack of balance between material and moral growth, a phenomenon given an already celebrated name: "cultural lag."

In giving a historical basis to the presence of the dictator, making it appear natural or inevitable, my explanation does not mean to justify or praise that presence, much less to diminish the enthusiasm of those who fight against tyranny. On the contrary, the history of Latin America easily shows that the appearance of the dictator was not in all cases inevitable. To give the stamp of inevitable fate to the Trujillo regime in Santo Domingo, for example, is to introduce a tragic element into the best carnival in the world.

This same history also shows us that little or nothing of the work of tyrants has long endured, even of the few with talent and generosity that we have had in our America, except, on occasions, for the pace they set. This is because the tyrant in general has had no other virtue but force, and experience has proved to excess that good works are not done by force alone, nor does force make the bad ones good. Child of impatience that it is, the work of the tyrant is hasty; it lacks the soundness and finish of lasting things. The child of violence, it engenders a hate which demands its destruction instead of a love that would watch over its preservation; the child of ignorance, it becomes an example of error rather than of good judgment. And as the child of demagoguery, it attracts the foolish and repels the wise.

There is another reason why the work of the dictator has little or no personal merit: the tyrant is merely an agent for interests alien to himself, which use him exactly as one may use an ordinary tool, a hammer to drive home a nail, let us say. Take the case of General Odría, present dictator of Peru. This man, who with a military uprising interrupted the only opportunity his country has had in a whole century to repair its political life, brought about this uprising and set up a whole system of authoritarian government solely to become the defender of ten Peruvian families whose full names I could set down right now if I so wished. And when General Odría on top of that calls upon Julius Klein to organize the economy and finances of Peru and on a sergeant of the Spanish *guardia civil* to organize the Peruvian police, what fields are left in which Odría may gather laurels of his own?

Because of all this, the impatient work of the dictator has had to be patiently redone almost from the point where he began it. And this second task, a really firm and effective one but slow and obscure, has been undertaken always by the other type of Latin American leader, the good one, which we have and always have had, to our comfort and good fortune.

It is not the purpose of this article to propose measures (above all the practical ones which hurried readers demand) to do away with all the tyrannies which darken Latin American skies today and to prevent their reappearance in the future. I have my own formula, but since I have not yet patented it, I cannot make it public now. Nonetheless, I can offer two simple bits of advice. We should advise our dictators that, since they already are omnipotent in the realm of brute force, they should also be omnipotent in the realms of ideas and deeds; and that they should attempt to achieve something which is new and which is theirs. We would not ask that it be good, for that would be asking too much of them. They would discover then that they could think of nothing, absolutely nothing, and that their force, unlimited in persecution and butchery, falls to pieces when they exert it to raise the well-being of their peoples as much as an inch.

And to the good Latin American leader (and to those of any other part of the world) we must give the rule never to allow the material development of his country to fall behind its political development. Both must move at the same pace, for if ever a serious imbalance develops between them, there will again appear the fateful figure of the tyrant, attempting to bring them back into balance.

THOUGHTS ON KOREA*

I SERIOUSLY DOUBT that Latin Americans have had the time or the inclination to meditate on the 38th Parallel. We have no taste for international affairs as a subject for serious and sustained thought, nor do we receive stimulus or help from a press that abounds in news and is poor in evaluation. We may even offer as a quick excuse our aversion to seeing with new eyes a series of problems apparently old, to discovering, understanding, and mastering new values which may save us from error or misunderstanding.

I shall suppose that the majority of the free people in Hispanic America feel that Korea is not worth their trouble as long as it remains a "local" problem. A smaller number must believe that Korea is a lamentable example of the bitter struggle between two imperialisms, as were Berlin and China before it. An even smaller group, the one most deeply concerned, will condemn Yankee intervention either openly or in private; it is all the more repugnant—they will say—because it wraps itself in the august mantle of an organization created to preserve the peace. And everyone (more so, of course, the women)

* First published in *Cuadernos Americanos,* Año IX, 6, November 1950, Vol. LIV.

will feel alarm and indignation at the mere idea that their sons or brothers could go to a war as alien to their national interests as it is distant from their borders.

God forbid that I should believe these people are not right in thinking and feeling as they do; moreover, in interpreting the attitude of these Latin Americans one must not disregard a multitude of considerations, obvious in a way but always worthy of our attention. One of them is the fact that our countries (again out of step with the times!) still are laying the foundations of their own nationalities when they are called upon to discard them, to act in and to see the present-day world from an international point of view. Another is that the United States, inevitably the standard-bearer for one of the theses in dispute, has not been able to dissociate that dispute from the stamp of regression and stagnation which it has for free minds. Nor has the United States succeeded in convincing us that its cause is ours, among other reasons because that friendship among equals which should give us a feeling of being participants in the conflict, and not mummers in a show, is taking a more and more phantasmagorical character. And yet, none of this—so real, so painful, so grave as it is—absolves us from the obligation of thinking and choosing our own course.

Whether it was the North or the South Koreans who began hostilities is quite secondary; for the mere understanding of the problem (not, of course, for its history) the same is true about the question of whether the North Koreans were instigated by the Russians, and whether or not they are using Russian weapons and officers. The problem is also easier to understand if for the moment we disregard the Yankee intervention and whether or not it is justified.

The essential thing is to understand that the conflict between North and South Koreans bears no resemblance, absolutely none, to the thousand conflicts that have occurred in Mexico, for example, between liberals and conservatives or Zapatistas and Carrancistas, in Argentina between federalists and unitarians, in Chile between Pipiolos and Pelucones. Those conflicts of ours were in fact civil wars, wars between the sons of one mother. Barbarous and execrable though they were, the victory of one or another faction never implied a loss of nationality, the end of Mexico as a nation or of Argentina as

an independent state. On the contrary, during the course of the nineteenth century they purified and strengthened our national independence. These civil wars of ours, furthermore, had a meaning, a reason
for being: to increase individual liberties or to recover them when
temporarily lost.

The liberal fought the conservative to liberate man from a government that was not his, from an authority designated rather than
freely chosen, from arbitrary and unjust taxes. The followers of Porfirio Díaz fought to free themselves from a generation of great men
who would not give quick access to power to a new generation of
anonymous men; those who followed Madero fought for liberty from
a tyranny that had destroyed all public freedom, and Zapata's followers to liberate the peon from the oppression of the great landowners. Without digging too deeply or resorting to history books, I
would be bold enough to say that there has not been a single civil
war fought in Latin America which did not have as a direct result the
assertion of our nationality, and whose origins or consequences were
not the enlargement of individual liberty.

The case of Korea is radically different: a North Korean victory
would not insure the Korean nationality but would make it disappear
instead; in the same manner, it would not extend individual liberties
but would suppress them. What would happen should South Korea
be victorious? Korea would not disappear as a nation; it would continue to exist, at least in theory. As for liberty, it could be had to the
extent that the Koreans desired it, for the concept of liberty would
not disappear, nor therefore the possibility of attaining it. The reason
for all this is new but simple: the North Koreans do not make war as
Koreans but as Communists, and for the Communists liberty and
nationality have no meaning; on the contrary, they consider these
ideals as obstacles to their cause. There is not nor can there be a
Communist who would dare give this statement the lie; to do so
would betray ignorance of Marxist theory or a childish desire to
deceive.

The Communist may defend the North Korean cause with many
other arguments, some of them valid and good; but it would be impossible for him to maintain that his system will strengthen the
Korean nationality and extend individual liberties. He may say, for
example, that nationality is real in the metropolis and a myth in the

colony; he may also say that individual liberties can be lost not only
in the Communist state but also in the bourgeois state governed by
any kind of tyranny. And to prove one and the other statement he
can without great effort amass example upon example, until he has
built an impressive mountain. But he will never be able to show
that personal liberty is absolutely incompatible with imperialism or
even with a temporary tyranny, while on the contrary the very concept of Communism excludes it. And this without dwelling on the
fact that for every historical example the Communist holds up before
us, another could be shown contradicting his thesis. More than that,
the examples most significant for us, those belonging to our history
and experience, would be contrary to the Communist thesis.

All Hispanic American countries lived under the rule of Spain or
Portugal; the only sure and final result, however, was that they over-
threw this rule, and twenty nations sprang forth where there had not
been one before. Another undeniable result was that in each nation
there came into flower an individual freedom hitherto unknown. The
Communist could answer that this was so because the general tone of
the Western World was nationalistic throughout the nineteenth century, while today the *dernier cri* is to diminish the importance of
nationality so that tomorrow it may entirely disappear. It is a good
argument, subtle and not ill-founded, but we shall return to it later.
In fine, the Communist may establish a doubt—and in a painfully
dramatic way—whether independence and liberty have any value at
all, especially when they are diminished by imperialism and occa-
sional tyranny, when man lives in penury and inequality. In fact, the
Communist sees this doubt resolved, assuring us that the sacrifice of
independence and liberty is a modest price to pay for material well-
being, and for the moral comfort of having ennobled man because of
his work and not because of the goods he may possess.

This is the great lure of Communism, its apparently irresistible
attraction. And in fact, who cannot confirm the existence of economic inequality, and who can fail to resent it? To these two facts,
within the daily experience and the proof of any man, one must add
the oversimplified argument that to attain equal and general well-
being all that is necessary is to distribute our present wealth, without
taking care to continue creating it day by day and every day with the
sweat of one's brow. It is unquestionable that, once loosed by con-

temporary civilization, the demon of wealth stole into the most intimate recesses of man's being, first to stir in him an exorbitant desire for wealth and then to engender in his breast envy and hate towards all who attain it in greater quantities than he or in a shorter time. That is why disparity of wealth has come to be the worst affront, and that is why man so easily accepts the plundering of his neighbor's substance. If he could be a bit more rational in this matter, he might doubt whether he would be permanently satisfied with a leveling which, like all averages, inevitably falls a little above the poorest but below the great majority. Because of that, and because man is man and not merely a brute, because he always has his noble side, he will in the end discover the comforting truth that he lives not by bread alone; and consequently he will consider whether it would not be better to be less rich, to be decidedly poor even, in order to be somewhat free.

A different question is how to resolve, thoroughly and without fraud or tricks, this devilish problem of heaping riches upon all men. One must, of course, discard the idea that everyone can be made rich with a wealth which by definition belongs to a few. Let us by all means distribute the wealth of the rich if in this way we can eradicate greed and rancor in the poor. But then this simple truth will make itself heard: if many are to be rich we must create much greater wealth. And I fear that not even in this way could we arrive at full satisfaction. This last may come from wealth in any proportion that one may wish to suppose, but it will also depend on our subtracting some of its value from wealth, on our not desiring it, not holding it as the only source of happiness, of honor, and of power. And in this respect let us confess, let us shout to the world, how miserably short has Christianity fallen, the religion, the philosophy, the code of morality invented precisely to exalt the worth of the spirit at the expense of material things!

We are not concerned with pursuing the matter; suffice it to establish a doubt in order to reach these important conclusions: Communism is death to national independence and to individual freedom. It makes us doubt that these can exist in a real and practical way in a world dominated by imperialism and in countries which are likely to fall under tyrannical governments. As compensation for our lost liberty and independence, Communism offers the advantage of an equally good life for all, whose permanent level and rewards may in time be equal or even superior to those of capitalism, but which cannot by any means be obtained with less suffering and fewer tears.

But let us return to the North and South Koreans; do not think we have forgotten them. So fleetingly important are the poor!

The United States and Russia are engaged in a power struggle without a doubt. Each side defends its interests, its predominance in the world, and perhaps some kind of opinion as well, and certain tastes. That struggle may today or tomorrow lead to a war, but not to an international war, between nations. The war will be one in which there will be nations allied with the United States and "classes" or factions on the Russian side. This is not the first time that a group of internationalist tendencies has opposed a nationalist war. The European socialists wanted to abolish war and thought that if French and German workers refused to take part the governments of France and Germany could not fight each other, even if they wished to do so. The socialists failed when the test came in 1914 because nationalist sentiment was stronger than class or group feeling.

In this cold war or frigid peace things may happen in a much different way, if Russia has time, ingenuity, and luck at its disposal. Messieurs Thorez and Cachin will not go to a red-hot war, and they will try to keep all the members of the French C.G.T. [General Confederation of Labor] from going. But they will not call sit-down strikes in recruiting offices and factories. To prevent the French nation from going to war they will attempt to seize power in France, and to do so they will provoke a civil war between the Communists and the nationalist middle class. They will seize the radio, the telephones, and telegraph; they will paralyze the railroads, automotive transport, and the airfields; they will abandon the factories, destroy the arsenals; they will fight the army and the police; they will deprive cities of water, light, and food; they will do all this and more until they succeed in taking the place of the national government. France will cease to fight, and then it will cease to exist as a nation; and naturally there will be no war between the French Communists and the Russians. Both will join fraternally to aid in the victory of their faction in the civil war which will have broken out in Italy and Belgium, in England and the United States. At the moment of conflict the Russian Communists will try to bring about simultaneously in all countries allied to the United States what has already occurred individually in Czechoslovakia and China, and what was attempted in Korea with the invasion and conquest of the South by the North.

This process invented by the Communist Parties explains why Russia, which as a nation produces only 10 million tons of steel yearly, can provoke the ire of the United States, which produces 105 millions. Russia is not gambling that it—together with Poland and Czechoslovakia and China also, in twenty years more—may one day produce more steel than the United States, France and Great Britain, Brazil and Venezuela. Its game is to have each national Communist Party paralyze the production of hostile nations by means of a surprise civil war. This achieved, the level of national production, be it what it may, will mean nothing for it will not be put into the country's service.

Russia's game then is to destroy the nationality of each country through the victory of the Communist Parties. It is to the interest of the United States to preserve the nationality of each and every one of the allied countries if possible, because if during the next ten to fifteen years nationalist sentiment remains as strong as it is today, the United States may emerge the victor in a war of nations against nations.

With this background, indispensable to an understanding of the problem, we may confidently essay the question about North and South Korea.

In the first place, it is worth asking Latin Americans if they still have a feeling of nationality for their respective countries, if they believe that feeling to be worth preserving, and what sacrifices they are willing to make for its preservation; or if, on the contrary, they judge that nationalism lacks or soon will lack meaning and value. In the second place, one should ask them if they love individual freedom, if they find it useful and valuable, if they still consider it, as they obstinately used to say, the very condition of human existence and human society. In the third place, we must ask them if their thirst for wealth is such that to slake it all at once, even though temporarily perhaps, they are ready to sacrifice their national independence and personal liberty, in the attainment of which they once spent so much effort, talent, and sacrifice.

I do not know what historians would say, of course, but it seems to me that from the latter part of the eighteenth century to the present the history of Latin America has but one interpretation which makes it intelligible: it is a tenacious struggle, bitter and cruel, to attain national independence and individual liberty. Peace, equality, and material progress have been secondary not primary goals—not, if you will, secondary in importance, but secondary in the order of their achievement. Mexican liberals, for example, thought that the independence and liberties attained in the War of Reform and the War of the French Intervention would bring peace and prosperity.

Our countries to date have not made a single contribution of the first order to Western civilization and culture; they are confused and disorderly; they flounder along not quite knowing what they want and where they are going, or they abandon ideas and goals, replacing them with others having no better claims to their attention; they let the most urgent problems drag on for years without ever fully solving them; they are neither powerful nor rich; and they choose or tolerate disgraceful governments.

In sum, they have in no way served as example or guide. In spite of this they have stood for something very important in Western civilization; they have always been a welcome refuge for the persecuted, for the nonconformist, for him who would better his fortunes. The great expanse of territory in our countries, their scanty populations, the limited exploitation of their natural resources, even the variety of climates and scenery have allowed each man to live in freedom, to his own taste, without the overwhelming pressure of the great masses of humanity found in Europe and the United States. Our Americans have always enjoyed air, light, and space in unlimited quantities, and for that reason—in spite of poverty, in spite of a thankless and changeful political existence—they have lived their own lives, modest and obscure but theirs. Our personal freedom has been the fruit of our geography rather than of our political institutions; but these last have seasoned it with a philosophy and law which has never had a permanent tendency toward oppression.

This constant struggle to enhance our individual liberties has had and still has in our countries another, innermost reason for being on which it is worth-while to meditate both slowly and long. Communism presupposes for its success what in its jargon has been called the "dictatorship of the proletariat," and what to date has been the tyranny of an extremely small group—an immense, an infinite sum of power entrusted to a ludicrously small minority. I am not going to argue that Lord Acton's maxim has such a universal application that it reaches even into that strange zone of the earth known as the Soviet Union, in which it would seem no human or divine law is valid except its own. But it does seem indisputable to me that in our countries there are no exceptions, perhaps because the clay from which we Latin Americans are made is simply human, and not heroic or divine. Lord Acton said that power corrupts and that absolute power corrupts absolutely. One needs to add only that undefined power corrupts man indefinitely, destroying him in the end because it breaks his backbone, and *homo* before being *sapiens* was *erectus.*

Keeping in mind our own history, both the recent and the past, doesn't it give us goose pimples to imagine twenty Mexicans with the sum of power possessed in Russia by the politburo? Shall we trade away our stock of liberty and independence? What shall we receive in return? Communism seems to offer but two goals (for the others are neither peculiar nor exclusive to it): quick economic prosperity (once the wealth is divided) and economic equality (partly attained by this division). A sense of social justice, the defense of the poor and subordination of the rich, the superiority of permanent over transitory values, the greater production and better distribution of wealth—all these existed already in liberalism and in the Mexican Revolution, and they still are preserved in British socialism. And behind them, as with so many a generous experiment of social reform, is Christian civilization, the spiritual fountain at which Western man has drunk for 2,000 years without diminishing its flow.

Compared to all this, economic prosperity and equality, the spiritual content of Communism—all of Communism itself—do not and cannot express anything that would turn the head of any serious and judicious man. And thus we come to the second grave problem revived by the North and South Koreans. The genuine liberal among us always has been a progressive spirit; with tender sensibility he has received and carries indelibly stamped in him the image of his America. Lashed by the plague of hunger and by the pestilence of injustice, when not full of the sores of tyranny, this America has by dint of so much effort and so much blood achieved a progress which disappoints him, not because it may be small in itself but because it

appears so compared to the immense road that America must travel
if it is some day to attain felicity.

It is many years since Viscount Brice said that democracy prolif-
erates in two ways: in one the transfer of power from the few to the
many arises from the wish to redress grievances attributed to bad
government, while in the other the transfer is born of a theoretical
conviction that the government belongs to all citizens by right. In
both cases there is a danger that democracy may decline from lack
of public support: in the first, once the grievance is redressed; in the
second, if the results obtained are disappointing. Neither "pre-
destined" for democracy like the United States, nor possessed of the
French creative genius for theorizing, or the English patience, which
accumulates and utilizes an infinite number of small experiences,
we have nourished our democracy more on explosive, intermittent
force born of unredressed injury than on the bloom of faith in an
idea or a theory.

It was fated to be so, since on the one hand our Brief of Grievances
—those *cahiers des doléances* as the French revolutionaries called
theirs in 1789—seemed to have no end, so infinite have been our mis-
fortunes; on the other, our best men have been attracted to political
action when they would have given their best fruits in the field of
thought. Thus disappointment in the practice of democracy has
grown, unmitigated by a faith in the idea, the theory of it. And because of this fact, things have run their course until a point has been
reached where our peoples are more interested in "good" government, in effective government, than in government which is their
own, belonging to all or to the majority—and they renounce it,
handing it over to the efficiency expert. And naturally, efficiency is
measured with the indulgent yardstick of public works, of material
progress.

This lamentable outcome of the long process of deception brought
about by democratic misrule and the lack of faith to counteract it has
created the illusion in some that Communism will be the radical and
everlasting cure for all their uncertainty and all their ills. The witty
definition of Communism given by the Marxist theorist Strachey, "a
deep movement for better plumbing," gauges the degree of blind-
ness to which grievances unsatisfied by democracy have led, for it is
clear that it no longer is easy to appeal to simple thoughts such as

this. If Communism is a deep, revolutionary, and subversive movement to better sanitary facilities, let us entrust the task of providing these facilities to the plumber or to the city engineer and not to the tyrant, for if not we shall violate the simplest rules of the division of labor, and we shall exchange our liberty and our independence for a mess of shining sewer pipes.

Such has been for the great masses the origin and the process of their disillusionment with democracy; but it should seem indisputable and evident to thoughtful men that not all our grievances at least are due to democracy, nor can democracy right all our wrongs. Aside from the fact, which I have tried to explain on another occasion, that we tried our hand at it prematurely and under the worst conditions possible, democracy has had to face a new and recent phenomenon which has caused it great and unforeseen harm.

There must have been other periods of history in which man rose in anger from the long stupor of an apparently assured tranquility, and, without even consulting his conscience, charged broadsword in hand to exterminate an enemy whose size and strength, whose very face he was not able to discern. These are periods when man becomes impatient, enraged even, when his only desire is to go faster and faster, so he may sooner return to his interrupted siesta perhaps. Everything must occur in a day, and what does not arrive immediately is considered tardy, slow, and torpid, and must be discarded or replaced. Greater industrialization, the creation of so many artificial products is like a wish to evade the "laws of nature," which require time, cycles, fixed and determined periods difficult or impossible to violate. Little has man achieved in reducing the five or six months which the seeds of wheat or maize require to grow and multiply; but he has achieved much, very much in the manufacture of bolts and nuts and of automobiles—day and night, night and day with men and machines perpetually exhausted.

Western man experienced a period of lethargy at the end of the Franco-Prussian war of 1870; he completed almost a half-century without wars, without serious international friction, enjoying the marvels of science and technology and joyfully planting the signal flag marking new distances traveled in the "forward march" of progress. The war of 1914 was a rude awakening for him, as was everything that came with it. Force could still prevail over reason; science and technology could be put at the service of evil as well as of good, of destruction as well as of creation; and man, after all, was not so much wise as vain. It was necessary to make up for lost time: to re- solve problems, overthrow obstacles, shorten distances, save time; to go directly to everything; to fly if necessary, today at one hundred kilometers per hour, tomorrow at three hundred, the day after at six hundred. And this was not only as regards the automobile, the rail- road, the ship, and the airplane, but—democracy too! It had been designed, more than for any other thing, to prevent the abuse of power! That democracy neither was nor is dead is revealed by its admirable recovery from this new and demanding surprise. This can be seen in the Mexican Revolution, in British socialism, in the New and Fair Deals, and also—should we need more forceful proof—in the victorious outcome of the second World War.

In opposing Communism the progressive liberal should not feel that he defends a negative, stationary, or regressive cause. He can and should advance—now in mind, now in deed—along the road of social reform, seeking always the good of others; he can and should repeatedly assert that his advance has only one just and necessary end: that reform shall come about through free consent and not be imposed by cruelty, violence, or intimidation, and not even by the sham of an overwhelming propaganda.

The other problem revived in Korea has to do with the company we keep. How many a Latin American has shouted, openly or in secret, "Not with the United States!" To our mutual misfortune, the animadversion toward that country becomes keener every day; upon its existence and dangers I allowed myself a small prophecy seven years ago. That animosity is fed with real facts, with true grievances; but it grows irrationally and it is being stirred up by the Commu- nists. It seems logical for them to stir it up, for such action is consist- ent with their ideas and their ends: but liberals go too far in inflam- ing it with thoughtless arguments under the pretext of defending their country. They harm the country instead of defending or strengthening it, and the harm may be irreparable.

In the first place, one cannot always choose his companions, either in international affairs or private life, with the added disadvantage— if we want to call it such—that in the former it is even harder to solve the problem by means which are of relative value even in the latter, that is by isolation or misanthropy. But over and above this consideration, which is after all a minor one and more dependent on logic than on anything else, there is another which must be stated with all possible clarity. Since when is the United States a den of corruption? Since when is it made up of conscienceless fakers, of bandits without scruples, of unbridled seducers? Not only do such suppositions lack all common sense, but it is a fact that one could make a careful and objective comparison of the international conduct of the United States and that of any other colonial power on earth—Holland, France, England, Spain—and the United States would come out the better.

Do we wish then to treat our peoples as if they were children and educate them with the holy terror of the bogeyman of our nurses two generations ago? The idea that the United States has done nothing but prevent our development, denying us help that would be our salvation and a mere bagatelle for them, could not be more inexact nor more harmful. Our governments have little sense of responsibility, and our peoples are too lenient in judging them. Should the day come when we are completely convinced that all our ills have their origin and their cure abroad, what future would be left for our countries? To seethe in resentment, to spend day and night rooted to the ground, eyes turned heavenward, waiting for the grace of God in order to move, to work, to make way, to grow and be strong, healthy, and virtuous.

In the task of making our own way and of growing and being strong, I would put at the head of the list the overthrowing of any obstacle that the United States might put in our road. We should grow and be strong in spite of it. Experiencing this struggle is in no way discouraging, not even for us Mexicans, who have found bad neighborliness so costly. With the passing of time it has been we Latin Americans, the weak, who have prevailed, who have succeeded in making right prevail over force. Just thirty years ago it was still possible for the United States to make an armed intervention in any of our countries; it made one in Mexico, in fact. That is no longer possible today. Frank Tannenbaum, for example, has made the perceptive and flattering remark that the birth of the Good Neighbor Policy is due as much to Carranza as to Roosevelt, for the stubborn, incorruptible firmness of Carranza (who has not had many imitators since) taught the United States to the point of satiety and obviousness that the "big stick" had lost its effectiveness. No longer able to intimidate, the United States must decide to make war or it must devise a radically different focus for its relations with Mexico.

During the last century the United States was a source of inspiration for all Spanish American countries as they searched, eager and confused, for better means to organize themselves politically, to gain freedom and equality. And this went on during a long period in which the United States was not a world power by far, nor even the country with the most promise on the continent. Then, full of respect and admiration, we did call the United States the "great nation." Time passed, and with an alarming synchronism, it might be said, the United States gained in material force until it alone is almost as influential as the rest of the world put together; but its moral force, its capacity to excite emulation and its role as arbiter have diminished more and more until they are limited to the important but narrow field of the knowledge and application of technology. In becoming a large nation the United States has become the most persuasive exponent of the worst faults of Western civilization and the weakest exponent of its best achievements.

In the last few years besides, the United States is beginning to be identified with the preservation of the grossest material interests, with a disconcerting political reaction, with the hastiest human incomprehension. It would not be surprising if, when the hour of danger strikes and there is a summons to battle, the United States should find itself alone, or accompanied by those who lack a faith of their own and who act with a delay and caution born of fear of the enemy's success. The position of the United States as leader of the world, or of half the world, will be precarious so long as it rests on material force alone and while its national life has a conservative political cast. And here is why and how we Latin American liberals have a task which it is a joy and a pride to bear, such is its urgency and magnitude. It consists in raising, high and unfurled, the banner of liberty and progress in our own countries, and to carry it some day perhaps, if it is needed, to the United States itself.

The best avenue for the undertaking would be a brave friendship; but a friendship between equals, with a critical, persistent, and frank understanding that would always recognize both points of agreement and points of disagreement, which would have both give and take. That is why, in the Korean conflict or in a wider one that may arise tomorrow, our course must be determined solely by the answer to the following question: does the United States defend interests which are similar or identical to those of Mexico or Latin America?

These thoughts attempt simply to provoke a thoughtful response.

POLITICS AND POLITICAL ECONOMY
IN LATIN AMERICA*

ＩN RECENT YEARS I have dedicated myself to history, that is to say, to the problems of dead men; and sometimes I must make a special effort of adjustment to consider the problems of the living. That may have been the reason why I awoke too late to a necessity later acutely felt: that our talks required of those who deal with the actual, the daily problems of economic growth, a previous exposition of a great quantity of facts illustrating the discrepancies between such growth and the laws, institutions, and political customs of Latin America. I feared that if we could not rely on a knowledge of the facts, our talks would develop on a plane of remote abstraction, or they would be limited to stirring up preconceived ideas.

I suppose that the point of departure has been our recognition that the Latin American countries were organized politically and have developed economically in accordance with the liberal philosophy, which at its most extreme point of abstraction pictures the state

* Written for a seminar on the social aspects of economic development in Latin America, convened by the United Nations, UNESCO, and CEPAL, 1960. Published in *Aspectos sociales del desarrollo económico en Americas Latinas* (Paris: UNESCO, 1962).

as having no other mission but to give the country internal and external security. Under this protection by the state the individual takes the initiative to such a degree that he becomes the true and the only motive force in political life. In this same theoretical extreme, individual or private enterprise—nonofficial enterprise, that is—plays an even more decisive role if possible in economic life. The state, far from intervening to impose or to suggest a new course, must create the best conditions possible so that private enterprise may move as freely as it likes.

Within this extreme and theoretical framework of the politico-economic philosophy of liberalism, the idea of a planned, programmed, or controlled economic growth—as we should call it the better to define the problem before us—has all the appearance and even the flavor of something exotic. Furthermore, it is an idea so difficult to join to the liberal philosophy that either we must abandon that philosophy or—persuaded that controlled economic growth is necessary and useful—we must modify the liberal political framework, making it not only logically compatible with the idea of this growth but favorable to its operation.

Thus outlined, the situation is purely theoretical and also extreme, for as a matter of fact no political thinker, no constitution, for that matter no head of a government, and no existing state has ever held to it. One must remember that the liberal philosophy coincided in great measure with a socio-economic transformation that, because of its magnitude rather than its suddenness, has been called a "revolution." Now then, the motive power of the Industrial Revolution was the railroad, which in no part of the world was constructed exclusively by individuals or by private corporations. On the contrary, the state always intervened in one way or another: with capital or credits on some occasions, with subsidies or tax exemptions on others, lastly with laws and regulations which encouraged or imposed conditions on private enterprise.

That same Revolution also brought about an extraordinary labor demand which soon included women and children, and which brought about an urban concentration of the population that unhinged the few public services of the time. The state intervened again, not to encourage private enterprise this time but to correct its excesses. It regulated the labor of children and women, in the end prohibiting the first and severely limiting the second. It intervened furthermore with public welfare laws, "poor laws" as they were called in England. Finally the Industrial Revolution in England, France, and Germany—though not in the United States—undermined the cornerstone position which agriculture had occupied until then in the economy of those countries. Again the state intervened, in England to bring about the near-death of agriculture, in Germany and France to "protect" it first and later to preserve it. The fact that this intervention on the part of the state was partial or late does not make it abstention.

If this has occurred in the countries that invented, defended, and still defend the liberal politico-economic doctrine as theirs, with greater reason should we expect the same in our countries, which as simple imitators of the doctrine have not been able to defend it as absolutely theirs, had they wished to do so (as once doubtless they did). Not only did our governments intervene in the construction of railroads, but to encourage such construction they rarely hesitated to commit their credit and even resources necessary to satisfy immediate necessities.

Let us then draw from history a conclusion which, though presented so sketchily, is nevertheless well-founded: there never has been a state so attached to the extreme concept of liberalism as to condemn itself to a total passivity; on the contrary, the state has intervened when it and public opinion have felt intervention to be necessary.

Why then do not the state and the public opinion which sustains it feel the necessity today of adopting measures for a program of economic growth?

I have a feeling that the necessity for controlled, programmed, or planned economic growth is based on valid considerations for all countries, but that this may be so in an extraordinary way for Latin America. The backwardness of our countries for one thing and their poverty for another compel them to be intelligent and far-sighted, for only in this way can they make up for lost time, and only thus will they be able to make maximum use of their limited resources. If the Latin American countries possessed the physical, human, and technical resources of the United States, the Soviet Union, or even of Canada, they could afford the luxury of trusting their economic progress to time and waste. Not having them—as certainly they do not, considered individually or as a group—they must be far-sighted and sober to an unusual degree.

It is curious however that Latin American economists, in spite of some laudable efforts by individuals or groups, have not been able to convey to the public consciousness a truth so vital to the ends of economic planning and so elementary and understandable that the public would have accepted it without great difficulty.

Another obstacle may come from the lack of comprehension of the only truth which, strictly speaking, is given us by economic science, the only one for which that science is worthy of study. The others are either mere elaborations of this truth or, what is worse, ways of concealing it, especially when entrusted to an incomprehensible jargon which has proliferated into an impenetrable and repugnant jungle. This truth is that no man, no country, no region, not even the whole world has sufficient resources to attempt the simultaneous solution of all the problems of economic progress. Stated in a negative way, this fundamental economic principle presupposes that if resource A is applied on day D in quantity C on objective O, the same resource may not be applied on the same day in the same quantity on a different objective. Political economy (as it used to be called), economic policy (as it was later named), economic planning (as we say today)—they presuppose then that the different choices possible will be discovered and weighed, and that the best and most urgent will be identified, in order that they may be undertaken and completed.

But here of course we become entangled in the involved question at the heart of liberal philosophy and of other philosophies which struggle to supplant it: who, the individual or society, has the keenest eyes to best discover the different possible choices; which of the two has the most sensitive and impartial balance on which to weigh the advantages and disadvantages of each of these choices; which of the two, consequently, will take this choice and reject that one; and who, finally, has the greater means and resolution to undertake and carry out the choices taken.

To see the possibility of different choices is, as it were, a function of the senses—of sight, smell, or touch; to evaluate them is the function of the intelligence; to undertake and complete them, that of the will. That is to say, each and every one of the organs and functions of man—of *homo sapiens*—comes into play in individual and collective economic life. For just this reason is man so sensitive to economic questions; that is why he will not yield to another the exercise of functions which he considers as distinctive of his human quality, whether this other be a concrete individual or—even more—the abstract entity of the state.

In communities under a totalitarian government, the individual has to renounce his freedom not only to make his own choices but even to debate whether he might not make better ones; moreover, in the end he loses the memory or notion that once he was able to make such decisions. And unless the regime is completely mistaken in the choices it makes, thus creating an adverse reaction that may overthrow it, such a society will go on existing; it is even possible and probable that it will progress economically, in some cases in an unbelievably fantastic way. In a democratic society the individual— the rich individual above all—often thinks that the state is not as qualified as he is, not only to decide what is convenient for the individual and the community, but even to suggest, let us say, another solution which is not his own. He refuses then to concede to the state the necessary authority to impose such decisions upon him.

The real situation however is not as desperate as it appears and as it would be made to appear by those who for one reason or another —often mere impatience—have a taste for "strong" heads of government and dictatorial states. In the first place, even when dealing with problems which apparently are "purely" economic, we should keep in mind noneconomic considerations, for as was said long ago, man does not live by bread alone. In the second place, though man—the rich man especially—is very much satisfied with himself and consequently thinks he knows it all, it is a fact that economic life has become so complex that only the state has the necessary information at its disposal to see all the aspects of the national economy as a whole. We will not speak of the individual, since, after all, in modern society he is a weakling compared to the state; but the richest private business is incapable of even making a study of possible markets for its products without using official statistics; let us not mention an obviously impossible task such as the making of a census of the population. But the state furthermore is the only one which, because of its very position *au-dessus de la mêlée*, can encompass the whole of the national economy. The individual and the business enterprise can see their own individual problems with greater accuracy than the state; but it would be effrontery for them to think they can see the problems of others just as clearly. Engaged in argument, the individual and the corporation—unless they are fools or hide behind ideological commonplaces—will end by believing the state, for it is the only one possessing the facts on which they base their arguments. In the third place, in any country the state in itself possesses great economic weight, in many the greatest of all. It has at hand the necessary resources to open certain channels and close others, to create favorable conditions here, adverse conditions there. The state, then, can play the role of leader or tyrant.

These are the possibilities for real and practical action open to a present-day state, but this is not to say that the situation must be the same in the actual case of the Latin American countries. If at the present moment we were to make an over-all evaluation, we would be more inclined to say that general opinion in Latin America is unfavorable to the idea of a frankly controlled economic growth.

For one thing, the memory of the economic—not to mention the political—excesses of seven or eight noisy and unbalanced tyrants is still very fresh. For another, many Latin American countries have suffered for years certain problems which, because of their magnitude and very persistence, have affected all social classes. Such have been, in the first place, the problem of one-crop economies, the loss of foreign markets, deficits in the balance of payments, and difficulties with exchange control and inflation. In all phases of these grave problems the state has intervened; it has not been able to do otherwise. But since it cannot be said that this intervention has been a happy one, and since we must say that in the majority of cases it has been ineffective or truly ruinous, a current of opinion has prevailed in the countries thus affected—confirmed on various occasions by the "expert" judgment of foreign economic missions—which is against state intervention and in favor of what is often called the "free play of economic forces."

But the factor that we should keep in mind here, the one that has done most to produce this opinion against state intervention, is that of economic growth itself. Each and every one of the Latin American countries has embarked upon it, willingly or by necessity, to greater or lesser degree. As far as I know, however, only one has done it, not with a plan or program at hand—that seems too much to ask—but at least with relatively clear general ideas about one or two questions which may be the keys to success—or to failure.

The most important of these questions is, of course, the role which the state may and should have in economic growth, and that which the individual and private enterprise may and should have. The complete lack of ideas on this key question has not prevented, as it is logical to suppose, de facto situations from arising, creating in their turn great interests whose future actions will be difficult to modify. Latin American governments seem to have accepted the fact that the state would not have all the economic resources, nor the political power, and perhaps not even the necessary legal faculties to shoulder the whole problem of economic growth, nor even the biggest part of the load. For that reason they have accepted the fact, in a somewhat unconscious way, that private enterprise must participate in it, perhaps as the most decisive factor. The state on the one hand has reserved to itself the riskiest and least productive fields of operation, and on the other it has offered maximum incentives so that private enterprise may operate confidently and on an increasingly large scale. The first has brought upon the state the discredit of being a poor administrator; the second has lost it its moral authority in the eyes of the nation.

Let us cite a Mexican case to illustrate the first situation. Before the Revolution private commercial banks financed the agriculture of the great estates, the most important economic activity of the time. They did it, strictly speaking, by lending money to the dealers in seeds, who in turn financed the *hacendado*. Rarely did the banks suffer a loss, and as for the wholesalers in seeds, they grew fat with profits. With the advent of agrarian reform, replacing with collective exploitation of the communal farm the individual property of the landed estate, private banks and wholesalers in seeds totally abstained from giving credit to the new agriculture, and the state then was compelled to do so. The natural conditions of the new agriculture were of course the same as before; and the former peon, now converted into a communal farmer, had tilled the soil for generations on generations. Thus the only two factors that truly were changed were the transformation of the peon into a proprietor and a manager of the business. In fact, however, one of these factors turned out to be more apparent than real, for since the rural Indian had never managed anything except his meager wage, the new administrator was going to be the state.

In theory at least, it was evident that the agronomists to whom the management of the communal farms was entrusted were much superior to the *hacendado* of the past, who never knew his business well and was not even a great lover of work, since he had been an absentee owner, delegating his powers to rude administrators. The second change had to be real, for if agrarian reform was to have any meaning it would be that the communal farmer would receive in the form of profits a greater sum than he formerly received as wages. And this really was a hazardous task, economically speaking, because nature imposes limits impossible to transcend on the productivity of the greater part of the land that passed into the hands of the communal farmer, this being so true that one may assert without any sort of demagogic spirit that the real origin of the profits from agriculture in the great estates had been the extremely low wages paid to labor. One must add that the true transformation of the peon into owner and manager demanded a persevering and costly educative effort.

Though no one seems to know for certain whether it is economically and socially possible to reach these goals, the fact remains that the Mexican state suffers discredit for not having attained them, at least as clearly, quickly, and dramatically as it was expected and believed possible. To this we must add a note that is at once tragic and comic: the state has never explained in a convincing way whether it has already attained what is possible of attainment, and what this gain has been. In fact, it has been so unperceptive and slow in this matter that it has not even cited in its own defense and justification the fact that, aside from what genuine economic progress he has attained, the new communal farmer, in contrast to the former peon his ancestor, already has the bearing, the expression, the gestures, and the language of a freedman and not of a slave.

The Latin American states, it seems, have been even less happy in their efforts to induce private enterprise and the individual to advance more vigorously along the road of economic growth, especially in industrialization. They have been clearly successful in that private capital has largely abandoned its traditional fields of investment: mortgages and routine agriculture. They have also been successful in inducing private capital to enlarge and strengthen banking and credit services. Lastly, the best of their victories perhaps is their aid in the education of a new type of investor and captain of industry— better informed, bold, quick, capable of risking investments in fields previously untouched.

But it is quite doubtful that national public opinion appreciates these successes as it should, and it is certain that it considers them too costly in any case. This is without taking into account, as has been said, that the general policy of stimulating private business works to the detriment of the moral and political authority of the state.

In the first place, private enterprise itself chooses the industrial activities where it will operate, guided naturally by the incentive of maximum gain. And the choice rarely coincides with what may be the most necessary or the most urgent from a national point of view. When one of these young captains of industry, for example, invests even the modest sum of forty or fifty thousand dollars in machinery to manufacture women's seamless hose, he is correct in judging the possibilities of profit, since such hose are very much in vogue and certainly they look better than other types. But from the viewpoint of the economic growth of a backward country, it is certain that those forty or fifty thousand dollars could have had a thousand preferable possibilities for investment.

In the second place, one of the incentives used to stimulate private enterprise is a favorable tax system. The ideal would be of course a nation without any taxes at all, in which the state and the government were supported by a wealth as free as air; but aside from the fact that administration of public affairs far from being gratis is every day more costly, in the same degree as the state desires to participate actively in economic development as investor and as manager, in that same degree must it have at its disposal more and more resources, the main origin of which—sometimes the only one —is the collection of taxes. The tax system of a country furthermore —the things to be taxed and above all the rates of taxation—should have for the public an aspect of indubitable social justice. The fact that the new captain of industry makes profits that always seem fabulous to the public requires from a social and moral point of view that he pay higher taxes in compensation. (This does not mean, however, that public opinion actively supports stricter fiscal measures, much less that it demands them politically.) Only a truly minimal part of public opinion—which one might call "enlightened," though not without irony—understands and accepts the fact that the object of low taxes is precisely that the "fabulous" profits of the captain of industry be reinvested in the business he already operates or in new industrial enterprises, thus contributing to economic growth. At all events, even this enlightened opinion feels that the incentive of low taxes is offered without any limits whatsoever, that it is excessive and indiscriminate and therefore unjustified.

Another usual incentive to private enterprise—one harder to manage in practice, though—is that of fixing wages as low as possible. Thus the state, though without making it an expressly recognized and proclaimed policy, places itself more on the side of capital than of the worker; and all its conduct takes on a conservative or even a reactionary air, weakening its popular support. As with taxation, the system of wages and social benefits has for the public an inescapable aspect of social justice. If the businessman's profits are today higher than before, he should raise the wages he pays.

Finally, to cap these and other stimuli—long-term credits at low interest, tax exemptions—the state adopts a general policy of public "tranquility" or "security," which is perfectly desirable in general principle but which may create sources of unrest if not of open protest and rebellion should it be translated into a resistance to reform and change or into the discouragement of free and spontaneous political and trade-union activity, thus giving the government a reactionary character and making it seem insensible to the problems of social justice.

A final consequence of this policy of incentives to private business is worth emphasizing, though it is implicit in what has been said up to this point. The new captains of industry and finance eventually form not mere pressure groups, as they are called in sociological jargon, but true oligarchies, which have taken the place of the old landed oligarchy in the Latin American social scene. Between the new and the old, however, there are two important differences, one political and one social. The old landed oligarchy ruled on its own in almost all Latin American countries throughout the nineteenth and well into the present century. Under these conditions it openly seized political power and made use of it, without a doubt for its own benefit. But at the same time it assumed the consequent responsibility. The new industrial and banking oligarchy wishes to influence and does influence government decisions, but without facing the responsibilities that these decisions inevitably involve.

The social difference is no less important. The old landed oligarchy in time succeeded in reforming itself, in becoming cultured and possessed of good taste, capable of understanding many general problems that had nothing to do with the exploitation of its lands, and for that reason it became the patron of education, literature, and the arts. The new oligarchy still is too crude and gross; it gives forth an unmistakable smell of money because it thinks of nothing else, and it seems to understand nothing which is not related in the most direct way to its business dealings.

These two characteristics of the new industrial and banking oligarchy—its tendency to rule in the shadows and to comport itself in a nakedly selfish way—also harm the government and the state, first because the public finds it difficult or impossible to know to what degree official economic policy, or even general policy, is the government's own creation and to what degree it is inspired by the advice or imposed by the pressure of the oligarchy. It is harmful also because the state becomes the protector of a type of man who appears to the public as interested only in the economic side of things, a lucky adventurer who gives nothing in return to the society in which and from which he lives, not a single disinterested act or a gesture even.

The final result of this inconsistent policy of incentives, which obeys no plan nor even any clear objectives, is the danger that public opinion may come to feel that the state, under the pretext of encouraging national economic growth, has done nothing but create a caste of "new rich."

But a great part of the difficulty which controlled economic growth may encounter comes from the ignorance or lack of a plan or program to guide that growth. The lack of a plan is understandable because official attention is given in good measure to the knowledge and solution of the most acute and immediate problems; little or no attention is devoted to those of a fairly distant future. And even the former are treated casuistically, that is to say, without general norms in mind, to the point that a psychology is created which sees in the solution of a problem what is peculiar to it, rather than the similarities which that concrete case may have with others.

In general this lack of foresight may be explained perhaps as due to a dearth of trained personnel to make the general plans of development technically and politically finer. But there also are other reasons, one of which is the fact that the Latin American politician avoids clear and firm positions toward any kind of problem because he feels that once he publicly commits himself to a certain solution or course he reduces his ability to maneuver. Another weighty motive is his desire to give the solution of a concrete problem an air of benevolence or service done expressly for the person or interests asking for that solution, thus obligating the petitioners to give some recompense, economic or political. With a program of economic advancement, the solution of concrete petitions or the pressure to resolve problems according to the desires of interested persons would have to conform to impersonal standards, and consequently the decision arrived at by those in authority could not be capitalized upon in a political or economic way. The Latin American head of state must dislike also the prospect of a long and painful task of persuasion and negotiation which would be necessary for the voluntary acceptance of a program of economic growth by all or by the main groups affected—public or private. And it is quite possible that he would dislike even more having to impose it upon the minority which objects to or rejects it.

Are the constitutions of the Latin American countries, the constitutional laws which govern them, a serious or decisive obstacle to the execution of a plan for economic growth, or can they become so? It seems that in principle the thesis that they are or may become so cannot be maintained, for since all of our countries—or almost all— live under a system of representative and popular democracy, it would always be possible to repeal constitutional measures which impede economic growth and to approve those which favor it. Constitutional reform is slow but not impossible if the majority groups or parties desire it. If one has in mind constitutional reforms which will give the state the power to impose a plan and to coerce its exe-

cution, it is possible to attain them; however, one must concede that
their approval will be politically difficult. And even more, it would
be fitting to ask whether reform of this type is really necessary for
planned economic development, and if it were, whether it would be
desirable for other reasons to go to this extreme.

In the first place a government, without resorting to constitutional reform, is given latitude through the recourse to administrative measures. As a matter of fact, Latin American governments have
abused the practice for less elevated purposes, to such a point that
many of their measures would be declared unconstitutional if they
were submitted to an impartial test in the courts.

Limiting ourselves to the constitutional framework, however, we
may consider Mexico, though it perhaps is an exceptional case in
Latin America. In fact, Article 27 of the Mexican Constitution gives
the "nation . . . at all times" the right to "impose upon private property the regulations which the public interest may dictate." This
article, like all constitutional texts, indicates an intention or assigns
a power, but always in general and sometimes in imprecise terms.
Regulative law should clarify, and in a certain way articulate, constitutional law; and at all events, judicial interpretation does this as
important and concrete cases arise.

In spite of the fact that Article 27, along with Article 123, represents the major novelty to be found in the revolutionary Constitution
of 1917, its judicial interpretation has been far from brilliant, partly
because of technical and imaginative incapacity and partly because
the judiciary has rarely felt free and distinct from the executive. In
spite of this, and even without our being sure, for example, whether
the "public interest" could justify judicially a plan of economic
growth, I believe that one may confidently maintain that the Mexican Constitution offers that possibility.

This is as regards the text of the Constitution, since in regard to
language and political habits it is curious to remember that in 1934
and 1940 two presidential campaigns were launched under the aegis
of two "Six-Year Plans," which incorporated the political platform
of the National Revolutionary Party. The framing of both plans was
elaborate and widely advertised, since among those invited to col-
laborate were not only the great organizations of workers, peasants,
and bureaucrats—that is to say, the truly political bodies—but also
distinguished university professors (economists, sociologists, edu-

cators, jurists). Those presidential candidates prided themselves throughout their campaigns on their respective "plans," and one of them must still preserve kind memories about his, because many years after his administration ended he referred to those better days when the Revolutionary Party had clear goals which were proclaimed to the whole nation. The truth of the matter is that there was no great reason to boast about those six-year "plans." They were at best mere ideological declarations whose high-flown language did not succeed in dissipating their vagueness; they did not even refer to the six-year periods to which they should have corresponded but referred rather to the whole revolutionary movement. Lastly, even within the scope of their purely declarative and ideological nature, there were obvious contradictions, the product not only of the many hands which took part in the original drafts but also of the lack of some supervisory group capable of collating such heterogeneous matter and fusing it into something passably coherent. But their main defect, the factor which kept them from deserving the name of "plan," was a complete lack of goals—either immediate or distant—and the absence of a reference even to the instruments which would have been used to attain the goals.

The experience of the "plans" was followed by another of great interest: two other presidential candidates sent out personal and appealing letters, asking a numerous but chosen group of persons their opinions about concrete problems on which they were supposed to be very well informed. Furthermore, in extremely extensive tours during their campaigns, in which they visited practically all the national territory, they called together to round-table discussions of a socio-economic nature those organizations possessing some degree of significance: labor, the peasants, university faculties, industry, banking, agriculture, mining, business. In these discussions, under the direction of the presidential candidate and his principal advisers, those invited presented, in writing or through the spoken word, their opinions about the most important problems in their own private businesses or in the unions or corporations to which they belonged. Not only were the national organizations affiliated with the official party consulted on this occasion (the General Confederation of Workers and the National Peasants Confederation) but also those not belonging to it, and not only those on a national scale but regional and even merely local ones. The end sought with this new

method—which quite accurately was called "national pulse-taking"
—was that the aspirant to the Presidency, aside from listening to all
political and economic sectors of the country, should later sift the
tumultuous avalanche of opinions and aspirations and formulate a
program of government that would satisfy those most justified.

Rarely perhaps has an inquiry of these proportions been
attempted, and though it was not planned with even a minimum of
care, to attain for example a certain uniformity in the formulation of
the questions and their answers, it is certain that the information
collected must have been priceless because of its abundance and
wide range. It became known that a committee had been named—of
experts let us say—to bring that chaos to order and thus to obtain a
picture, if not of the purposes at least of the complaints and the
economic aspirations of the country. Nothing more was ever heard
of the work of this committee, so that the presidential candidates,
once they were in power, worked out their governments as best they
saw fit.

Aside from their intrinsic interest, I have cited these examples with
two principal ends in mind: on the one hand, to emphasize that
public opinion in Mexico never was scandalized by the idea that it is
advantageous to have a certain order in the future economic life of
the country; and on the other to point out what seems to me to be
the true origin of the "political" difficulties which truly are obstacles
in Latin America to the idea of channeling economic growth within a
plan or program.

That idea—and even more its attendant purpose—does not have
sufficient popular support at the present time, or to be more exact it
has no popular support. Furthermore, in spite of vainglorious and
repeated statements to the contrary, the political parties and the
government leaders of Latin America are not sufficiently well-
informed truly to understand this idea and accept it and to make of
it, as it were, the central axis of their preachment and their practice.

Let us explore first the matter of popular support, and to do so let
us begin by substituting for this expression the less compromising
one of "public opinion," or, if you will, "informed" public opinion.
The truth is that outside of the Communist countries and those that
are ruled by dictatorial governments—whatever may be the political
label in the latter case, left, right, or simple opportunism—I do not

believe that one can talk of the "popularity" or general acceptance of the idea of a plan for economic development. It is scarcely necessary to mention that in the United States it is, as a principle, a veritable heresy, and this in spite of the fact that the great North American corporations plan very carefully, and with great success, their future activities, as may be seen by the enormous sums which they spend on applied scientific research. In England, cradle of abstentionist liberalism, as a consequence above all of the two world wars the idea that the state can and should intervene in economic life when exceptional circumstances demand it has won general acceptance; but one may say that the political weakening of the British Labor Party has robbed economic planning of its best opportunity. In France the situation is quite peculiar, for while in metropolitan France both theory and practice are very much those of private enterprise, in the former African territories, in Algeria above all, there is concrete and detailed talk about a controlled economic development. In Italy such planning is limited to partial projects, such as the reclamation of the South and of Sicily. Perhaps it is in the small European countries (in Holland first of all, and in Belgium in the near future), which have had to readjust their economies in a very thorough way because of important historical vicissitudes— wars and the loss of a colonial empire—where in a rather silent way and at least for the present only in an advisory scope economic planning is a current idea. And yet, in no way could it be said that the Dutch economy is developing according to a plan or program.

Of the countries leading a democratic life, the only one strictly speaking that has openly accepted development plans is India. Its exceptional situation should be attributed to various reasons perhaps —the main though not the only ones, of course: for one thing, the intellectual training of the principal leaders of present-day India, which ranges from the vaguely socialistic to the definitely Marxist; for another, their character as rebels against colonial rule, which without a doubt has led them—as the Latin American countries were led in respect to Spain 150 years ago—to reject in principle the patterns of the mother country and to seek new ones. Greatly influential too must have been the dramatic situation of the giant with feet of clay: India, with its truly continental territory and its numerous population multiplying at a dizzy rate besides, turned out to be a basically weak country, in its capacity to support itself as well as in its political and social organization. I imagine that this tragic disparity between a poor and circumscribed reality and an almost limitless potential must be a cruel spur. In India, besides, favorable political conditions are present for the acceptance of an economic plan: master of the government from the first day of independence, the majority Congress Party has two rivals—the Socialist and the Communist Parties—which aside from their weakness could with difficulty disagree on the point of a programmed economy.

This rough and rapid review may lead us perhaps to a conclusion not entirely lacking in interest: even though the idea of a planned economic growth does not seem to find general acceptance in a democracy, the two concepts decidedly are not mutually exclusive or incompatible. This fact is revealed by the many partial attempts, by the determined effort in India, and by the beginning made in Colombia. From this point of view, then, the situation in Latin America may be judged as bad but certainly not as unusual as might seem at first sight.

Let us return to the Latin American politicians and government leaders, who are not very enlightened we have found (and who are excessively opportunistic we could now add). It is not easy, of course, to judge the intentions of men in public life, even those best known and nearest to us; for that reason, even in speaking of Mexicans, I dare not go further than to make conditional statements. Nevertheless, in regard to Mexico's "Six-Year Plans," it seems to me that they were intended more to give the presidential candidates some sort of inspiration that would make up for their political inexperience at the time than to give the country a plan, that is to say to set it goals and give it the procedures to attain them. As regards the socio-economic round tables, I have believed for some time now that at bottom they were nothing but an ingenious form of publicity. If this is all we can expect of the few Latin American leaders who have talked of economic plans and who have boasted of having adopted them or of having laid the foundations for their adoption, what may we expect of those others who have been mute before such an important problem!

The strange thing, however, is that in the last twenty or twenty-five years no Latin American government has failed to construct great public works, nor has any head of government failed to boast of having made them in greater number and at greater price than his predecessors, and his successors even. Those enormous signs reading "Perón Keeps His Promises," which used to appear even before the first spadeful of dirt was removed in a project, and which always were the most visible signs of it, captured in an ostentatious but faithful way the desire to make the country progress, and the vanity of having attempted and succeeded in doing so. The annual reports submitted to their legislative assemblies by heads of state are full of figures: the mounting sums budgeted for appropriations and expenditures; money invested in public works, in kilometer after kilometer of highways, railroads, telegraph lines, sewers, or in more schools, or hospitals.

There is, then, no Latin American government leader who has escaped the experience of planning some public works: the divine pleasure of creating them from nothing, contemplating them first in plans or sketches; the anxiety of seeing them fail to progress at the desired pace or of finding that the funds destined for them are exhausted; and finally the pride in unveiling the commemorative plaque in which his name is eternally linked to the work. Nor is there at this point a Latin American head of state who has not had a predecessor with public works to his credit, whom he wishes to emulate and to surpass. There has come to be then a clear notion of continuity and the desire to pass from one stage to the next, that is to say, a notion of progress rather than simply of development.

What is needed to arrive at a general plan with an established system of choices, with stages of achievement both in the near and distant future, so that the heads of state of today may undertake the first and those of tomorrow the second?

A plan for economic growth cannot be brought forth by technicians exclusively; it must be their child and also that of political judgments, criteria, convictions, and decisions, and even of an image of how the society of the future should be. If, as I believe, this is a truth (and in some ways an obvious one) perhaps we may reach with it the real core of the problem. The technicians who should contribute to the establishment of the plan of development are many and of the most varied kind: geographers and geologists, engineers (civil, hydraulic, highway, chemical, industrial, electro-mechanical); but the major contribution will be made by the economist—from the initial postulates to the general assembling and final reconciliation of the partial opinions of the specialists.

Now then, if Latin American economists are convinced of the necessity of channeling in a more rational way the economic growth of their respective countries, can we be sure that they have tried as hard as is necessary to make this idea viable? These economists have two principal functions: to know and to advise. And they have failed in both, it seems to me, as regards the problem of a planned economy. I doubt very much that there is in each country even one economist with sufficient information and clear ideas about this problem. And the reason is simple after all: each economist works in a very limited area—in foreign trade, expenditures, income, or monetary policy. To very few, or to none, has it been given to climb up on an observation point high enough to see the whole field of the national economy. Too, small and immediate problems take up so much of their attention and time that today passes without their having had the time or the energy to think of tomorrow and to foresee what will happen then.

There is however one thing which is of greater substance and gravity: the Latin American economist (and simply the economist) is not as a rule a man of strong convictions, and one must agree that the idea of planned economic development cannot succeed if one is not convinced about it, and with a degree of firmness and enthusiasm which bring to mind religious or political mysticism. Even more, if one is to judge from the more direct view that each one of us has of his own country, it is to be feared that the great majority of Latin American economists have turned out to be more opportunistic than the politicians whom they serve. The politicians, after all, have a good excuse for their inconsistencies; it is they who—because they handle them directly—are responsible for the results of political forces, so much so that history records more than one case in which a politician paid for a serious mistake with his own hide. The Latin American economist has not done more than to be the daemon of Socrates, and it was the latter who drank the hemlock. Once Socrates was dead and buried, the daemon flew to another philosophical ear, in which to whisper his complaints. There is, after all, a simple explanation for this lamentable state of affairs, which all of us would

like to believe is transitory. Precisely because of economic development, and above all because of the popular longing—irrational and
explosive even—for material betterment, the Latin American economist has overnight ceased to belong to a profession as obscure as
that of the homeopath or the veterinary, becoming the magician
whose spells can create universal wealth and happiness. This has
given our economists what they did not have before—political
power; and in general they have not made good use of it.

If in general the Latin American economist sees only a limited
area of the national economy, if his time and energy are consumed
with problems which are always immediate and of small import, if
in fine he is not a man of strong convictions and if he has surrendered
to the giddiness of political power—is it at all strange that he should
be an ineffective adviser to the politician and the head of state,
incapable of inculcating in them the idea of a planned economy,
unable to kindle the faith that would make them standard-bearers
of this idea?

Not all the blame should fall on the economists; as much or greater
yet belongs to the politician and the head of state, the other necessary half for a planned economy. It may not be entirely incorrect
perhaps to say that the best leaders of government in Latin America
were produced during the long epoch when the liberal philosophy
reigned supreme, that is to say when economic planning was not
even talked about. Since the world in general began to lose that com-
pass, heretofore so sure, not one of our leaders has been equal to
this epoch of perplexity and insecurity, let alone superior to it. If we
study the problem carefully, we should find nothing strange in the
fact that Latin American politicians and government heads, con-
sciously or not, have avoided committing themselves to the idea of
an economic plan, and even more to its faithful execution. In fact,
the old metaphor that a statesman is the helmsman who guides the
ship to a safe port has ceased to have even the most remote reality.
For some time now the twenty Latin American ships of state have
been adrift, floundering this way and that, be it as a consequence of
exterior forces which they cannot control or of interior ones whose
true origin and extent they rarely understand. To adopt the notion
of controlled economic growth and to commit oneself to carrying it
out involves returning to the helm—grasping it with a firm hand—to

guide the ship of state, to force it if necessary to follow a predetermined course, braving the angry seas and the fury of the storm. And if in rapid review one gauges the climate of discouraging uncertainty which prevails in the world, the magnitude and the rapid pace of change, the great and intrinsic difficulties in drawing a plan of economic development and carrying it out, one has to recognize that it is sweeter and more comfortable to be adrift, because in this way one at least is ignorant of the nearness of disaster.

LATIN AMERICA AND THE UNITED STATES: TODAY AND TOMORROW*

$\mathbf{T}$HE UNUSUAL WORLD SITUATION and the equally unusual conditions prevailing in Latin America today make it advisable to return once again to the old question of the relations that Latin American countries have with each other and with the United States—what they are and what they should be.

What is the present situation of Latin America, with the exception of Cuba which must be considered separately? Unfortunately, it is not satisfactory from an economic point of view. Since all Latin American countries have set out to develop their economies as fast as they can, their imports have greatly increased in quantity—especially imports of capital goods—and perhaps even more in value because they must be paid for at prices higher than those of ten or fifteen years ago. Their exports, on the other hand, have had an uncertain and not very profitable market during this same period. This keeps their balances of payments in deficit, or very close to it. [The International Monetary Fund cannot remedy such an imbalance, which seems permanent or at least of indeterminate duration;

---

* A different translation of this essay was published in *Change in Latin America: The Mexican and Cuban Revolutions,* the University of Nebraska, Lincoln, Nebraska, 1961.

and investments by foreign capital usually do not make up for the loss of foreign currencies suffered as a result of the decrease in exports.] The final outcome is that the economic development which they need so much and almost wildly desire stagnates; or it does not attain the pace necessary to create the clear and convincing impression that they are moving without pause toward the great goal of a material well-being definitely greater and more general than heretofore. Hence their restlessness, their pessimism, or their feeling that they must try other methods, copy other models, or perhaps embrace a new political philosophy in order to attain their objectives.

The political picture is better today than it was a few years ago. With the disappearance of the shameful dictatorships of Perón in Argentina, Rojas Pinilla in Colombia, and Pérez Jiménez in Venezuela, and the destruction of the parent stem of the Somoza dictatorship in Nicaragua, the only really disgraceful one that remains is that of Trujillo in the Dominican Republic. But the governments of Stroessner in Paraguay and of the little Somoza brothers in Nicaragua certainly are to be condemned; furthermore, it will not be possible to postpone much longer the fundamental socio-economic changes which are needed at least in Guatemala, El Salvador, and Peru.

On the other hand, there exists a very disheartening situation in two of the three countries which have succeeded in establishing popularly elected governments after having suffered under the yoke of dictatorship. The excessive influence of the army in Venezuela and Argentina forces the civilian governments of Betancourt and Frondizi to follow an uncertain and sometimes tortuous path, which at all events does not express the wishes of the majorities as they are represented in the parliaments of those two countries. One may assume that without the harmful influence of the armed forces Betancourt's government would attempt bolder and more basic reforms. And in the case of Argentina the interference of the armed forces has, among other things, the certain effect of undermining the prestige of civilian authority and making the country believe that it must return to a government by the military.

Nonetheless, what is most discouraging is that there is not a single Latin American government which can be said to enjoy evident and, above all, active popular support. Those with the best democratic tradition—Chile, Uruguay, and Costa Rica—certainly do not have brilliant governments which could attract the burning loyalties of the governed; much less could they be regarded as a hope for other Latin American peoples, and even less as a model.

Brazil, with its superior physical and human resources, is a country of surprises, but not always pleasant ones. Coupled with President Kubitschek's clever trick of launching Marshal Lott as *his* presidential candidate to free the country from the threat of a high-ranking militarist, and with the exaggerated though bold impulse to create a great capital overnight, we have a Brazil which lives in chronic administrative disorder, complacently spending more than it has, so that it also lives in a state of chronic inflation, which enriches a bold minority while impoverishing the people.

Colombia, which has never lacked at least a nucleus of government leaders of exceptional intellectual and moral caliber, still has not awakened from the nightmare of Rojas Pinilla, nor has it succeeded in eliminating the irrational hatreds which divide liberals and conservatives. In spite of all that, Colombia progresses; but one has anxious doubts whether new generations are being created which will succeed the great liberal and conservative figures of today, and which will have the sensibility to measure the urgency and perceive the shape of the new problems of the country and of Latin America.

Mexico, which led by many years the countries not only of Latin America but of the world in reforming its economic, social and political structure, shaking off the lethargy of an economic progress that was undeniable but not general; Mexico, the intrepid pioneer of so many good causes, has failed in this crucial hour for Latin America. For some time now the United States has been engaged in presenting Mexico as a model to its sister states. This—says the United States—is a country which, after making a revolution to shake off the burden of a useless and cumbersome past, has set its house in order in a quiet and determined way. It lives in peace; it has gained in political stability; the civilian leader has succeeded the military man; it has made spectacular economic progress, and the lower classes are rising into the middle class in greater numbers and with a degree of ease. All this is true, and yet we Mexicans believe that Mexico could have done more, a great deal more than that, and that by not doing so it has lost the initiative in Latin American eyes for true and just social reform.

The situation in Latin America, in spite of the flaws that have been pointed out and a few that have been passed over, was at least tolerable, if not good, and better than it had been in recent times; but one must confess that the Cuban revolution has thrown it into almost complete confusion.

No one, of course, would now venture to predict how and under what circumstances this revolution will end. Even so, and supposing that it should end in total failure at this very moment, its leaders being relaced by a governing group entirely different in men, aims, and methods, it would leave a legacy and exercise an influence that no power on earth could obliterate. Some of its lessons have already been stated firmly and clearly; that is to say, they belong in the inviolable realm of history.

The first lesson—and an important one—is that everything and anything can happen in Latin America; or, to put it in another way, that in Latin America nothing is firm and stable, nothing is based on solid rock but everything seems to rest lightly on a powder keg that may explode at any moment. The second lesson—which is the reverse of the first—is the incredible power of the fiery word, a power all the greater in proportion to its recklessness. This leads us to the sad conclusion that man in the mass loses much of his individual reasoning and judgment, which give way in him to blind and violent emotion.

It is better however to single out two other concrete and impressive lessons. One of them is the fantastic vulnerability of the United States: Cuba, formerly its docile slave and a small, poor, and disunited country to boot, has backed the United States into a corner, leaving it speechless and immobilized. The other is that, apart from its deep political significance, the Cuban revolution has appeared as a determinedly popular movement which has stopped at nothing to better the lot of the masses. That is to say, the two characteristics which impress Latin America more than any others are determination and firmness, especially when they serve a good cause.

For the last ten or fifteen years, the "realistic" concept of international politics has been fashionable in American academic circles. According to it, man in his national and the state in its international political life are motivated solely by a desire to better their positions of power at any cost. And even though the theorists who defend this concept are very careful to emphasize that physical force is not the only element which creates and increases power, they always put it in first place. Well then, Cuba is a living example for all the world to see that physical force may be successfully opposed by other forces, even that of the spoken word, whose fate according to the popular saying is to be carried away by the wind.

If Latin Americans were intelligent and perceptive, they would be profoundly impressed by this incredible vulnerability of the United States; first, because they have discovered it—rediscovered it, a good historian would say—at Cuba's expense; second, because everything in this world is relative, and the weakness of the United States strengthens Latin Americans, again at someone else's expense; finally and above all because the weakness of the United States is of a good kind, worthy of unstinted praise: the strong who do not resort to force in order to resolve their difficulties inspire confidence and sympathy.

The other lesson, perhaps more interesting than the first, is that the admiration aroused by the Cuban revolution in Latin America is due more than anything else to the fact that it has tried to benefit the people boldly and directly. It is probable that not all the methods used in Cuba could be applied in other Latin American countries, and more probable still that their application would be undesirable even when possible. But what cannot be denied is the following: the longing for self-betterment in the poor of Latin America and of all the world can no longer be contained. The poor man is tired of being told that his condition will improve, only to see that it does not improve; he is tired of bettering himself today but not tomorrow; he is also tired of bettering himself both today and tomorrow but only a little bit. He wants, in sum, to better himself a great deal, quickly, and all the time. It is quite possible—and from my point of view desirable—that man may change his mind some day; but for the present and for a long time to come he believes and will continue to believe that he can live by bread alone, and in order to obtain that bread present-day man is capable of selling his soul to the devil or his freedom to Communism.

And this is the most disturbing element of the Cuban revolution for Latin America. Granted that the Mexican revolution was the last one which could be snow-white and innocently nationalistic, and that all others which have followed it have had to stain themselves with some international "ism"; granted that it was logical, natural, and inevitable that the Cuban revolutionaries should have believed and should still believe that the United States will crush their revolution; granted that the fall of Arbenz made an indelible impression on Fidel Castro, and even more on Che Guevara, who witnessed it with his own eyes; granted, finally, that no revolutionary movement has failed to feed on mistrust and hatred and that for Cuba the United States was the closest and easiest target. And in a friendly disposition to understand, let us make one concession more: granted that the policy of resisting and fighting a great power is a hard game, in which almost any weapon may be considered fair, and that the Cuban revolutionaries might flirt a little with the Soviet block.

None of this can prevent an impartial observer from concluding that—aside from strategy and tactics, from intentions and words— the Cuban revolutionaries have imported Communism into their country and into Latin America, and that they have set up a Communist system and a Communist government. The same observer also must conclude that this is an absolutely new event, of incalculable importance and destined to profoundly disturb relations among the Latin American countries and between them and the United States.

The relations among Latin American countries have never been as intelligent and beneficial as they can and should be; but they have always been based on a tacit understanding which has seldom been disturbed, and then only temporarily. The dominant tone of these relations has been similarity, not difference, much less an insurmountable difference. For the first time in one hundred and fifty years of independent life, Latin America is presented, in Cuban Communism, with a difference that may become insurmountable. Should the Cuban leaders allow ideological loyalty to prevail over Latin America's common historical background, not only will Cuba tend to withdraw from Latin America, but it will end by looking on Latin America with inevitable hostility as still another obstacle in its path. And to the extent that the other Latin American peoples and governments feel that friendship with Cuba depends on an indiscriminate acceptance of all that Cuba does within and without its borders, to that extent will they consider Cuba at best a black sheep which should be left to its own fate, and at worst an insufferable burden from which they must free themselves.

But the Cuban revolutionaries have presented Latin America with another problem of equal gravity, that of choosing between Cuba and the United States, since they maintain that their differences with the latter are irreconcilable. No Latin American country loves the United States; and perhaps no nation has ever loved another. In spite of this, there will always be people in the Latin American countries with sufficient common sense to recognize in the clear light of truth that not only is it impossible not to have relations with the United States but that our relations should be good, strong, and close. It is one thing that these relations should be conditioned by respect for the rights of others, that they should benefit the poor and the weak more than the rich and the strong; quite different is the fact that it is literally impossible and undesirable to do without them or to base them on recriminations and constant quarrels. Thus Communist Cuba places Latin America in a real dilemma.

I am convinced that the Cuban leaders are perfectly aware of the problems they have created for the Latin American countries in their relations with each other and with the United States. It happens that as true revolutionaries, as people who seek to subvert everything, to turn everything in the world upside down, they believe that the Latin American people are on their side and that only the governments are against them. That is why they treat the latter with silent scorn or insult them openly, and why they encourage the people to overthrow them. So firmly do they believe in this idea that they have carried it to the deluded extreme of assiduously cultivating the Negro population of the United States in the certainty that it will soon embrace their cause. Thus, in addition to gaining some sympathy for their cause, they would deal the United States a blow by planting in the very heart of its territory a Trojan horse from which would burst forth at the proper moment eight million armed rebels.

At this stage, no thinking person can disdain a priori the destructive force not only of a whole revolutionary doctrine but of a simple isolated tactic carried out with sufficient determination. In the particular case of Cuba, moreover, one must recognize and admire the fact that the revolutionaries have up until now played their cards not only in a splendidly effective way but grandly, on a truly universal stage. So much so that a poor Mexican conspirator scarcely can suppress the doubt whether the Cuban revolutionaries really are playing the cards, or whether they only move them about.

At any rate, it is a great shame that man, so willing to make laboratory tests when looking for the secrets of chemistry or biology, does not want to carry out similar tests in human affairs, though they may involve the fate of millions of men. For the truth of the matter is that I would give anything if Fidel Castro, Guevara, and Raúl Roa would decide to try out their ideas on Mexico. The experiment or test would be made under ideal conditions, for if any country in the Western Hemisphere is sympathetic towards the Cuban revolution it is Mexico, and in no other is the ground better prepared for dislike of the United States. As for the Mexican government, it is as vulnerable to the attacks of demagoguery as those of Ydígoras and Trujillo. The experiment would be that the Cuban revolutionaries would carry out a public campaign of insults to the Mexican government for just one month, applying to President López Mateos the same epithets that Castro, Roa, and Guevara have spat in the face of Eisenhower, and now of Nixon and Kennedy, and to Foreign Secretary Tello the adjectives which Roa—not in Costa Rica, of course, but in the safe refuge of his own country—has used on the foreign ministers of Chile, Argentina, and Brazil. This propaganda of insults to the heads of the government would alternate with another of glowing praises of the Mexican "people," and of exhortations that they overthrow their government. Well then, I would bet two to one that Mexican sympathy for the Cuban revolution would evaporate as if by magic, and I would also bet that even as staunch a friend as General Cárdenas would not defend it again, at least not in public.

What, then, is the make-up of Latin American sympathy for Cuba? I do not speak, of course, of the sympathy which Communists have for it, since they, by definition, are mere coreligionists; nor do I speak of the radicals who project their domestic dissatisfactions into internationalist sympathies, those sympathies being a clear-cut case of the grass being greener on the other side of the fence. I refer to the spontaneous sympathy of the ordinary man and woman without prejudices or ideological ties. Knowing that it is both risky and unpleasantly pedantic to make an attempt at collective psychology, I would say that this sympathy has one or two principal elements and perhaps a secondary one, and no more. The principal element of popular sympathy is the fact that the Cuban revolution has sought to benefit the poor, the helpless, those who form the majority in every society, including that of the Soviet Union. The second principal element is the conviction—still in force —that the sole aim of the Cuban revolutionaries is the welfare of

their people, and that they pursue this end so sincerely and honestly
that they will put it before any other. And the secondary element is
the natural sympathy which is aroused by any David struggling
against a Goliath.

As deep and enthusiastic as this sympathy must be, gushing forth
as it does under the influence of these elements, it may turn out to be
perishable. Because it is not enough to seek the welfare of the
people; this welfare must be achieved truly and effectively, for
otherwise the whole business will end up as one of those many good
intentions with which the way to hell has been paved a long time
since. Up to the present the struggle and the annihilation of economic imperialism and the amoral middle class have seemed glorious;
but there is already a legitimate doubt: can the revolution proceed
from its task of destruction to that of creation and construction, using
only the instrument of the spoken word and the televised image?
And other doubts, already felt by some, are bound to become general. One of these may destroy the second element of sympathy:
what interests Cuban leaders more, improving the condition of their
people or making trouble for the United States? No one, I believe,
can boast of having read the complete works of Dr. Castro; but it
perhaps is not far from the truth to suppose that 80 percent of the
words they contain are dedicated to defaming the United States, and
a modest 20 percent to a discussion of the problems of the Cuban
people. (I refer solely to the words, since I ignore what actions may
have taken place and how they have been employed.) And there are
doubts even about the secondary element of sympathy, because from
the beginning our David called for help from the Chinese and
Russian Goliaths in his struggle against the North American one.
Thus David's gallantry is considerably diminished.

The position of Latin America as regards its relations with the
United States is even more delicate—were it possible—than its relations with Cuba. All the Latin American governments must realize
that as Cuba becomes more insistent and bitter in its recriminations
against the United States, the situation becomes more precarious and
the crisis more imminent. But it is absolutely impossible for them to
sustain any other thesis than the negative one of nonintervention,
and with even greater vigor than before. In the first place, because
Latin America has already had more than its share of North Ameri-

can intervention. In the second, because Latin America has with great difficulty convinced the United States that intervention in the long run is more harmful to the intervener than to his victim, and all this painful work would fall to pieces never to be resumed as something useless. In the third place, because the lethal power of modern weapons—even those ironically called "conventional"—makes even a symbolic defense ridiculous. So weak peoples are left no other choice than to fall abjectly to their knees in order not to disappear from the earth.

But there is a reason more decisive still, though it appears to have been overlooked until now, which will put to the test the intelligence of the United States, its ability to resolve the Cuban problem without resorting to force. After announcing several times—and to the four winds to boot—that he would use his intercontinental missiles to defend Cuba from a North American invasion, Khrushchev explained to a Cuban journalist that it must be understood that he never has considered anything but a symbolic defense of Cuba; that is to say that he would defend it by setting off beautiful Roman candles in Moscow's Red Square.

What does this apparent withdrawal mean? Not weakness, for heaven's sake! But a maneuver that I shall refrain from describing in all its ramifications—in spite of its almost irresistible fascination—in order to stick to the pertinent point. It is a trap so that the United States will carry out an armed intervention in Cuba, in the certainty that Russia will make no military movement in its "defense." Many of the cards that the Russians play seem stupid or eccentric at first sight, but they are surely mischievous in their long-range effects. And in this case Russia hopes that the United States will do itself irreparable harm, not only in Latin America of course but also in Africa and Asia, today's field of discord.

Presumably the Latin American governments are fully aware of the situation—already difficult of itself—in which the United States has been placed in regard to Cuba, and of the truly cosmic complications which the Cuban problem has brought with it, since for the United States, with interests all over the world, there can be no "local" nor even a simply "continental" problem. This problem of Cuba, moreover, has arisen at the worst moment in its history, when Russia has certainly surpassed the United States in political skill, and when rightly or wrongly many have been convinced that she has also done so in physical strength. The United States, then, cannot postpone making a decision for very long; and as the fatal moment draws near, the apprehension increases that the decision may be unwise.

What can a truly unhappy Latin America do now, caught as it is between the devil and the deep blue sea? One thing only: mediate, conciliate, or rather try doing so since up to the present the Cubans have not shown the slightest desire even to be approached. Not only have they failed to express any such desire, even by implication, but their conduct must be interpreted as one of complete intolerance. We may be certain that the United States would respond to a call for a discussion, though we should expect that its demands would not be small. So for the moment there seems to be nothing left for Latin America but to pray that God be with it in this crisis, and to hope from the bottom of its heart that those who are involved in this problem will recognize before it is too late the existence of an eternal principle: that everything, absolutely everything in this world—and in the next one as well—has a limit or end.

As for the United States, what course of action can it take? To examine this problem one must begin with a clear understanding of the North American position not only as regards Cuba but in respect to the whole world.

The United States is the leader of the so-called Western world, which is confronted by an apparently irreconcilable enemy, the Communist world. Between these two camps, scattered and disunited, is a group of countries that take no active part in the struggle, that desire to take no part in it and even consider it unnecessary, but who nevertheless may be drawn into that struggle. Any conflict between personal or national interests—more so a conflict of this magnitude and depth—may be resolved by war. One of the contenders would disappear or would be left in such a state of material or political inferiority as to convert him from rival into slave. Or the struggle may be resolved through a series of compromises and provisional agreements which would indefinitely postpone a declaration of war by clearing each obstacle as it appears. Even with this alternative— certainly the better of the two—the danger of war would always exist. And considering present-day armaments, it is no exaggeration to say that this danger exists at every instant of our lives.

Now then, one must admit in all honesty that to be in real and con-

stant danger of war, not as one of many soldiers but as the leader in
a military, technical, and financial sense, to be in danger of a war in
which no trick or weapon is considered dishonorable or unnecessary,
to be in danger of war without clear hope of victory, knowing that
even the victor must suffer irreparable harm—all this inevitably
creates a psychology that is little disposed to patience, tolerance, and
understanding. And matters are even worse for the United States
when it is defied and offended by Cuba, a small country traditionally
at its beck and call geographically located at its very doors, not in
some remote place as, for example, Bolivia.

The United States, therefore, must do something about this Cuban
business, but, to repeat, what can it do? From a juridical point of
view, we must discount a solution by means of an international court
of justice because we cannot be certain that Cuba would submit to
the findings of the court. The United States could bring Cuba before
the tribunals of the Organization of American States or the United
Nations. It would gain nothing and might perhaps lose by this,
because Cuba knows how to defend itself, and it does not stand
alone. The dispute would only increase tension and bring forth
recriminations, leading us away from rather than toward any kind of
agreement. Another recourse within the law would be for the United
States to make a formal declaration of war on Cuba with the knowledge and approval of the Congress of the United States. Such a solution is wholly unrealistic. Though it is easy enough to find some sort
of justification for any formal declaration of war, a state making such
a declaration seeks to justify it on moral grounds. In the case of Cuba
it would be literally impossible to establish such grounds, first
because the acts of the revolutionary government of Cuba—censurable though many of them may be—could not be presented as a
real *casus belli*, even if the facts were twisted beyond all recognition;
and second because the unequal strength of the two would prevent
us from seeing any justice in the actions of the United States.

Left without lawful recourse, what may the United States do? If
we have rejected a formal declaration of war as legally and morally
unjustifiable, we must reject with greater reason a *de facto* invasion,
no matter how it may be disguised. The United States could attempt
the solution suggested in an unfortunate moment by Senator
Kennedy during his presidential campaign: to encourage the Cubans
opposed to Castro, to give them money and the implements of war

so they can invade Cuba and win it back into the friendship of the United States.

This was exactly the method used to overthrow the government of Jacobo Arbenz in Guatemala. Cuba's island position would make such a maneuver as clear as day, and the truth is that in Guatemala the whole thing was so evident that attempts to cover it up were like trying to obscure the sun with your little finger. This may be seen in the fact that the best men in Guatemala refused to work with Castillo Armas, considering him a traitor to his country. Shortly after assuming power, he was assassinated under truly mysterious circumstances that seemed, however, to imply national approval.

But this is not the lesson taught by the Guatemalan episode. If North American intervention made any sense at all, it was as the necessarily violent act of tearing out Communism by the roots so it would not sprout again, either in Guatemala or anywhere else in Latin America. Well then, Communism has shot up in Cuba and to such an extent as to make Guatemalan Communism look like child's play. Let us remember that in Guatemala the straw that broke the patience of the United States was a declaration made by Arbenz that his country would receive a few pistols and rifles from Czechoslovakia. Cuba, on the other hand, has made no bones about receiving quantities of weapons not only from Czechoslovakia but from the Soviet Union itself.

To my way of thinking the only solution is for the United States and Latin America to attempt a reconciliation at once, a course which may have the unexpected effect of laying the foundations for a new concept in American solidarity.

MEXICO'S LEGENDARY WEALTH*

A FULLY EXECUTED ESSAY on Mexico's natural riches should be made, I believe, of three principal parts. The first would be the answer to the question: is Mexico really a rich country? If, as I think, the answer is negative, one must pass to the second: why then does the notion persist that Mexico possesses great riches? The third part, to a great extent a consequence of the other two, would be an attempt to set forth a true concept of our national wealth.

The second and third parts are the theme of this article, which could not be completely understood, however, without a summary of the conclusions which I have reached on various occasions in regard to the first.[1]

The first thing to consider is our territory, which is far from ideal. It is not outstanding for its size; its mountainous surface underscores man's neglect in the erosion of the land, impedes agriculture on a large scale, and makes communications costly and difficult. Along the coasts, where the best lands are found, the climate is unhealthy; on the central and northern plateaus the climate is good, but there the

---

* First published in *El Tremestre Económico*, VI, 1, April 1940.

[1] See, for example, my course in Mexican Sociology (1924–1925); "La importancia de nuestra agricultura," in *El Trimestre Económico*, I (1934), 112–130; and others.

154

soil is mediocre or downright poor. The lack of large and navigable rivers is a decided disadvantage; rainfall in the central and northern plateaus, above all, is scanty and unreliable, while in other regions, in the Tehuantepec Isthmus, for example, it is excessive. In case of the first, irrigation is necessary, in the second, drainage; but both require additional effort and expense. The best measure of the conditions of Mexico's territory is seen in its own population, which is small in an absolute sense and unequally distributed. Its mean density is low, while in regions like Baja California and Sonora it is extremely low. It has a very high rate of reproduction, which is nullified for the most part by an appalling infant mortality. In spite of all this, Mexico's population increases at a steady and perceptible pace, leading us to conclude that in some way the soil of Mexico has become better suited to support it. There is no doubt that such has been the case. The new industries, with all their limitations, have absorbed part of the new population; the broad net of highways, begun in 1926, has created a good number of businesses and services which employ considerable numbers of people; the concentration of the population in urban centers intensifies commerce and enlarges the bureaucracy, both private and official. In spite of all these facts, sure and favorable though they are, we see in the very neighborhood of the Valley of Mexico great deforested zones whose steep slopes have been quickly occupied by new farmers; and we get the impression that at least part of the new population is living off the old natural resources, the end of which is clearly in sight. In fact, some of those slopes first lost the trees and then the farms; now the only thing that meets the eye is the living rock, or the dismal, yellow subsoil.

Agricultural production, as well as agriculture itself, would have to be examined from two different aspects: those of the products of the temperate zone and of the tropical and semitropical. Whether one compares with the corresponding data of other countries the total production or the area planted, the yield per acre or the importance of trade, the per capita consumption of wheat, corn, beans, oats, rye, rice, or potatoes, the conclusion is inescapable. Our production is shamefully low. The situation is somewhat more favorable in regard to coffee, sugar, and cotton, and obviously good for tropical products such as bananas and some fibers. In regard to stock raising, it is useless to think that Mexico some day could do as well as Argentina, Uruguay, Australia, the United States, or Canada. Our saltwater fishing resources are great perhaps, as we are often told; but with few exceptions such is not the case with the fishing in our rivers and lakes, because we have so few of them if for no other reason.

It is true that in the future very important changes may be achieved in Mexican agriculture. In the temperate zone, these may include the general application of fundamental techniques: the use of fertilizers and machinery, the rotation of crops, the selection of the best varieties of seed, the construction of new irrigation and drainage works, the full realization of agrarian reform, a relocation program that would relieve the central plateau of part of its excessive population by settling it in more appropriate areas such as La Laguna, the Yaqui Valley, and in general in the North Pacific zone. In the tropical regions, let the main problem be solved: the control of living conditions.

The very fact that up to the present these fundamental techniques have not been applied to crops like wheat, corn, and barley (though they have been employed on sugar cane, cotton, and citrus fruits) shows that the true reason why they have not become general practices is not the "ignorance of the Indian" (since he did not take part in agricultural management until after the Revolution) but the fact that the high costs involved would leave no margin for profit. This means that the present condition of our agriculture in the temperate zone cannot be made more modern and productive without the introduction, among other things, of two main incentives: a much higher yield per acre (three times the present one, let us say) and a higher price for the crops raised. It is conceivable that the yield could reach such heights, even though any sane person would express some doubts about it. As for better prices, however, one must agree that our cereals have never been cheap, so that the margin for improvement cannot be very large; not to mention the fact that the very possibility of paying better prices to the farmer of tomorrow presupposes a nonagricultural population with an income decidedly higher than the present one. We must accept the fact that the problems of obtaining higher yields and getting better prices for the more abundant crops are truly vicious circles, which may be broken somewhere, somehow, but which for the present are in fact circles which imprison us.

But both reforms, as far as they may be achieved, will produce a series of consequences, the main one being a correlative increase in the population. It seems fair then to conclude that agriculturally Mexico at the very best could produce enough to feed a larger population well; but it is not easy to imagine, no matter how great our faith in progress may be, that Mexico will become a major exporter of foodstuffs, as are now for example the United States, Canada, and Argentina for cereals, Cuba for sugar, and Brazil for coffee and cotton. We would face natural obstacles that could never be completely overcome. The North Pacific zone, and parts of some other areas, could not produce all the cereals which would be needed by a population of, let us say, forty million, if we are to assume a nutritional level equal to that of the Scandinavian peoples. It would be necessary to continue using land in the central zone, which no matter how well cultivated would always produce relatively scanty yields.

The obstacles in the way of the unlimited development of semi-tropical and tropical agriculture may perhaps be more of an economic than a natural sort. There are several countries as well endowed as ours which could offer the world what we could offer. The experience Mexico has had in foreign markets in respect to its coffee, bananas, other fruits like pineapples, and henequen would make us think so. This difficulty, though serious, could be overcome. Better working methods, better means of presentation and sale could give an individuality to Mexican products, like that possessed today for example by the coffee of Costa Rica, where quality and not quantity has been made the strong point in competition. The domestic market would solve part of the problem, for if we assume that the whole population of the country is raising its standard of living and that the privileged working groups already have sufficient means, the Mexican's ordinary diet will in time include products which now he buys only on feast days, or which he dreams of buying on the day he wins first prize in the national lottery. There are also the big-little advantages provided by technology or plain skill: canning the fruit or converting it into juices, using coffee as raw material for the manufacture of plastics, obtaining cellulose from sugar-cane bagasse or from the henequen plant. In the agriculture of the semitropical and tropical zones, in spite of serious and complicated problems, the road seems clearer; or at least it does not give the impression of leading into a blind alley, as does that of the temperate zone.

As regards industrial resources and productivity, it is easy to show and to judge the present situation, but much harder to evaluate that of the future, partly because little is known in truth about Mexican resources, and partly because it is very difficult to predict the industrial course of the world, given man's unpredictable genius. Some things are clear, however, especially for our purpose, which is not to quantify with precision the industrial possibilities of Mexico, but simply and roughly to form some idea whether it is possible for Mexico to become a great industrial country some day, as Germany, England, and the United States are now.

The first thing to consider is that all great industrial countries in the past have had to depend on iron and coal. Mexico's known iron deposits are few and poor, and I believe that by this time all those that exist are known. Their poverty is marked as regards to quantity; that is to say in respect to the number of deposits and the possible tonnage that they contain—between 94 and 273 million tons. In some cases our deposits are qualitatively poor, though in general they are rich in this respect, the average for all deposits being about 60 percent iron. Finally, there exists in regard to iron that tragic or Biblical curse that all things Mexican seem to possess: the deposits of highest quality and greatest yield are on the Pacific coast, in the states of Guerrero, Michoacán, and Jalisco; not only are they situated almost at the diametrical extreme from the only coal field known in Mexico, but in a location where their use (be it in raw form or in finished product) would demand their transportation across the crags of the Western Sierra Madre to the plateau, where the population that can use and pay for them is to be found. Under these conditions it would be more logical to export the iron to Japan or to the west coast of the United States, where there already are important steel plants; but then, what would become of the Mexican steel industry? It is true that economic theory tells us that in exchange for this exported iron ore Mexico would receive from the buyer countries some other "useful" product; but are we sure that in return we will not get brilliant silk kerchiefs from Japan and "Catalina" bathing suits from California for the Creole tourist's morning dip?

In respect to coal, our prospects are far from brilliant, or at least they are far from certain or secure. The only field known to date is that in the state of Coahuila; and even though the country has got along on it without any great difficulties, we know that exploitation on a greater scale and in a more reasonable manner would require technical installations as complex, as complete, and as costly as those in Germany, the United States, and Czechoslovakia. We have some coal, at all events, and for Mexico's foreseeable needs it will be enough, not counting the use that may be made of lower grade coals, and even peats, which may be utilized on a lower scale for industries that are not as demanding as the making of steel. In any case, we can be absolutely sure of one thing. Mexico will never be outstanding as a producer of coal; on the contrary, it must use what little it has with a great deal of economy.

Many people are easily convinced that if our coal resources are limited we may count on other sources of fuel and energy: charcoal, electricity, and petroleum. We must discount the first; in fact what would we not give if we could replace charcoal in domestic use with some other fuel in order to conserve the few forests that remain to us on the plateau. The great tropical forests will not serve this ignoble end, for they are too far from the manufacturing centers, and communications are precarious and expensive.

Mexico's circumstances may not be completely bad in respect to electrical energy, though I fear that the situation is not as good as popular imagination and political demagoguery would have it. The country is mountainous (who could doubt it), this being the first condition necessary for waterfalls. But we must not forget that in the central zone of the country, where most of Mexico's population lives today, there are few rivers with a permanent flow, the majority being of the "freshet" type, which carry water only during the summer. This means that the second condition would be lacking for the most part, namely that there be water which will fall over the "waterfalls." The best Mexican rivers are those that flow along the watersheds of the two oceans, in zones which are less populated than the central area and which have an unfavorable climate. Consequently the utilization of electrical energy produced there would presuppose great plans for colonization to shift part of the population of the plateau into the coastal regions. This is without taking into account the fact that electricity, which has so many industrial and domestic applications, has been used to date in the steel industry only to make fine steels, which Mexico for the present needs the least.

It is more probable that we may count on considerable petroleum resources, and that it may not be impossible for us to resolve on our own the inevitably great problems presented by an industry whose technical and financial requirements are so great. The existence of these resources will allow the country a very ample development of its communications system, railroads, and airlines as well as automotive transport. This alone is an advantage that could well be judged invaluable, considering the fact that rapid and efficient communications are almost synonymous with modern economy, and on the other hand that Mexico, because of its unfortunate topography, requires even greater facilities than most countries to insure good communications. Furthermore, petroleum has many industrial and domestic applications—and it generates electricity. All this, however, should not make us forget that petroleum is more limited in its uses than is generally admitted. To date its best uses have been for railroads, automobiles, airplanes, and in lesser degree for ships; that is, as a fuel of light weight and small volume, capable of producing great speeds; but one could not mention many important cases where petroleum has replaced coal in a strictly industrial field. This is without taking into account the fact that the countries which possess coal and lack petroleum—Germany and England—are finding a number of uses formerly unthought-of for coal.

These notes were not meant as an attempt to evaluate all of Mexico's natural resources, nor even its principal ones. We are speaking in a general way, and even though certain resources are pointed out specifically, it is always with the intention of investigating not Mexico's degree of wealth or poverty but whether the country is as fantastically, as exceptionally, rich as so many foreigners have said it is, and as the majority of Mexicans believe it to be. That is why I made immediate though broad reference to our mineral resources; these more than any other thing have been what awakened the greed of the conquistador in the past, and that of the capitalist today. Mexico has, in fact, considerable mineral resources; because of their individual importance and their variety and quantity they could perhaps arouse the envy of the greater part of Latin America and of a good number of European countries. Mexico produces in appreciable volume and value silver, gold, lead, zinc, copper, mercury, antimony, manganese, tin, arsenic, bismuth, vanadium, tungsten, molybdenum, cadmium, graphite, and iron. Hope has not been lost for the discovery and economic exploitation of nickel, cobalt, titanium, chromium, selenium, uranium, beryllium, and others. A rough estimate of Mexico's total mineral production in 1939 would be as high as some 700 million pesos. On the other hand, mining employs a very small number of workers (some sixty thousand), though they are among the best paid in the country. In sum, mining provides the greater part of the freight of our railroads, and it is one of the most important sources of official income, especially for the federal government.

In spite of all this, Mexico's mineral wealth is not fabulous, nor even exceptional. If one makes up a list of the world's ten highest producers for each mineral, it will be seen that our country will not be among the first ten in iron, nor in manganese, tin, arsenic, bismuth, tungsten, or molybdenum. It is in first place only in silver, a precious metal without important monetary use and for the present with only limited industrial application, with a falling price and an even more uncertain future. Mexico occupies second place in the production of cadmium and antimony, but its cadmium production is barely a third of what the country in first place produces, though in antimony it is 85 percent. It occupies third place in the world's production of lead, though with barely 69 percent of the best producer. In mercury and vanadium it has fifth place, but with a production which represents respectively 7 and 13 percent of the producers in first place. Mexico takes sixth place in zinc, but it produces only a fifth of what the country in first produces; seventh place in graphite but also with a fifth of the highest; eighth in gold and copper, but again with only 16 and 6 percent of the highest production. It seems to me that this information, summary though it is, should be enough to support the conclusion noted above: Mexico's mineral wealth is varied but modest. In no case can it be classed as fabulous or exceptional, whether judged as a whole or by the evaluation of each individual mineral.

We are on surer ground if we turn to the comparative ratings that have been essayed by various authors, the latest one being Herman Kranold.[2] Using a series of coefficients ingeniously devised and combined, Kranold comes to the conclusion that the fifteen countries with the best natural resources for industrial purposes are the following in ascending order of wealth (the column at far right gives the coefficients for the wealth of each country):

[2] *The International Distribution of Raw Materials* (London: Routledge and Kegan Paul, Ltd., 1938).

Rank	Country	Coefficients
1	China	0.1
2	India	0.4
3	Poland	0.5
4	France	0.6
5	Japan	0.7
6, 7	Brazil, Holland	0.8
8	Italy	1.0
9	Germany	1.3
10	Great Britain	1.5
11	Russia	1.6
12	United States	4.4
13	Union of South Africa	6.0
14	Australia	7.5
15	Canada	8.3

It would be interesting, of course, to apply Kranold's coefficients to Mexico; but for our purpose the conclusions are enough. Mexico does not figure among the fifteen richest countries in the world, and consequently cannot be thought of as being extraordinarily rich.

If, as it seems, Mexico is not a rich country, why has it always been considered so? Foreigners and Mexicans alike have thought it rich. Even more, my experience in teaching is that the foreigner is merely amazed to hear the contrary, while the Mexican offers a peculiar resistance to the idea, his rebellion at times reaching an irrational point. I would not hesitate to believe that the Mexican would brand as antipatriotic, though silently perhaps, the assertion that our resources are limited and perhaps even the innocent expression merely of a doubt that they are not thus limited.

The reasons for this attitude are many and varied, besides being confused one with another and, therefore, difficult to discern. Their discovery, study, and classification would furnish material for a beautiful essay.

It is advisable to follow this clue: in very good measure the foreigner has been the source and the encouragement for the legendary concept of our wealth. From Cortés in his *Letters* to Charles V to the little Texas schoolteacher who will visit us this summer and write her own letters to her parents, all foreigners have proclaimed the richness of the Mexican soil and the Mexican sky. It is the same with the objective Bernal Díaz as with the subjective Acosta, the historian Solís and the scientist Humboldt, our friend Soustelle and our adversary Simpson. All have described, praised and overvalued our wealth.

One cannot suppose that all of them were moved by the same motive, nor that the reason in all cases may be the very simple one of ignorance; but it would perhaps not be too far from the truth to believe that our neighbor's eyes are by necessity different from ours.

This is extremely curious, for example, in Humboldt's case. This man, extraordinary in the variety of his knowledge, the equilibrium of his judgments and the authenticity of his investigations, in his instinct as a discoverer-traveler, even in his faith in and affection for our country, summarized thus his opinion about Mexico's wealth:

The vast kingdom of New Spain well developed would by itself produce all that commerce goes to seek in the rest of the world: sugar, cochineal, cacao, cotton, coffee, wheat, hemp, linen, silk, oils, and wine. It would provide all the metals, not excluding mercury; its excellent building timbers and the abundance of iron and copper would favor the advance of Mexican navigation, though the condition of the coasts and the lack of ports from the mouth of the Alvarado River to that of the Rio Grande present obstacles that would be difficult to overcome.[3]

In the first place, the exaggeration of the first statement has been sufficiently verified by the later history of Mexico to make unnecessary much speculation about its lack of factual basis. It can only be attributed to the infinite hope with which men of that period looked upon "developed real estate"; great and determined effort on the part of man was the lever that would work miracles. It may also be attributed to the incomplete knowledge which Humboldt acquired of New Spain, and which easily made him believe that if what he knew was good how much better must be that which he had not seen. Secondly, a good part of Humboldt's vision—if not all of it— was that of a foreign eye. He saw Mexico as a source of foreign supply, or better said, as a colony supplying the metropolis with raw materials which the latter required. Humboldt's allusion to the poor quality of Mexican ports confirms this, and it is more clearly apparent in the list of articles he mentions: metals on the one hand and

[3] Alexander Von Humboldt, *Ensayo politico sobre el Reino de la Nueva Espana.* 5 vols. Sexta edicion Castellano, Vito Alessio Robles, ed. (Mexico: Pedro Robredo, 1941), I, 368.

on the other agricultural products and fibers. The only exception is wheat, a foodstuff produced in Europe. But precisely in respect to wheat, Humboldt was mistaken, because though Mexico exported or could have exported the other articles, it was not, is not, and never will be able to export wheat in competition with "new" countries that are well suited for its production, such as Argentina and the United States.

The idea that if a country can export what it produces it also can import what it needs belongs not to the theory of international commerce but to simple common sense. Yet the idea has two faults when applied to the so-called colonial countries. The foreigner forgets the first and is ignorant in general of the second. The economic history of the nineteenth century (and that of the present, though in lesser degree) shows that what in technical jargon are called "conditions of interchange" favor the metropolitan, industrial country and are unfavorable to the colonial producer of raw materials, with the consequence that the benefits of the division of labor and of international commerce are not shared equally by both types of countries. The second fault (also proved by the economic history of the past century) is that if a country does not possess the type of resources which will permit it to satisfy its primary necessities in a direct and abundant way, the effort to produce these necessities is such that little means are left to buy imported industrial articles. What its citizens can buy must be produced by the national industry, to which is soon granted the protection of tariffs, with the consequence that the benefits of international commerce are not enjoyed in the colonial country by all social classes, but preferentially and exclusively by the highest. This means that from the Industrial Revolution to the present time (even though in lesser degree in recent years) it has been more advantageous to be an industrial country than a producer of raw materials. Consequently the judgment made of his own wealth by a Mexican should be made with a different viewpoint from the accurate but alien view of Humboldt.

A further exploration of this idea and of the author of the *Political Essay* himself may prove worthwhile. It is curious that he should cite the abundance of iron solely as a cause for "the progress of Mexican navigation" and that in judging Mexico's industrial possibilities he should have failed to associate with iron the existence or lack of coal. It may be an exaggeration to suggest that the reason for Humboldt's oversight was that he judged our future through a foreigner's eyes; but we would not go too far in rejecting the hypothesis that he lacked the knowledge to make a valid judgment. Humboldt was an admirably informed man; and at the time he wrote, the idea that the coexistence of coal and iron create a brilliant industrial future for the country possessing them had already been accepted. The substitution of coal for coke in the process of separating the metal from the ore came into general use about the middle of the eighteenth century and was the reason for the already apparent superiority of England.

It is true that it was difficult to imagine how a country without accumulated capital could be launched into industrialization, even if it possessed coal and iron. From this point of view Humboldt was right in pointing to navigation and foreign trade as perhaps the only means to secure the needed capital; they had served this function in succession for Spain, Holland, France, and England. We know, in fact, that commerce was the primary source of capital, as industry and finance later were. Nevertheless, it is not certain that this consideration was what prevented Humboldt from associating iron with coal. Happily for him and for ourselves, he was no economist.

The foreigner judging our wealth has been blinded not only by the lack of focus in his foreign eyes but also by the distortion arising from greed, the celebrated "profit motive" on which economists have speculated so much. The discoverers and conquerors of the New World were thus misled. Recent historical investigations (including those of our countryman Silvio Zavala) have helped establish that the early Spanish enterprises of discovery and conquest fell within the legal forms of private law; in short, they were contracts among various individuals forming a society and contributing capital in different amounts, expecting profits which would be distributed among the members proportionately. Diego Velázquez was an important capitalist in the three expeditions to Mexico, while Bernal Díaz del Castillo, like the soldiers and sailors who accompanied him, was an industrial associate. The latter contributed their arms and their abilities as soldiers. There is nothing strange then that the judgment of both should be influenced by two general factors: the hope, the expectation of obtaining great profits from the enterprise, which reality failed to confirm; and the practice of exaggerating the infinite possibilities of the undertaking in order to get others to join it, thus making it stronger and more viable.

I choose Bernal Díaz del Castillo to illustrate these ideas because the objectivity which he brings to bear in his celebrated chronicle is extraordinary, and because the enchantment of his account easily silences all national resentments.

In Bernal are found thousands of examples of the first attitude, the expectations of the speculator in the face of the facts which will decide the success or the failure of his undertaking; but there is none better than what happens when Cortés and his men arrive before Zempoala.

And it seems that our scouts, who were on horseback, reached the great plaza and the courtyards where the dwellings were, and it seems that a few days before they had whitewashed them so that they shone, which they knew well how to do; and since it seemed to one of the horsemen that the white which shone was silver, he returned at a gallop to tell Cortés that their walls were made of silver, and Doña Marina and Aguilar said it must be plaster or whitewash, and we had a good laugh at his silver and his frenzy, so that ever after we would tell him that all white things looked to him like silver.[4]

The anonymous soldier of Cortés' expedition was so eager to find silver and gold to compensate in full measure his dangers and hardships that he saw a wall of silver in a freshly whitewashed wall. Is not a psychology of extreme exaltation—of veritable "frenzy," as Bernal calls it—necessary to believe it possible that in any town of the globe or in Mexico there could be ordinary houses (not altars or temples even) with silver-covered walls or with walls made solidly of the precious metal?

When the Spaniards obtained permission from Moctezuma to raise the first Christian temple in the Great Tenochtitlán, Bernal describes thus the scene of the finding of great treasures:

. . . and when they opened the foundations, to make them more firm, they found much gold and silver and emeralds and pearls of various sizes and other stones; and likewise another inhabitant of Mexico, who occupied another part of the same lot, he found the same . . . and they said that it is true that all inhabitants of Mexico of that time put into the foundations those jewels and all the rest.[5]

[4] Bernal Díaz del Castillo, *Historia verdadera de la conquista de la Nueva España*. 2 vols. (Madrid: Espass-Calpe, S.A., 1933), I, 142.

[5] *Ibid.*, I, 329.

That is why Moctezuma in his first interview says to Cortés with a heat that makes his words truly a formal plea:

. . . you have also been told that my houses had walls of gold, and that the mats of my rooms and other things in my use were likewise of gold, and that I was and called myself a god, and many other things. You see the houses yourself, that they are made of stone and lime and earth.[6]

At this distance the reality of those events may provoke in us a benevolent smile; but in that age the psychology of the adventurer, of the conquistador, was not only an individual reality but a collective one. Great groups of men abandoned the impoverished lands of Extremadura, leaving homes and families behind them to come to the conquest of America, an enterprise bristling with labors and with dangers but the only undertaking which would yield a hundredfold return on the capital invested.

The second general factor we have mentioned played its part in the make-up of this psychology: exaggeration of the possibilities in the undertaking to get others, from the king on down, to take part in it. Examples of this sort also can be found in abundance in the chronicles of the Conquest. According to Bernal, for example, Pedro de Alvarado returned to Cuba in command of the second expedition to the coast of Mexico and conversed with Diego Velázquez, principal associate in the enterprise, about the riches discovered by the expedition:

And when the king's officers took the royal fifth which was due His Majesty, they were all amazed at the wealth of the lands we had discovered . . . and since Pedro de Alvarado knew very well how to tell it to him, it is said that Diego Velázquez embraced him again and again, and for eight days did nothing but to rejoice in tilts and merriment.[7]

Not everything is profit in this world, of course, but it is curious that the foreigner, even after deception and disillusion, will not believe in the poverty of Mexico, continuing to think it extraordinarily rich. If he did not obtain these riches, or did not obtain as much of them as he hoped, it was not because they did not exist but because of some other reason, which in general was thought to be man himself.

[6] Hernán Cortés, *Cartas del famoso conquistador Hernán Cortés al Emperador Carlos Quinto* (Mexico: Imprenta de Escalante y Cª, 1870), p. 114.

[7] Díaz del Castillo, *Historia verdadera*, I, 49.

Bernal Díaz del Castillo came to Mexico to make money; he does not hide the fact. On the contrary, he says it with such great clarity that insistence on the point is unnecessary. Perhaps because his purpose was such a simple one, he is not easily moved. He took part in three expeditions to Mexico, and he was in Cortés' from the first day to the last. Hundreds of times he witnessed the already familiar scene of the arrival of the conquistadors at each town, the reception they were accorded by chiefs and principal lords, the giving of presents dictated by the fear and mystery which was felt toward the *teutlis*. But Bernal thinks the gifts are paltry, calling them such, or valuing them at low sums: "And they brought a gift of gold worked in jewels which could have been worth two hundred pesos." [8] So Bernal does not tremble until he reaches what he surely felt was his goal: The Great Tenochtitlán. The first time that one may discover some emotion in Bernal's account is in his description of the great Plaza of Tlaltelolco and the neighboring marketplaces, and again when he sees the temple of Huitzilopoxtle. But his great emotion comes when the Spaniards discover behind a walled-up door the treasure of Moctezuma's father, King Atzayácatl:

> And when it was opened and Cortés, with certain captains, entered first within and saw numbers of jewels, of gold in bars, and many disks, and emeralds and other very great riches, they were transported and did not know what to say about so much wealth . . . and when I saw it, I will say that I was amazed, and since I was then a youth and had not in my life seen riches like those, I was certain that there had never been in the world others like them.[9]

This wealth does convince him, but it does not become his until Moctezuma (the Great Moctezuma, as he calls him) surrenders it to the Spaniards. This was the terminus, the end of the undertaking.

> . . . Moctezuma sent his majordomos to deliver all the treasure of gold and riches which was in that whitewashed chamber; and examining it and removing it from the jewels in which it was set took us three days, even though to remove it and melt it down there came Moctezuma's silversmiths from a town called Escapucalco. And it was so much that after it was melted down there were three piles of gold, and they must

[8] *Ibid.*, I, 337.
[9] *Ibid.*, I, 334.

have weighed more than six hundred thousand pesos, not counting the silver and many other riches, and I do not count among it the disks and bars of gold and the gold nuggets from the mines . . . After it had been cast into bars, they brought another present as part of what the Great Moctezuma had said that he would give; and so much gold was cause for amazement, as were the riches in other jewels that were brought, for the native emeralds were of such high value that among the caciques themselves they were worth great quantities of gold.[10]

But this immense wealth had to be divided, and not in equal parts; to the greater must go the greater share, to the lesser the smaller, or as Cortés says, "according to the manner, the service, and the quality of each." [11] And though it was so great, it did not satisfy everyone, not because it was not enough, but because of the principle by which the division was made:

First was taken out the royal fifth, and then Cortés commanded that another fifth part be taken out for him as for His Majesty, for we had promised it to him at El Arenal, when we made him Captain General and High Justice, as I have said in the chapter which speaks of it. After this he said that he had done certain things on the island of Cuba, that he had spent on the armada, and that this must be taken from the pile; and besides this that there be taken from the same pile the expense made by Diego Velázquez on the ships that we had destroyed, for all of us had been involved, and then for the envoys that were sent to Castile, and for those who had remained at Villa Rica, who were seventy, and for his horse that died, and for Juan Sedeño's mare, that was stabbed by the Tlaxcalans; then for the friar of La Merced and the cleric Juan Díaz, and the captains; and those who were mounted received a double portion, and musketeers and crossbowmen likewise, and other tricks, so that very little was left to be divided, and because it was so little many soldiers there were who refused their part, and Cortés kept it all, for at that time we could do nothing but be silent, because to demand justice about it was useless. Cortés would give secretly to this man and that . . .[12]

Faced with the wonders of Mexico, Cortés himself wavers between an attitude that it is impossible for him to describe them and a feeling that he has exaggerated, going on immediately into assurances that such is not the case, that on the contrary he has not

[10] *Ibid.*, I, 383.
[11] Cortés, *Cartas*, p. 410.
[12] Díaz del Castillo, *Historia verdadera*, I, 385–388.

gone as far as he could. This passage from his second letter is typical of the first attitude:

Because to give an account, most powerful lord, to Your Royal Excellence, of the greatness, of the strange and marvelous things of this great city of Temijtitán, and the dominion and the vassals of this Muteczuma, its lord, and the rites and customs that these people have, and the gold, which may be found in that city as in the others which belonged to that lord, much time would be necessary, and many narrators and very expert ones; I cannot tell one part in a hundred of the things that could be said.[13]

This other passage belongs to the second attitude: "And let not Your Majesty think that what I say is fabulous, for it is true." [14] And concerning the reaction of this attitude on the first, here is another passage:

But your Majesty may be assured that if there be some fault in my account, it is that it falls short and not that it goes too far, in this and in everything else that I give account to Your Highness; for it seems proper to tell the truth to my Prince and Lord, clearly and without adding things that will diminish or enlarge it.[15]

But in the course of time Cortés is disappointed, as were Bernal and his fellows before him: "It is true," he says, "that there are neither jewels of gold or silver, nor plumes, nor any rich thing as there used to be, although a few small pieces of gold and silver do appear, but not as before." [16] But it is not that the gold and silver are exhausted; it is the fault of Diego Velázquez, the Bishop of Burgos, the India House at Seville, and "especially Juan López de Recalde, its cashier."

This takes us by the hand as it were to the analysis of the second cause, why in spite of so many facts to the contrary there has persisted and will persist for a long time to come the opinion that Mexico is a rich country. Mexico's wealth has been taken for granted or defended as an obvious fact in order to discover the source of all our ills in the moral poverty of the Mexican himself. Nature, it is argued, has been bountiful with the Mexican. It has given him all

[13] Cortés, *Cartas,* pp. 140–141.
[14] *Ibid.,* p. 139.
[15] *Ibid.,* p. 141.
[16] *Ibid.,* pp. 508–509.

varieties of climate, from the tropics to the eternal snows, it has
given him an agriculture and minerals, a wide territory, a long coast-
line, rivers, a sky that is always blue and clear. But the Mexican is
ignorant, lazy, undisciplined, wasteful, lacking in foresight, quick to
take offense, rebellious. What can be done with this human material?
Is it any wonder that the country is backward, that there is poverty
and even extreme want in the midst of so much wealth?

It is not necessary to say that this manner of relating Mexico's
physical wealth to its moral weakness has been done for the most
part by foreigners, by all those who, anxious to obtain a higher interest for their money, have come to invest it in these parts—in
mines, railroads, electric plants, government loans. The interest has
always been collected during the first years, but not later, invariably.
Why not forever, as had been expected? Ah! Because of the ignorance, the lack of discipline, the laziness and lack of foresight, the
rebelliousness and prodigality of the Mexican.

Of course it is not only the foreigner who has made political use
of this fable. We ourselves are the ones who have encouraged it
most. The general line of reasoning is this: why, in this land of
wonders, is there so much trouble, so much poverty? Why do the
United States and Argentina progress while we do not? "Ah!" says
one, "because of the priest." Another says, "Because of the military
man." Some say, "Because of the Indian." Others, "Because of the
foreigner, democracy, dictatorship, science, ignorance." And finally,
"It is a divine punishment." Naturally, for the past few years the fashionable answers have been these: "Because of agrarian reform, the
syndicates, and labor legislation."

There is an abundance of examples, but two magnificent ones are
given us by a man as perspicacious as Lorenzo de Zavala. He says in
a passage of his *Historical Essay on the Revolutions of Mexico*:

Cortés in his letters to Charles V painted flattering pictures, so poetic
and extraordinary, of the things he had seen and conquered with his brave
companions, that he found it difficult not to feel transported into a new
world, to a land resembling and even superior to the imaginary Atlantis,
or to those lands of gold, incense, and perfume about which Oriental
writers tell us. Magnificent palaces covered with gold and silver, kings and
emperors richer than the most powerful potentates of Europe, temples
comparable to those of ancient Greece, rivers that instead of sand contained the most precious metals, and emeralds and diamonds instead of

pebbles, extraordinary birds, monstrous quadrupeds, climes in which man breathed a fiery atmosphere, or in which perpetual spring resembled the nearest image possible of Paradise.[17]

"But how different were these same things when seen from within those same countries," exclaims Zavala. Why? For various political reasons: "The conquest by the Spaniards left the Indians in slavery. . . . There were only masters and slaves . . ." What was the true result for the Mexican people in the midst of their wealth? Zavala points it out: "There are not five [Indians] in a hundred who own a change of clothes." [18]

In another passage he examines conditions in Mexico in the first years after independence and says with more modesty than Cortés:

> The mines prospered to the point that La Valenciana and the mine of Rayas, the richest, were sufficient to support two thousand families and to enrich the owners; the haciendas breeding cattle and sheep were princely estates, for they contained from twenty to thirty thousand head; those dedicated to farming, in spite of the backwardness of agriculture, produced immense quantities of wheat, corn, barley, beans, and other edible grains. In the hot lands were cultivated, as in the present day, sugar cane and coffee; and these valuable commodities constituted the wealth of the owners, the greater part of whom were Spaniards and friars. Estates of much importance were accumulated in their hands, establishing the inequality of wealth and with it slavery and aristocracy. In the midst of this wealth . . . the mass of the population was sunk in the most frightful misery.[19]

Again, why? Because of political reasons: "The terror inspired by the authorities with their troops, their despotism and pride . . . because of the religious superstition of clerics and fanatics, without any sort of education . . . because it was impossible to obtain justice against the will of the viceroy." [20]

It is not only the critic or opponent of the regime, the political organization, party, or person who presupposes our great natural wealth in order to find the cause of all ills in his adversary. The same thing is done by the candidate, the planner, the magician, the mes-

[17] Lorenzo de Zavala, *Ensayo histórico de las revoluciones de Mexico desde 1808 hasta 1830.* 2 vols. (Mexico: M.N. de la Vega, 1845), I, 10–11.

[18] *Ibid.*, I, 14.

[19] *Ibid.*, I, 30–31.

[20] *Ibid.*, I, 32.

siah in politics. All of them say, "Mexico would have everything if . . ." The ingenuous add, "if we irrigate, if we drain, if we campaign against malaria or the mange; if we encourage tourism." The very grim and the very clever say that we could have everything "if . . . we had a great dictatorship, or a great social revolution."

That a whole political regime and even more a whole historical period of Mexico has been condemned by manipulating the idea of Mexico's fabulous wealth can be proved to a rare degree of perfection by this passage from *Barbarous Mexico* by Turner:

Mexico has [a territory covering] 767,000 square miles. Acre for acre it is as rich or richer than the United States. It has excellent ports on both coasts. It is almost as close to international markets as is the United States. There is no natural or geographic reason to prevent this people from being as prosperous and happy as any other in the world. It is not overpopulated. With a population of fifteen million [Turner was writing in 1911], it has eighteen inhabitants per square mile, just less than the United States average. And, nevertheless, seeing the heart of Mexico it is inconceivable that there could be a more extreme poverty in all the world. India and China could not be worse because if they were acute starvation would depopulate them. Mexico is a starving country, a prostrated nation. What is the reason? Who is to blame? [21]

And the answer, though given in the next chapter, in reality follows immediately after:

The slavery and the peonage of Mexico, the poverty and illiteracy, the general prostration of the people, are due in my humble opinion to the present government of Mexico, in a word, to the autocracy of Porfirio Díaz.[22]

There is of course nothing absurd in the idea that part of the wealth or poverty of a country must be ascribed to man and not to nature, to man in his social behavior, in his social achievements, one of which obviously is the kind of political organization that he chooses. And Mexico's political organization has been one of the main reasons why the notion of our great wealth has persisted for so long.

A social organization of such radical inequality, in which great

[21] John Kenneth Turner, *Barbarous Mexico* (Chicago: Charles H. Kerr & Co., 1911), pp. 118–119.
[22] *Ibid.*, p. 120.

and humble, luxury and misery, have always lived side by side must perforce create in an undiscerning eye the view that there would be riches for all if certain things were changed.

Cortés described the luxury quite well, and called it furthermore by its right name, "African."

There is jewelry of gold and silver, and stones and other jewels made of plumes, as well executed as any found in any place or market in the world. There is a great deal of pottery of all kinds and very good, such as the best in Spain. They sell much linen, and edible and medicinal herbs. There are houses where the head is washed, as do our barbers, and decorated. There are baths. Finally, there is all manner of good order and police among them; they are a reasonable and harmonious people: and such that the best of Africa does not equal them.[23]

The view that everything would go very well if certain things were changed, is reflected in the title of a recent North American work: *The Ejido: Mexico's Way Out.* Moreover, this Mexican characteristic of contrast, of inequality, has been noted by everyone who has wished to show the character of our country—the only one, it is said, in which one finds both the magnificent cathedral and the blue sky, sole shelter for so many Mexicans, the latest model airplane or automobile on the one hand and on the other the bare foot, full of cracks and calluses from so much trotting up and down the byways of the world.

And precisely to bring some order into so much confusion, an old Mexican economist, Don Carlos Díaz Dufoo, invented a formula which enjoyed a degree of renown. "We are," he used to say, "naturally rich but economically poor." By this he meant that we possessed wealth in its natural state, but that to make use of it in an economic way we needed techniques, organization, an enterprising spirit, and capital.

Díaz Dufoo's formula already is a step forward; but neither does it clear the obstacle nor to my mind is it complete. If we are to form the best opinion as to the extent of our wealth, we have to consider not only our natural and economic possibilities but our social and political ones as well, all those factors which can enter into the transformation of a society, not only to increase its wealth but to distribute it in a better fashion.

[23] Cortés, *Cartas,* p. 81.

It also seems to me that Díaz Dufoo's formula puts too much faith on techniques. Granted that if we take a quick look at the economic transformation the world has undergone since the last third of the eighteenth century, in particular during the second half of the nineteenth, it is easy to feel an enraptured admiration for technology and to believe that if all the technology the world now possesses were applied to our little Mexico, our country would grow so much, would change in such a manner that even we would not recognize it except after rubbing hard at our eyes.

This is not the time to predict how far technology might transform the natural resources of any country. The point rather is to indicate the possible limitations which technology may have as a transforming element. For one thing, it faces in Mexico obstacles which will be impossible to overcome, or which may be overcome only in part. No technology imaginable could make of our territory what the United States is—truly immense, level, rich, where everything seems to be advantageous and nothing seems difficult. For another, techniques are not developed by countries like Mexico but by great countries, countries already rich in resources or organization, for whom the choosing, developing, and utilizing of techniques is a traditionally familiar process. In general we have three types of techniques in Mexico: first, local invention, which is good enough only to get by, substituting for good, solid invention from abroad, the sort of thing which any chauffeur or mechanic can do; second, good and stable techniques which came into the public domain at the turn of the century, and which we apply in order to bridge a backwardness of many years. The third type is that brought in by foreign capital invested in Mexico—in transportation, petroleum, aviation, and some industries. Study of the conditions under which Mexico has sometimes initiated important techniques (processes in the mining of metals or in the construction of machinery to extract the fiber from henequen) supports this view. At that time our country was the most important producer, or the only one, as was the case with henequen at the end of the last century and the beginning of this one. It is in the great industrial countries, in which life is creative simply because it is intense, that techniques are invented.

And naturally those countries devise their techniques to meet their own needs, as answers to their own problems. For that reason much of the technology of the industrial nations destroys the natural resources of countries like ours. Such is the case with synthetic dyes and fertilizers. This is not all; sometimes we do not find the borrowed remedy abroad, and our interest in foreign things leads us to mistaken solutions. This was the case when we abandoned for the most part the cultivation of cacao, replacing it with the banana, only to discover after a while that we had acquired a wealth of the most precarious sort.

Nothing is farther from my intent than to belittle the urgent need for good techniques to exploit our natural resources; but I cannot agree that technology will give us everything, first because it does not give everything and second because we do not have it for the most part.

All this seems to require some modification of Díaz Dufoo's formula, to express it thus: "by nature we are relatively poor; from an economic standpoint we are poor, though we could be somewhat less poor; from a social viewpoint we are also poor, even though we could be much less so." Then may we hope that some day Mexico will be as it has been imagined by Gonzalo Robles, the man who has studied and thought most upon the subject of our national wealth: a country modestly endowed but well-balanced, healthy and happy, living in equal parts from its agriculture, its industries, and its mines.

THE CHAPULTEPEC CONFERENCE
(February 21–March 8, 1945)*

$\mathbf{T}$HREE POINTS would engage the attention of any person who wanted to form an opinion about this
Conference from the few printed documents that exist about it.
First, documents are such a poor basis on which to make a history
that either such a history is not made or it is made by mixing with
them a good dose of imagination; second, the Conference was not
attended by the statesmen of genius who could have helped America
to emerge from the crucial situation in which it finds itself; finally,
there is an enormous distance, or rather there is no connection at all,
between public opinion and the acts and words of the American
governments.

Printed sources are a poor basis on which to write the history of
the Chapultepec Conference because up to the present they have
been confined to the fifteen (daily) numbers of the *Journal* of the
Conference and to the Mexican press reports for those same days.
The *Journal* contains an enormous number of announcements and a
quantity of useless information, or data, which could be used only
to compile empty statistics: for instance, the disconcerting number of

* First published in *Cuadernos Americanos,* Año IV, 3, May 1945, Vol. XXI.

newspapermen who attended the Conference, and the no less extraordinary number of delegates and advisers—three hundred and thirty. It contains the *ponencias* or documents with which the committees began their labors, and the final form given to them; but not always can one follow the changes that were made, much less the reasons for them. There are no records of proceedings *in extenso*, showing the statements and actions of each and every one of the delegates, much less any account of the private conversations in restaurants and night clubs, places which apparently are propitious for the handling of international politics.

The Mexican press reported on the Conference as it has reported no other happening in or out of Mexican national life, not even the war itself. Day after day news of the Conference filled the first pages of our major newspapers, and many items were continued on page after page, down to the very last. But this profusion of news, and the sensational tone which it was given, produced the impression of an orchestra in which only the wind instruments play. Never had we experienced the extraordinary noise which can be made by three daily newspapers, and the degree of deafness and confusion in which they can submerge the public opinion of a country. It is not strange that public opinion, surprised and frightened, should seek some explanation for such a strange and moving event.

But even so the conclusion is inevitable; in this Conference we did not hear the piercing voice of the prophet, the anguished tones of the sinner, nor even the passionate voice of him who, with blind zeal, defends his country's interests. It is a fact that the causes, the true significance, and the legacy of the war became objects of repeated allusions; but these allusions were limited to mere phrases, the major part of which had been cast into bad Spanish years before by the Associated Press and the United Press. Thus we have the trenchant division of the world into two sectors: ours, which is formed of the *"pueblos amantes de la paz* (for "peace-loving countries") and the other, in which are included the strengths *("poderes")* and not the powers *("potencias")* of evil.

It is true that in his inaugural speech the Mexican minister of foreign affairs, after suggesting that "in the course of our labors we remember that an invisible world of immolations and sacrifices blazes over our heads," asserted that "this war is above all a social revolution, the greatest in history" (*Journal* III, p. 25). But read that speech and you will see that the same things had been said—and more than once in fact—by President Roosevelt, by the head of an enormous industrial democracy where the unforgettable spectacle of 12 million unemployed and living on charity has already occurred. For a country like the United States or England "security" can in fact be the primary goal, or even the only one; but the situation is much different in the Spanish American countries, where the economy is semifeudal and static. They have barely heard the echo of the "greatest social revolution in history," the Industrial Revolution of the eighteenth century.

It was not only that the Conference failed to provide a serious and exhaustive analysis of new situations in American foreign affairs; it did not even express the apprehension that arises from a failure to understand the final consequences of a grave and pressing problem. One can go through the pages of the *Journal* in vain, seeking to find someone who has given voice to the anguish of Latin America, a formless mass tied to the coattails of the United States, which was already determined to enter into a highly dangerous game of world politics. In the Conference itself it was the North Americans who pointed this problem out, with that last-minute joy which has come over them as they assert that now they are at last "global-minded." Secretary of State Stettinius himself pictured the history of the change in this way:

For many years we [the North Americans] depended for our protection on the oceans which surround us. Today we know that neither the sea nor the air nor the earth are impregnable barriers . . . We have come to know that it is not enough to keep a war from our shores nor to confine it beyond the seas which bathe our coasts. We have discovered that we must annihilate it at the source, wherever that may be on the face of the earth (*Journal* III, 28).

This is not the only paragraph in Stettinius' speech that came as a rude blow upon our doors, a blow that should have waked us brusquely; here are two others, also very significant. "The United States will not evade its responsibility in seeing that this fundamental proposition is carried out: the reestablishment of a world in which the right of each nation shall prevail to create institutions of its own choice" (*Journal* III, 28). That is to say that the United States, going against its centuries-old political tradition, will intervene in all aspects of international politics. That is why the Secretary of State reached the logical conclusion that "concerning war and peace there are no problems which are properly European or exclusively American" (*Journal* III, 27). And Senator Connally, with the cunning of a furtive hunter who suddenly stumbles and reveals himself, said, "We do not disregard international organizations for peace, nor the security of nations; we simply postulate the national integrity of our continent" (*Journal* XI, 158).

No one has even paused to reflect, even by accident, that Latin America's situation has changed radically from one World War to the other, nor to wonder what may be the fate that the next war will bring. In the war of 1914 some of our countries managed to remain neutral in a decent and honorable way; in this last none was able to do so. In the next war, shall we not be forced to participate in an active way, with all human and material resources at our disposal? But what can this matter to men like us—broad-chested, strong-hearted and ready "to die like the gladiator, with our faces to the sun"? There should be created a real and workable apparatus which would insure that the United States would not make any decision that might drag us into war without consulting us first. But that is a matter that perhaps some other Conference will consider and pass on to the remote Inter-American Juridical Committee of Rio de Janeiro. The ministers of foreign affairs can only make great declarations. And they made this one: "In case of aggression against any of us, we shall make war together, and none shall conclude a separate peace" (*Journal* X, 153).

But there is another conclusion which cannot escape us. The United States was not this time the villain of the piece, nor was it imperialistic, nor did it nourish devious designs. It presented no major obstacles to the desires or the demands of the Latin Americans. The Yankee delegation, mediocre and unprepared, turned out to be a faithful reflection of the deep crisis through which North American foreign policy is passing. Not even the great publicity given it by the daily press could help it, nor the more modest publicity given it verbally within the Conference, of which the following gem is a good example: "Mr. Edward Stettinius, Jr., officially opened the sessions [those of the Second Committee], emphasizing the importance of the work which is entrusted to it, of which he said one may expect results as beneficial as those obtained in other meetings over which he has presided" (*Journal* IV, 41).

The North Americans refused to commit themselves only when there were clear and legal facts that prevented them from doing so: they did not wish to compromise themselves by condemning export subsidies because it is a fact that they have one on cotton; neither did they support the extension of contracts to buy strategic materials because the powers possessed by President Roosevelt were limited to the duration of the war. But they stood with the Latin Americans in everything, even in their desire that the United States send troops to a Latin American country which tried to play the "aggressor." They even committed themselves to raise the price of coffee, though the Yankee government refused to do so eight days after the end of the Conference, alleging that it did not wish to aggravate the ills of inflation suffered by the producer nations.

The major demands made by the United States appear to have been centered on the verbal acceptance by our countries of a hackneyed economic philosophy which the United States exports to foreign countries but which it consumes less and less at home. There were also repeated efforts to convince the Latin American countries that they should "endeavor to eradicate the discriminations which are imposed by reason of their nationality on foreigners or their abilities [*sic*], or against foreign capital" (*Journal* VII, 108). The economic philosophy revealed itself boldly on various occasions, such as in the condemnation of official government aid for the new industrial enterprises recently founded by Latin American countries (*Journal* VII, 108) and of the creation of government-owned companies that would compete in any way with those privately owned (*Journal* VII, 108). But it was in the Economic Charter of the Americas that it had its most organized and ambitious efflorescence.

It is in itself absurd to think that countries with economic characteristics as diverse as those of the Latin American nations—both in respect to the United States and to each other—could live by a common economic decalogue. And because of that, one may very well think that the United States has taken up this idea merely because it is advantageous for itself in its dealings with the great countries of

Europe and Asia. The Economic Charter is not redeemed either by the grandiose paragraphs or the trite commonplaces which it contains. On the contrary, it is to be condemned for its inconsistencies and its unreal character. It is inconsistent, for example, in not distinguishing between the raising of living standards, which is an end, and economic freedom, which is a means. It is also inconsistent in exalting economic freedom in the "Declaration of Objectives" and asking for international intervention to resolve the problem of surpluses in the "Declaration of Principles." It is a commonplace (and as such a half-truth) to affirm that "work is more productive if it is concentrated on the production of those things which nature has endowed us with, and if it is founded on an advanced technology" (*Journal* vii, 108). And there is little to give us a feeling of reality in the exclamation: "The economic strength of the Americas, based on the raising of living standards and on economic freedom, and attained by means of cooperation in order to give a feeling of security and liberty of opportunity, will be a beacon of hope for the world" (*Journal* vii, 108). And it is unrealistic, politically speaking, for official representatives of the United States abroad to advocate a lowering of barriers against international commerce (among them, of course, the tariffs) as long as the North American Congress has as one of its essential characteristics a membership that represents partial or regional interests. In the same manner it is unrealistic to expect that private initiative will be the leader of economic progress in the Latin American countries, where the governments have the best resources in power, intelligence, and money.

The economic philosophy of the United States which is really consistent with the actual economic, political, and mental realities of that country is pictured with greater veracity in this paragraph from the draft of a resolution presented by the North American delegation:

That the special control which has been indispensably imposed on international commerce because of the war situation be eliminated in the interests of the expansion of private commerce in the post-war period as soon as it is possible and in a measure compatible with the most efficient prosecution of the war, with the understanding that on the cessation of hostilities the temporary continuation of such controls may perhaps be necessary, but that this continuation shall be solely for general ends related directly to the transition from war to peace (*Journal* vi, 90).

How rightly did Guillermo del Pedregal observe, from his real experience in Chile in the task of giving impetus to one of our economies:

I have noted in this conference a certain desire not to talk about plans, about coordination. There is perhaps a fear of controlled economies, of dictatorial systems, of the regime of the *caudillo*, of personal government. That is very well; but under no circumstances should one believe that it is the same thing for a democracy to orient its actions within the common interest as to make plans whose only goal is to debase the human personality (*Journal* xii, 194).

And the delegate Pedretti from Paraguay made an even more acute observation:

We can conclude that there seems to have been created an atmosphere of confusion and contradiction about the economic policy most convenient for our Republics . . . While, on the one hand, statements are formulated about better continental coordination and about plans of inter-American economic cooperation, on the other hand, recommendations are approved which tend toward a reconstruction based on liberal principles of doubtful efficacy in our time (*Journal* vii, 95).

That is why I said in the beginning that one of the three things (to the other two I have already referred) that would be noted by anyone forming an opinion about the Chapultepec Conference would be the enormous distance between national public opinion and the acts and statements of the American governments. The North American press has said that one of the reasons why President Roosevelt finally gave up his attempt to secure three votes on the Security Council for the United States was that Latin American public opinion was decidedly against it. That is possible, but it was not the official opinion, if one may judge from the clear statement made by the Mexican minister of foreign affairs: "The small nations do not aspire for equality of participation in a world of unequal responsibility" (*Journal* xii, 200). Nor may one expect that Peruvian public opinion (to the degree that it may exist) would agree enthusiastically with its minister of foreign affairs in this statement: "I am not going to refer at this time to the problems of war. It is the great leaders of the struggle who are fully entitled to tell us what is the effort we should make and how we should lend our aid" (*Journal* iv, 37). Nor is it easy to imagine that the Cuban taxpayer (not to say the patriot) would approve of this statement proposed by his delegation: "When an American republic's own resources are not sufficient to carry out with its own capital the projects necessary for improvement of its economy, citizens of other American republics should be preferred in the investment of the required capital" (*Journal* vii, 119). And it is doubtful, to say the least, that Brazilian public opinion is sufficiently mature to agree with its delegation in this proposal: "No American country will appeal to the Security Council nor to the General Assembly of the international organization without first using all the conciliatory means which the Inter-American Permanent Commission may impose" (*Journal* vii, 106). And I am bold enough to think that Mexican public opinion would disapprove of the language (since it is not a question of ideas) of the draft of the Resolution on the Attendance of Women to the Conferences: "That woman, in all functional orders of the universal mechanism, is the proved determinant of half of the total available human energy" (*Journal* vi, 85). And again, it does not seem that public opinion in the Americas is yet ready to look with pleasure on the revolutionary measure which the Mexican draft of the Women's and Children's Charter advocates: "That there be dictated [*sic*] an inter-American agreement by which there shall be established for each of the individuals of the conglomerate [*sic*] the obligation of lending a proved [*sic*] social service in favor of minors" (*Journal* vi, 92). Nor do I believe that even the Catholics would approve the Pan Americanist rapture of the Costa Rican minister of foreign affairs: "If we are illuminated by the most profound sincerity, and if the God of America is with us, we can give Europe an example of concord" (*Journal* ii, 12).

What were the origins of the Chapultepec Conference? They are obscure, not to say dark. It is true that the American countries had very important problems to talk about. On the one hand the promoter of the Conference, and its President, after all, on asking himself in his inaugural speech, "What does America expect of this Conference?" gave the following strange objective: "The first thing it expects is practical resolutions, resolutions which will alleviate to a great extent the misery, the forlornness, and the lack of safeguards of our masses" (*Journal* iii, 25). On the other hand the agenda of the

Conference contained both pressing topics which could justify the cloaking of its convocation in that air of urgency which a meeting of twenty ministers of foreign affairs presupposes, and long-range matters with goals whose full attainment lay in the very distant future. Among the first there appeared with all propriety and logic the examination of the world political organization and its relations with what is now called the Inter-American "System" (not "Organization"); economic cooperation during the war and in the period of transition; and the case of Argentina. Also part of the agenda was the theme (as vast as it is vague) of the "consideration of the economic and social problems of America," and the distant, and therefore permanent problem of raising the living standards of our populations (*Journal* i, 2). On the subject of the Inter-American Organization and its relation with the world organization, what took place in reality was a compromise on the question of Argentina. But these were part of the same subject which has been studied all along, at least since the Montevideo Conference of 1933, and whose definitive solution—as was inevitable—was postponed until the Bogotá conference of the coming year (*Journal* xiv, 255). The subject of the general organization of peace had been explored for months, in conversations between the Secretary of State and the Latin American ambassadors in Washington.

The Inter-American and World Organizations

In any case, those discussions and the study of the subject at the Chapultepec Conference had as their point of departure what has been called the Design or Plan or Proposals of Dumbarton Oaks. On few occasions, one must agree, has humanity had to cope with a document as unfortunate as this one: poorly thought out and poorly written, timorous and mutilated, it presents a text which is frequently interrupted by suspension points . . . marking quite clearly the lack of agreement on the part of the four powers which framed it. It anticipates a world organization, charged with creating and maintaining the peace, made up of a unique organ of government— the Security Council—and an Assembly devoid of any authority. To the Assembly are destined the small and middle-sized powers, the great ones belonging in the Council. The Assembly is so lacking in power that it provoked in the Chapultepec Conference the only stroke of humor which was noted there, and for which we must be grateful to the delegation from Honduras. This delegation submitted a text in which appeared some observations on the Dumbarton Oaks design, one of which was the following: "Without any desire to criticize, it could be suggested that the General Assembly should have the authority purely and simply to elect the Secretary [of the organization]. The sense of this would lie in an attribute peculiar to the *exclusive* character which the General Assembly should possess" (*Journal* xi, 180).

Such an unequal division of powers proved to be an unfortunate circumstance for the study of the Plan in the Chapultepec Conference because the majority of the remarks of the Latin American delegations were directed toward that point, which though it was important was not a central one. All asked that the Assembly have some authority and that the Latin American countries as well as the great powers be given permanent representation on the Security Council. And it cannot be but strange and significant that the North American delegation, at whose head was the "architect" (as one would say in English) of the Dumbarton Oaks plan, did not make the slightest effort to defend it, either from this or from any of the other criticisms of the Latin Americans. From a realistic point of view it should not surprise us that Russia asked for only three votes.

On the other hand the matter of the relationship between the inter-American and the world organizations—to me that of the greatest interest, without a doubt—did not receive all the attention it deserved. Nevertheless, marked differences arose among the Latin American countries. On one extreme could be placed Colombia, which declared flatly that "the inter-American organization is of more direct application than the world organization because its most frequent problems [those of Colombia] are also inter-American. Therefore, the American Republics should resort to the inter-American organization rather than to the general organization" (*Journal* xi, 169). In addition, it proposed that in the final document there be made "an explicit declaration concerning the inter-American system, similar to that found in the League of Nations pact concerning the Monroe Doctrine" (*Journal* xi, 169). At the other extreme one might place Uruguay, which clearly and repeatedly opined that "it accepts regional organizations such as the Pan American one, but in a character complementary to the world organization, acting within its orbit, incapable of creating opposition between continents or regions, and not representing the isolation of the nations of one region in respect to those of another region" (*Journal* xi, 171). And as if this were not enough it added, "The countries which make up a regional system will have the power to resort to the jurisdiction of the international organization, and they shall participate in the legal guarantees, the security plans, and cooperative systems of the international organization" (*Journal* xi, 171).

Brazil leaned toward the Colombian stand, though not with as much consistency. On the one hand it declared:

The solution of questions of exclusive interest to a regional group already organized, as is the case with the inter-American group, shall be left to the methods employed among the components of said group, so that the intervention of the Security Council [of the international organization] shall be justified only when such questions could endanger the peace in another group of nations (*Journal* xi, 173).

Nevertheless, we have already seen that Brazil, in another proposal (which it finally withdrew) to create a Permanent Inter-American Committee somewhat similar to the Security Council, suggested that a Latin American country could resort to the international organization as a secondary recourse. Venezuela more clearly took the middle position, for while proposing too that regional conflicts be resolved by regional bodies, it also suggested the possibility of resorting directly to the international organization "when the regional process has failed and there results from that failure a threat to international peace and security" (*Journal* xi, 173).

Peru and Chile, in a joint declaration, proposed the same thing, but with a special turn of extraordinary interest: "If a conflict affecting another continent or region occurs outside America, and if it does not endanger the general peace of the world, the American States will not be obligated to participate in the military operations agreed upon by the duly authorized body of the international organization" (*Journal* vii, 177). Chile and Peru looked into the problem of military operations which might be dictated by conflicts outside America;

Bolivia, on its part, considered the problems originating from inter-American conflicts, proposing that they be resolved "jointly with the Security Council of the general organization" (*Journal* vii, 113). This would truly be a signal exception to the regional thesis, and no less signal an exception to the universalist thesis as well.

The Mexican delegation was the only one which submitted a special proposal concerning this matter, and it was a meritorious one (*Journal* vi, 78). First, it noted the necessity of transforming the Pan American Union into a political institution, without which there would be no way to connect it with the world organization, whose political character is its very essence. Then, in its plan of reorganization of the inter-American "system"—a plan which is commented upon later—it suggested that the latter be able to count on a military force charged with handling the problem of coercive sanctions, whether these emanate from the Pan American organization or from the world organization, as one should suppose. Unfortunately, the character of mere "resolution" which the Mexican delegation chose to give its proposal forced it to be limited for the most part to a declaration of general principles: general consent to the ties to be established between the inter-American and the international organizations; the reservation that these ties should not restrict the liberty of action of any country in problems which did not require a regional or continental solution. The Mexican plan left for a later decision points as important as the determination "of exclusive, conjunctive, or alternative competences," and, what is so important, the mechanism that would resolve jurisdictional conflicts. Lastly, the Mexican delegation, among the statements it made concerning the Dumbarton Oaks text, asked that that text should expressly declare that the inter-American organization is compatible with the world organization (*Journal* vii, 175). Is it—and above all—will it be compatible? Is it and will it be desirable that it be so?

The Pan American Union

In the agenda of the Conference was included the question, barbarously presented, of the "furtherance of the existing inter-American system" (*Journal* i, 2), which gave rise to debates and agitated measures. Concerning it there were submitted two proposals, one

North American (*Journal* vi, 73) and the other Mexican (*Journal* vi, 71); and three resolutions, the first Paraguayan (*Journal* vi, 74), the second and the third Venezuelan (*Journal* vi, 74 and 75). The North American proposal (in which there is still used the early name for the Conference—"Conference of the American republics cooperating in the war effort") is somewhat more watered down than the Mexican one, but in any case its nature is clear. It attempts to improve the existing system without, however, changing its main features or, above all, its internal character. The Mexican proposal, on the other hand, asks for more fundamental changes, many of which represent aspirations of long standing among several Latin American countries. It suggests, for example, that the members of the Governing Council be *ad hoc* delegates of their governments and not, as they have been, the ambassadors directly accredited to the government of the United States; this change would give them greater liberty in respect to the North American member of the Council, who is the Secretary of State. Besides this, the Mexican proposal, with an exaggeration that was not very wise indeed, suggested that the meetings of the Council take place by rotation at the different capitals of the American republics, "to accentuate the continental character of the organization"; and that each of the Council's components, which are known as "complementary bodies," be located in a different country. Along the same lines, the Mexican plan proposed that the Secretary General be named for a term of ten years, that he be barred from serving another term, and that he always be succeeded by a person of a different nationality. The Mexican proposal, furthermore, reveals an even greater desire for modification, for it sets dates and outlines procedures to carry out its suggested reforms.

Yet the two proposals have many similarities, among which are vagueness and lack of serious thought. Both included the three organs of government that exist at present: the International Conferences of American States, the consultative meetings of the ministers on foreign affairs, and the Governing Council. The only difference —and not a small one, to be sure—was that the North American proposal sought to make of the consultative meetings a more permanent and standard body with a jurisdiction as broad as that of the Conferences, while the Mexican plan wished to give the consultative meetings the function of "dealing exclusively with those emergency questions for which they were instituted, basing their functions on Resolution XVII on consultative procedure as approved in Havana" (*Journal* vi, 72).

In the bodies of administrative rather than governmental character, there are also great similarities. The North American proposal envisions the creation of two councils (so called no doubt to distinguish them easily from the Governing Council), the socio-economic and the educational-cultural councils, which the Mexican proposal accepts, though without giving them special names. The latter, however, envisions the creation of other bodies which are lacking in the North American proposal, particularly of an organization of military character, "which shall have among its functions that of anticipating the measures of inter-American cooperation for the defense of the Continent and the preservation of peace" (*Journal* vi, 72).

The resolution finally approved by the Conference, the result of a compromise, gained in clarity and precision, and even in diction—though a *"supervisar"* did slip into it, which would have been readily hunted down by Alfonso Reyes, the Mexican delegate who worked with so much distinction on this project, had he not left the Conference by that time. Respected was Mexico's wish that changes be made in conformity with procedures and within time limits well established beforehand, even though some will have 1960 as their beginning date; that the Governing Council be composed of *ad hoc* delegates beginning the first of May of this year; that the Director of the Pan American Union maintain his post for ten years, and that it not be possible for him to succeed himself, or to be succeeded by a person of his own nationality; that the "extraordinary" consultative meetings deal exclusively with unexpected questions, though the ordinary annual meetings will deal with "situations and disputes of all kinds that may disturb the peace" (*Journal* x, 144). On the other hand, it was resolved that the seat of the Pan American Union and of the Governing Council should continue to be in Washington.

The resolution as approved is far from satisfactory; all that was accomplished was to establish, and not as clearly as possible, the hierarchy of the three organs of government; but not their respective functions nor their jurisdictions. In respect to executive and administrative matters, this inconsistency is painfully apparent. For that reason it was wisely decided to present the definitive proposal at the Bogotá Conference of 1946.

Economic Questions

The economic problems were in fact the most numerous problems discussed at the conference, possibly the most important, and without a doubt—unfortunately—those most keenly felt by Latin American countries. The greatest problem, one which seemed to be the result of the inflation that has affected these countries for the past three or four years, involved the wise application of the monetary reserves which have been accumulated during the war. Also discussed were the prolongation for as long as possible of the purchases of strategic materials which the United States has bought in our countries since the autumn of 1940, for with the cessation of hostilities in Europe, at least, these purchases may end suddenly and almost completely; the possibility that Latin American countries may buy, once the war has ended, all the equipment they need, not only as replacements for that worn out during the war but also for new industrial, agricultural, or communications projects which are under study or in the first stages of execution; and finally, though with less urgency, the relationship that shall exist between the prices paid for raw materials—principal or sole item of Latin American export—and the prices paid for the manufactured products which they import. The Conference also examined, in general, the new forms which international commerce may take in the near future.

In the Chapultepec Conference all these problems and a few others were examined; in fact, of the seventy-odd committee reports presented at the opening of the Conference, somewhat more than twenty-five referred to economic questions. (For a list of these reports see *Journal* VI, 68–69; for the texts of the main ones see *Journal* VI, 76–82, 84, and 87; VII, 113, 115, 116, 119, 125, 126, and 127.)

I believe that even the most casual historian of the Chapultepec Conference will have to point out the notable fact that in all of it, apparently, the words *inflation* and *rise in prices* were not even pronounced; at least I do not believe they can be found in the *Journal* of the Conference. Could there be more forceful proof that the voice of officialdom does not always coincide with the voice of the people?

On the problem of abnormal monetary reserves scarcely anything was said. The Cuban delegation was the only one that presented a concrete draft of a resolution on this important problem (*Journal* vii, 119), a draft which unfortunately was not fully developed, and which did not propose a complete solution. In its introductory clauses it clearly defined the problem: the Latin American countries have accumulated extraordinary gold and dollar reserves because they have either maintained or increased their exports in the last few years, while imports have diminished markedly with the closing of the European source of supply and the curtailment of the American one. Instead of imports they have received gold or notes. With the end of the war the opposite will take place; exports will diminish and imports will increase, the result being that the Latin American countries will have to pay with their accumulated gold and notes for the imports which they may be unable to pay for in full with their exports. The possibility exists, then, that these reserves will be lost, an event which not only would endanger the monetary stability of our countries but would presuppose that these reserves would be spent on unneccesary imports or imports frankly in the luxury class instead of being used for the replacement of industrial, transport, or agricultural equipment worn out or lost during the war.

The Cuban draft proposed that the countries met at the Conference recognize the necessity of regulating imports in the period following the end of the war, and that of protecting their accumulated reserves; but the proposal was deficient, not only because monetary control would in fact be more effective but because neither monetary control nor the control of imports would be sufficient to maintain the reserves, or rather to make the best use of them, if the prices of our exports go down while the prices of our imports rise. Furthermore, the other Cuban recommendation, that of stimulating the sale of machinery and equipment "to develop new sources of production," will not easily be efficacious since to be successful it should precede by a good deal the decrease in exports.

The problem of monetary reserves was also touched upon by the North American delegate William L. Clayton in a statement which to my thinking was the best speech of the Conference, with the exception of Alberto Lleras Camargo's (the first in *Journal* vii, 101–103; the second in *Journal* xv, 273–274). Mr. Clayton saw the problem clearly—and better so from a North American point of view—

when he declared: "We recognize, furthermore, that the buying operations which we have carried out during the war cannot be terminated until you have received from our country, or from others, the equivalent in products or in services" (*Journal* vii, 102). He added that the United States was interested in seeing that "you use, as you wish, a considerable part of those dollars [those accumulated during the war] to adequately develop your industrial, agricultural, and mining resources, since in this way you will raise the standard of living of your peoples, which in turn will give better markets for our own products" (*Journal* vii, 102). But aside from offering the vague hope that Europe and Asia would become our immediate customers, in reality Mr. Clayton went no farther than to recognize that Latin American countries would be justified in resorting to the control of the rates of exchange to clear the obstacles they may face in their just desire to use those reserves wisely.

The problem which perhaps preoccupied the Latin American countries most was the approaching end of North American purchases of the so-called basic products and strategic materials, partly because in some cases (characteristically Bolivia and Chile) these represent the determining item in their exports today and in normal times as well; in part because, even when such is not the case, the Latin American countries fear that if they stop selling these products before they can sell their usual exports in Europe, they will suffer serious economic difficulties and disorders; and partly also because some of our countries have deceived themselves that in one way or another they could maintain these new exports in addition to those of normal times. The problem was and is a difficult one, since after all the United States in principle plays the role of a mere commercial buyer, who of course reserves the right to suspend his purchases when he judges it convenient. Then, besides the fact that the North American government has the authority to make these purchases only while the war lasts, many of these basic products and strategic materials either have no application except to warlike ends or they are produced by our countries under conditions which for one reason or another are not the best. This is the reason why it would seem absurd to the United States to buy things for which it no longer has any use, and unprofitable to acquire those it can use at high prices when it can obtain them on better terms outside the continent.

The problem has another side, of course, one which was well

emphasized by the Peruvian delegation on the one hand, and by North American delegate Clayton himself, on the other. The Peruvian delegation declared that in economic demobilization there should be "shown the same earnest endeavor present in 1942, when the mobilization of production for the war effort was discussed" (*Journal* vii, 116). Clayton more bluntly described the situation thus:

This is an important sum [the five billion dollars of North American purchases in our countries during the past four years], and there are persons in my country who considering such transactions from a petty and prejudiced point of view would say: "Just imagine the billions of dollars that we have poured into these countries! They should be extremely grateful to us for having given them such a lucrative market for their products." And also in your countries there must be people who will say: "The United States would have lost the war if we had not given it millions of tons of essential materials, and they should be grateful to us forever" (*Journal* vii, 101).

Chile, Mexico, Peru, Ecuador, Bolivia, and Costa Rica presented draft resolutions on this problem; but the truth is that none of them went far enough, either in stating the problem or in offering solutions. Peru offered the most ambitious plan in its Resolution on Economic Demobilization (*Journal* vii, 115–116), for it went so far as to suggest the creation of a special Pan American institution, modeled on the Bank of Reconstruction and Development of Bretton Woods, which, although of short duration, would undertake the purchase from Latin American countries of their excess exports, and the placing of them in markets, preferably markets which appeared to be permanent; but the Peruvian delegation did not go beyond this first outline, necessarily vague; and it fell for that reason into the chronic vice of asking that the Inter-American Financial and Economic Advisory Committee study the problem and draw up the plan, adding besides the requirement that it be done on extremely short notice: the Committee should submit the plan to the governments by April 1. This unfortunate circumstance, and the fact that the other countries did not go beyond proposing completely innocuous solutions, permitted the United States to obtain approval of its recommendation, according to which the countries affected by the termination of the purchases, and the purchasing countries (that is to

say the United States) "will adopt, by means of bilateral agreements, measures tending to reduce to the minimum during the period of transition adverse consequences to the economies of the countries in question" (*Journal* XIV, 259).

Once the war ended, the problem of acquiring industrial, agricultural, mining, and transport equipment, and in broader terms the problem of industrializing our countries, would be of great importance and immediacy. It was logical, then, that it should engage the Conference's attention. Chile presented an industrialization plan (*Journal* VI, 77), whose dominant theme was a wise one: the necessity that the Latin American countries industrialize not only according to their national wants and desires but with a general inter-American view. For that reason it recommended that the location of new industries should depend not only on the availability of raw materials and power but also upon the geography of the country and "the necessity to maintain and increase a balanced and remunerative intercourse among the American countries." The Chilean plan, however, showed a great weakness; it did not even touch upon the sore point raised by an inter-American industrialization coordinated to an international point of view, namely whether or not the economy of Latin America should be merely complementary to that of the United States. Then, it fell into the outright simplicity of supposing that organizations as transitory and formless as the Inter-American Financial and Economic Advisory Committee and the Commission of Inter-American Development are capable of embarking on a complex study such as this plan would require, and that they have the clear authority to "take all necessary measures in carrying out the objectives of this resolution."

The Mexican delegation also presented a plan dealing with industrialization (*Journal* VI, 79–80), whose introductory clauses are clear and expressed with logic and order, even though the plan is excessively repetitious in its attempt to show that industrialization of Latin American countries will not harm North American commerce; on the other hand its recommendations do not deal directly with the means to attain industrialization, but rather with a series of disparate phenomena, which do in fact have some relation to it: that the price of equipment should not be raised, that measures be taken to prevent the reduction of monetary reserves below prudent limits, that dumping be condemned, and that some specialized, long-term credit organization be created.

The Ecuadorian delegation also submitted a plan for the acquisition of industrial equipment, and in it reference is made to industrialization itself (*Journal* vII, 127); this plan recommends that a definite program be formulated; the conditions are outlined which an industry must meet before it can be considered viable. But it goes no further. Finally Brazil, in a plan concerning the removal of export restrictions (*Journal* vII, 127), recommended that the industrialized and creditor nations lower their tariffs so that the less developed and debtor countries could increase their exports and thus obtain the means for industrialization. The resolution that was finally approved (*Journal* xIV, 266) improved by far on all the drafts, and it goes without saying that in this as in other things the North American hand is apparent. The idea of continental planning was abandoned, and even that of mere coordination; the protection of new industry by means of high and permanent protective tariffs was condemned; the idea of a credit organization to serve the Latin American countries especially was discarded, the recommendation being made instead that the Bretton Woods agreement be quickly approved; industrial enterprises of governmental origin were condemned; facilities were demanded for the investment of foreign capital and equal treatment for national and foreign securities; dumping was ignored; and the principle of the Atlantic Charter, of equal access to raw materials, was reaffirmed.

Non-Intervention and the Case of Argentina

The case of Argentina was first in importance among the political problems of the Conference, in spite of the fact that it was placed last on the agenda, with the addition even that it would be considered "once the preceding subjects have been finished with," that is to say at the very last (*Journal* I, 2). Of course it was not the case itself which made it so important, but the deep feeling it had excited: here again was the old problem of intervention, continual theme in so many Pan American conferences, a theme which, it was believed, had been taken care of at Montevideo. That made it a disconcerting problem, complex and impassioned. And that was what made so many people fall into mistaken, contradictory, and even ingenuous opinions.

On the one hand there was the long and painful effort of the Latin American countries to establish judicial precedents that would prevent the United States from intervening in their domestic and foreign affairs. One of the most common forms which this intervention has taken has been the denying of diplomatic recognition to a government and the granting of it later, conditional to the acceptance of certain commitments. This practice had been repeated so often in the recent history of Mexico and Central America that Genaro Estrada, one of the few foreign ministers our country has had, formulated the doctrine that bears his name, according to which a change in government did not create a problem in recognition, diplomatic relations not being interrupted for an instant by the change unless a country, in a deliberate move, decided to break them by withdrawing its diplomatic representatives. Imperfect though it was, the Estrada Doctrine represented the long-standing aspirations of many Spanish American countries, and because of that it was accorded general respect.

On the other hand there was the war itself, that war in whose sixth year we still found ourselves. The nations that later called themselves United waged it in support of democracy and against a very peculiar form of tyranny which was called Nazism, or Nazi-fascism. This meant that if the political regime or the government of a country was classed by the United Nations as Nazi, not only was it impossible for them to have any diplomatic relations with it, but the most elemental logic made it inevitable that they should declare it an irreconcilable enemy, an entity with which they could not coexist, and which on the contrary it was necessary for them to exterminate even at the cost of extreme sacrifice, as the Hitler regime was being exterminated in Germany and the Mussolini regime in Italy. To the degree then that one seriously believed in the reasons why war was being waged, to that precise degree was the Estrada Doctrine inoperable; and not because it was a poor one but because it had not been conceived and proposed for a case like that of the military regime of Argentina. In the cases of Germany, Italy, and Japan—to see the problem more clearly—no one ever thought that the question was to seek a form of peaceful coexistence; rather, the question was simply and purely one of making war upon and exterminating an enemy.

Logically, the problem which was presented by the Argentine military regime was whether it was a nazi government, in which case it would be impossible to coexist with it in any way; or whether it was not nazi, in which case according to the Estrada Doctrine it was automatically necessary to tolerate it, for otherwise we were in fact intervening in the affairs of a sovereign state. Colombia, for example, through the words of its minister of foreign affairs, and even through those of President López, has maintained that there is no logic at all in denying recognition to the Argentine government because it is not democratic while maintaining life-long relations with other governments which are far from being democracies. The weakness of the Colombian thesis is that in order to judge the Argentine regime it has made use of one of two opposite terms, terms which in theory are irreconcilable. This term is "democracy" or "democratic," whose definition makes us think about political regimes like those of England and the United States. To illustrate the error, look at Russia: while many would deny to Russia the name of democracy, no one would be so bold as to call it nazi. And the truth is that there are many political systems which without being in a strict sense democracies are not nazi either. Our sadly celebrated Creole *caudillo* is a well-known example, and the one that interests us the most. The other error in the Colombian thesis, judging it pragmatically, is one immediately noted and resented by liberals in America: since some of us are sheep and others goats, let us all be classified as goats.

Is the Argentine military regime nazi in truth? Even supposing that we had all the necessary information to judge, one would expect a great difference of opinion on this question, although I personally have reached a decision on the matter a long time ago. But we are dealing here solely with a problem in international politics. And from this point of view one must agree that there have been at least two American governments which have publicly and repeatedly accused General Farrell's regime of being nazi. These are the governments of the United States and Mexico. When some Jewish newspaper was suppressed in Buenos Aires, President Roosevelt—whose death saddened all of us democrats of the world—clearly pointed out that an act of that nature identified a regime. And the foreign minister of Mexico, no later than October 17, 1944, declared in Havana to newspaper reporter Flora Lewis:

We are applying economic sanctions to Argentina and we will isolate it form the rest of the world. Argentina has been accused of obstructing the Allied political effort. This problem is already an old one. The grave problem now is the peacetime role of Argentina, and the present organization of the country endangers the peaceful development of the Continent.

On being asked whether Mexico would support the sanctions against Argentina, Padilla called the Argentine government fascist and declared that it was a menace to the rest of the continent, as well as to its own people.

"The rest of the American republics," he said, "are sorry to see that one of the principal countries of the continent has turned away from democracy. Argentina is sufficiently advanced and well prepared to be a democracy," the foreign minister said, "but the present government constitutes a regression to dictatorship and we are fighting fascism throughout the world."

This—and no other—is the picture that logic would draw; but the Spanish American countries know, having felt it keenly in their own flesh, that there is little logic in international politics, especially as it is practiced by the great powers. Because of this, all of them asked that the recognition be given Argentina, even if this meant the sacrifice of the most fundamental political decency, and even at the cost of denying the democratic Argentines the only weapon that they had possessed. Furthermore, several of the Spanish American countries, those geographically closest to Argentina, took this course knowing that it was more than just words to say that with the consolidation of the Argentine military regime they would lose much of their tranquility. Another reason, an important one, which compelled the Latin American countries to seek a solution to the Argentine problem at all costs was the fact that—whatever they might actually think—their conduct in the eyes of the world was unmistakably stamped as imposed by the United States. For that reason, all the delegations on arriving and being questioned by reporters declared in one form or another that they would like to see the Argentine problem resolved;

for that reason the President of Mexico lamented the absence of Argentina in his opening address to the Conference; for that reason the Paraguayan delegation proposed that the subject of Argentina be not the last but the first on the agenda; and for that reason, in fine, Argentina was recognized and soon after became an Associated and United nation. It is difficult to decide which was more surprising, the solution arrived at in Chapultepec or the Argentine government's ready acceptance of it.

In any event, even with the case of Argentina out of the way the Conference still could not escape its lasting significance: the old problem of intervention. On one side Ecuador presented a draft of a trenchant resolution entitled "On the abolition of the recognition of *de facto* governments" (*Journal* vii, 129). On the other the Mexican delegation submitted one which could very well have been called "On organized intervention" instead of "Relations among the American governments founded on the solidarity of Continental democracy" (*Journal* vi, 82–83). The Ecuadorian draft proposed the signing of an agreement that would abolish the custom of recognizing *de facto* governments; but the preamble on which it was based was an extremely vigorous repudiation of this form of intervention. It said in fact that to deny recognition was "a serious blow to a government's right to sovereignty in foreign affairs, the enjoyment and exercise of which do not admit interruption of any kind," and that the custom of recognition or nonrecognition violates "the right which is theirs to substitute or constitute governments according to the dictates of their completely free will." The clause in the preamble which was the most pointed and which brought the problem best into focus was the fifth:

That the facultative character of diplomatic recognition confers upon foreign governments the power to meddle in the inviolate orbit of domestic affairs of a state in which a new governmental entity may have been established, to pass judgment on it and qualify it before the world according to their whims, and it consequently gives them the ability to exercise a sort of moral coercion, forming thus an imperative interference that corresponds to the typical forms of intervention (*Journal* vii, 129).

The Conference could not digest such a strongly flavored dish and resolved to send it to the Inter-American Juridical Committee "so that it could formulate the pertinent rules" (*Journal* vii, 138).

The Mexican plan concerning the organizing of intervention into the domestic and foreign affairs of other states is remarkable for more than one reason: first, because it forgets Mexico's most recent history—the nonrecognition both of *de facto* governments such as those of Victoriano Huerta and Carranza and *de jure* governments such as that of Obregón—second because it goes against the diplomatic traditions of Mexico and the historic role which Mexico has played as interpreter and standard-bearer for the Spanish American countries; finally, because it has such a childish air, its weakness is so manifest, its political unreality so evident, that one is amazed that such a document should have stolen into a Conference attended by real men, tangible beings of flesh and blood.

The preamble generously bestows on our America the patrimony of "the liberties and philosophic ideas which together constitute the democratic system." For which reason there is "imposed" on the American countries "the unavoidable obligation not to limit the effects of their actions solely to the orbit of their *domestic* manifestations, each one of them being obliged to consider as their own problem a threat that may exist against the Democratic Institutions of any one of them." Consequently

the American countries should organize a system of *exclusively international nature* which without affecting *in any way* the principles of respect toward sovereignty and nonintervention, *so many times asserted by them,* may watch over the creation of a continental and international atmosphere which will permit each American government to be and to constitute the true expression of national sovereignty.

And then the "system" is created, a simple procedure: 1) when any change occurs in the government of an American country, it shall be provisionally accepted by the others during a "security period" of a month; 2) if during this period no government objects to the newly born, "all the American Governments *ipso facto* will accept as definite the existence of the new government"; 3) but if one of them expresses an adverse opinion, it will propose a conference "to arrive at a collective agreement . . . in respect to the suspension or denial of international status of the new government, *as well as to the political, diplomatic, and economic effects which the American states shall seek to give their joint action.*" This proceeding shall apply whenever any new government is established, when a government already established shall "modify its internal politics," and when revolutionary groups "at any given moment may attempt to constitute a government."

All of these monstrosities have to be reconciled with the principle of absolute respect for the sovereignty of the American States—a simple task of course. When "any American State expresses an adverse opinion in regard to the new government" it shall be understood that it is done solely "in its international aspect." And if all agree in nonrecognition, it shall be understood that "in no case may their accord include a judgment of any sort on the legality, legitimacy, or internal constitutionality [*sic*] of the new government." So much so that

from the moment of its being constituted and *even before there exists any statement* from the other American States in regard to its international status, the new government *has the right* to defend the integrity and independence of the State in which it has been constituted, to watch over the preservation and the prosperity of its people, organizing and legislating concerning its interests, administering its services, and determining the jurisdiction of its tribunals.

It is to be supposed that once an adverse declaration was made the new government lost these rights, as generous as they were provisional, which were granted by the other governments. Should there be any fear that this might constitute intervention, it would only be necessary for the signatories of the resolution proposed by Mexico to "recognize" that "the internal political existence of a new government is independent of the collective opinion that other nations may adopt in respect to it." And how independent!

The Mexican draft was withdrawn "in view of the fact that the Mexican delegation had prematurely announced on the 27th of February its intent of submitting it for the consideration of the Conference, and for that reason it was published before it had reached its definitive form" (*Journal* vii, 13). From this we may assume that the Mexican draft for the reorganization of the Pan American Union did not attain its definitive form either, because in its Clause *f* there is very clearly outlined the procedure to be followed in conferences "dealing with cases such as changes in a government, which are alluded to in another of the resolutions of this conference" (*Journal* vi, 72).

At all events here was a procedure which would eliminate all possibility that the revolutionary groups of a country might constitute a government. And to imagine that this could be applied to Mexico some day, through the initiative of Mexicans, must have shaken Madero, Carranza, and Obregón in their graves. But they may continue to sleep in peace, knowing that those who might seek to imitate them in the future will be safe, thanks to a providential circumstance: the Mexican draft did not attain its definitive form.

INDEX

Acapulco, Mexico: 80
Acción Nacional: 25–26
Acosta, José de: 163
Acton, John Emerick Edward Dalberg-Acton, Lord: 46, 113
Africa: 150
agrarian colonies. SEE agrarian reform; cloister; *ejidos;* land grants
agrarian law: 14
agrarian reform: as revolutionary objective, 4, 6, 13, 18; strategy of, 14; failure of, 14–15; processing of products under, 15; results of, 15–16, 126–127; crisis in, 22–27; and Acción Nacional, 26; role of state in, 126–127; communal farm credit under, 126–127. SEE ALSO agriculture, Mexican
agriculture, Mexican: during Díaz regime, 13–14; teaching of, 14; experimentation in, 14–15; and Mexican Revolutionary Constitution, 16; financing of, 126–127; profits in, 127; evaluation of, 155–157, 176. SEE ALSO agrarian reform; banking, Latin American
Alemán Valdés, Miguel: 29, 51
Algeria: economic planning in, 135
Altos Hornos project: 47
Alvarado, Pedro de: 167
Alvarado River: 163
America. SEE Central America; Latin America; North America; United States
—, Spanish. SEE Latin America
Americans. SEE Latin Americans; North Americans
Americas, the: vastness of, 75
antimony: in Mexico, 160–161
Antioquia, Colombia: 80

113; and democracy, 114; and liberalism, 116; in India, 136; in Guatemala, 153. SEE ALSO Communist bloc; Russia

Communist bloc: steel production in, 111; economic planning in, 134–135; as enemy of Western world, 151. SEE ALSO Communism

Communist Party. SEE Communism; Communist bloc; Russia

Congress, Mexican: in revolutionary era, 11–12

congresses: as models for Latin America, 11–12

congressmen: criticism of, 12

Congress Party, Indian: 136

Connally, Thomas Terry: at Chapultepec Conference, 180

conquistadors: 160, 165, 167

conservatism: in Latin America, 93, 107, 143; in United States, 47, 118. SEE ALSO conservatives

conservatives: in Mexico, 11, 106, 107; political power of, 63; in Colombia, 143. SEE ALSO conservatism

Constitution, Mexican: and labor, 16; and agriculture, 16; derived from Declaration of the Rights of Man, 61; generalities of, 132; and regulative law, 132; and economic planning, 132. SEE ALSO constitutional reform

—, United States: 35

—, Virginia: 35

constitutional reform: 131–132

constitutions: in Latin America, 101–102

copper: in Mexico, 160–161

Cordova Island: and Chamizal problem, 28 n

corn: in Mexico, 155

Cortés, Hernán: 162; expedition of, 166, 168–170; letters of, 171–172

Costa Rica: demographic growth of, 75; tyranny in, 94; democracy in, 142–143; coffee of, 157; at Chapultepec Conference, 184, 194

cotton: in Mexico, 15, 155

crafts: compared to factory production, 82

credit, foreign: 14, 98. SEE ALSO capital, foreign

Cuba: democracy in, 94; Latin American relationship with, 141, 146, 147, 149; revolution in, 144–145, 148–149, 149–150; and U.S., 150–151, 151–153; and Russia, 150, 153; armament of, 153; and Czechoslovakia, 153; Communism in, 153; Velázquez in, 167; at Chapultepec Conference, 184, 192

Cuernavaca, Mexico: 80

culture, national: Mexico's pride in, 7

Czechoslovakia: Communist conquest of, 111; and Cuba, 153; and Guatemala, 153; coal mining in, 159

Darío, Rubén: 56

demobilization, economic: Chapultepec Conference on, 191–196

democracy: in Mexico, 9, 12, 52, 100, 197; in Latin America, 9, 12, 52, 89, 92–93, 94, 100, 114–115, 131, 142–143, 197; in U.S., 71–72; disillusionment with, 89, 114–115; definition of, 92, 99, 198; types of,